Featuring Phenomenal Women with Amazing Stories

100 Most Successful Women Around World

Build Success From Scratch

100 Most Successful Women Around World Build Success From Scratch

Maria Renee Davila, Founder of 100 Most Successful Women Around the World
Al Otero, President of Global Trade Chamber

Dr. Caroline Makaka, Conclusion

María Angélica Benavides, EdD, Publisher
Dr. Randi Ward, Editor

Maria Renee Davila * Al Otero * Caroline Makaka * María Angélica Benavides, EdD *Randi D. Ward

Eva Maria Davila * Viola Edward * Vee Escarment * Amelia Fjellvard * Ella Ford Mthethwa * Kandee G.

Daisy Gallagher * Monica Gomez * Dr. Sherri Henderson, Dr. Violet Howard *Tamara Hunter

Vaneese Johnson * Preeti Kachroo * Dr. Real N. Kunene * Dr. Virginia LeBlanc * Amber Ann Lyons

Mimi Mala * Rose marok * Tonya McNeal-Weary * Susie Mierzwik * Shamila Mooloo * Milenia Nazaret

Yaima Osorio * Hatice Ozalp * Ines Elvira Pardo * Nutan Patel * Eline Pedersen

Nareshini Ranganthan * H.E. Dr. Desiree Richardson * Rodeline Robinson * Karin C. Rodriguez

Laylah Rose * Merete Stangeland * Patricia Tanner * Tia Tatem * Cheryl Thibault

Hope Philips Umansky, PHD. * Dr. Joy Vaughan * Jo Wiehler * Madeleine P Wober * Beatrice O. Yesufu

100 Most Successful Women Around World
Build Success From Scratch

Published by B-Global Publishing.

Copyright © 2022

DEDICATION

"I dedicate this book to the person that has always been there for me, and with me through this amazing journey as an international entrepreneur. Ruth Garcia de Davila, my supportive and encouraging mother. From an early age, she believed in me and saw my heart as an entrepreneur. She helped me to start my first company at 17. With her wisdom and experience as an entrepreneur herself and an educator she guided me through all the stages of starting and growing a business. She is still there by my side giving me advice, encouraging, and often helping me through the challenging times.

Thank you, Mamita!

ACKNOWLEDGMENT

Every successful project or idea requires the support and contributions of a team of amazing individuals that believe in you and your project. This book is proof that it takes a team with wisdom, vision, and the desire to help others. The support from Robbie Motter, Angela Posillico, Caroline Makaka, Dr. Randi D. Ward, Shamila Ramjawan, and especially the Publisher of this life-changing book Dr. Angelica Benavides has turned the dream and vision of putting together amazing stories of success to inspire other women around the globe, a reality. We want to express our sincere gratitude to all the phenomenal women who dare to share their challenges and ultimate success to support and empower other women around the world.

Table of Contents

FOREWORD

"The power of women comes from other women that inspire, empower, and motivate."
Al Otero, President Global Trade Chamber

If you are a woman in business or thinking about going into business, this book is filled with wisdom from women who have overcome great odds to achieve their dreams, succeed, and help other women on their road to entrepreneurship. This book will have a life-changing impact on your life.

There are two ways to grow in life; we either learn from our trials and errors, or we learn from the experiences of others and their achievements. Life balance is a big challenge for today's woman, family, career, entrepreneurship, children, home, health, personal development, and so much more.

This book is like having personal mentors and coaches and successful women from many sectors and cultures that have achieved balance, daily routines, and priorities and see challenges as opportunities. These amazing women are making a positive impact on the world in many ways. This book will enable you to find out how you can also make an impact in your community and succeed in your vocation, enterprise, or career.

After working for over 15 years with Maria-Renee, the author of this book and Founder of the 100 Successful Women in Business Network, I have come to learn much about women in business, their challenges and incredible strengths, resilience, and tenacity. I admire and respect Maria-Renee and the impact she is making to empower women around the globe.

I am a huge supporter of the 100 Successful Women in Business Network and all the activities and initiatives, such as this book, to educate, connect, and empower women.

This book will make a great addition to your library and will make a wonderful gift for any woman.

I invite you to join the 100 Successful Women in Business Network, the 100 Successful Women in Business Annual Convention, and many other initiatives to maximize your potential and reach new heights in every area of your life.

"The quality of your connections and relationships determine your ability to open new opportunities."

Register today at www.100swb.com and receive a free special gift from an amazing global leader!

Al Otero
President/Global Trade Chamber
www.globaltradechamber.com
Chairman of the 100 Successful Women in Business Conference & Expo

"Greatness is a lifelong mission. Create a mission to serve millions, and gently with love, shake the world."

María Angélica Benavides, known as Dr. B

Milenia Nazaret
MJ Globus, LLC
West Palm Beach, Florida, USA
mglobusllc@gmail.com

Chapter 1
A Road from Pitfalls to Success

I grew up in Kazakhstan. I have two bachelor's degrees in (Architecture and Economics). I am bilingual (English and Russian). I have excellent communication and customer service skills, have coordinated communication strategies with Global 500 companies, and have worked with product teams on multicultural marketing and private development. I am a blockchain enthusiast and international real estate broker located in West Palm Beach, Florida. I work with a big group of investors around the world. I have specialized in off-market luxury 4-5 stars hotels, office buildings, apartment complexes, businesses, and shares of big companies in the US and Worldwide. Most recently I have spent time connecting buyers and sellers of commodities including BTC. I have a very good network of buyers and sellers across Asia, Europe, Africa, North and South America.

Mission and Vision

I am in the business of helping connect buyers and sellers. As a licensed broker, I am involved in commercial real estate, mines, commodities, and cryptocurrency. We work with ultra-wealthy individuals and provide them with solutions with off-market opportunities. We create value for our clients and work with discretion and a high level of integrity and ethics. We always try to find creative ways to help make a difference for good.

Starting from Scratch
Introduction building from scratch

Sometimes starting over just happens. For me, I was enjoying life and enjoying success, and then life changed very quickly when I was involved in a serious car crash. Thankfully I was able to make a full recovery, but the journey to do so was illuminating and I learned much about myself, what is truly important. I reflected on my purpose and how to reframe my world and my own dreams. This led me to make some major changes that ultimately opened up doors and opportunities that never would have been available to me or my family had the accident not occurred. There is a silver lining in the troubles we experience in this life.

Car Crash Transformation

In April 2004, I was invited by the government of Karaganda to represent my country and traditional Kazakh costume in Hannover-Messe 2004, Exhibition in Hannover, Germany, as the leading model of Kazakhstan in the name of Nurasem agency. It was a big honor for me at this time to be recognized by the most influential person in my country and to cut the red ribbon during the opening of the

A Road from Pitfalls to Success

Hannover-Messe 2004 ceremony. It was quite an experience to be part of the Ceremony with the President of Kazakhstan, Nursultan Nazarbayev, and Gerhard Schroder, the Chancellor of Germany After this trip, my life changed. I made a significant number of valuable contacts with businesspeople from different countries during the exhibition. My artistic skills, creativity, critical thinking, and leadership prowess played a substantial role in my success during the event. During the Hannover-Messe 2004 ceremony, I researched women in power, and I concluded that women are less represented compared to men. I evaluated the information I received from businesswomen and what was shared is that they had fewer opportunities for economic participation than men and less political representation.

I had a powerful desire to become a civil rights attorney and focus on cases involving issues such as equality, human rights, social freedom, and discrimination. However, a severe car accident changed my plans, and it took two years to recover from the injuries that I incurred during the crash. The car crash led me into creating my own model agency, which ultimately led me to the United States and created an entirely new life for myself in Real Estate and ultimately what I am currently doing with my company, MJ Globus, LLC.

Big Why
Why, What, and How

Why am I here, what is my purpose, and how do I get to where I am called to go? Why did I get in this car crash? What do I need to accomplish for myself and my family? How do I get to America and a new start? These were questions I was pondering. Now, I challenge you to ask yourself, what is your big why that leads you to your big dreams.

Why are you doing what you are doing? Engage the reader
My passion is people. And I love to help them. I have found the best way to succeed is to help solve people's problems. I love working on deals and engaging with others as we work together to accomplish something that will benefit many. I want to have a positive impact on people's lives, in the life of their families, and contribute to their success so that they can have a more influential and positive impact in their community. I absolutely love life and am so grateful for each and every day.

14

Aha Moment Epiphany
From Employment to Business

When I first started in business, I spent time working for others and realized that my greatest call was to create something that I could help bring to fruition that would have a far more reaching impact than being limited by the thinking of others. I am grateful for their contributions to my success, but I do not need to limit myself. I have God-given ability and talent that I need to use. I need to dream big. I wrote down my goals and kept them in front of me daily. They are very big, and it is amazing how God is helping me achieve them. My life is different in so many wonderful and beautiful ways. I am greatly blessed. When did you have that aha moment of creating? Take time to reflect on your aha moment and go after your big idea!

When I was working for others, I always questioned what I could do to improve their efforts. This expanded my thinking beyond my current circumstances and the horizon upon which I viewed my life. Since I was a little girl, I always felt called to something big but didn't understand exactly what that meant or how I was to proceed with my life. Along the way as I grew up and experienced life, it led me to go deeper into myself to question and to envision a plan that was not on my immediate agenda. I am also grateful for the hard times that cause me to become a better me. Life is often not easy, but the end result of staying positive and not being afraid of big changes or challenges has been a family, and those that mean the most to me.

Secret Formula

God opens and closes doors for me. He gives me discernment on what deals I should work on and then how to help solve people's problems. He opens up doors for me, and I have clients that knock on my door. I am very blessed. I give Him credit for my success.

We have been involved in deals that have been heading in the wrong direction. Fortunately, I have been able to step in and facilitate the discussions between principals to turn the deal around. This is a skill that I have been able to hone over time, and I greatly appreciate the discernment that God gives me to understand the timing and means by which to communicate to the parties involved.

Steps to Build Success from Scratch

Attitude and Faith are critical for success. You have to believe and stay positive when dealing with people. The business I am in is extremely demanding, and there are many interesting characters and personalities. I listen, I stay positive, and I try to meet the needs of my clients in a professional, timely, and creative way. This works for me.

First Sign of Success.

Success has been a difficult journey. There has been a road full of pitfalls and missteps. The breakthrough happened by building trust with clients. When trust is established, then doors open. My partner, Jeff, has helped me. He has weathered the storms with me, and he believes in our ability to get deals done. We complement each other, and I am very grateful for our journey together.

Ultimate Solution Name it

Mentoring is important– the road I am on has required many different mentors from different backgrounds. I know what I don't know, and I am confident I can find the answers to problems if given the time and opportunity. Confidence and staying positive and believing for the best make a difference in the success of our company and our partners and clients. Working with successful people from the same industry helps a lot. I learn by my mistakes, and it takes time for me to find the right people to work with to accomplish my goals.

Free Gift (Advice)

Listen, stay positive, and work to solve the problems of your clients while reassuring them and doing all you can to act in a professional and timely manner. Use wisdom when communicating; sometimes your client does not need to know all the gory details of what is happening in the process to get a deal done. Just let them know you are their advocate and are working to solve their problem as expeditiously and appropriately as possible.

A Road from Pitfalls to Success

Accolades and Achievements

I have been recognized as one of the 10 most beautiful people in my country. I was able to be a trailblazer for women's rights in a Muslim country, and I have restarted my life with very little in a new country learning a new language.

I am a member of many organizations: Global Business Alliance NAR 2022; Woman's Counsel of Realtors; and Global Business Committee 2022 NAR. I am a Certified International Property Specialist (CIPS); a Global Real Estate Practitioner (GREP); AREAA Global New Construction Specialist; and Dubai International Property Consultant (DIPS). I have an At Home with Diversity Certification (AHWD) and a UNIC Security Token Strategy (Blockchain Certification). I am a member of Global Commercial Investors Network in (USA, China, Spain, Portugal, UK, France, Switzerland, Monaco, Germany, Dubai, Greece, Mexico, and the Dominican Republic).

See What They Are Saying...

"Milenia is a Queen. She is one of the most gifted and extraordinary women I have met in my life. Her ability to effectively communicate complex business transactions and keep everyone moving forward to closure is exceptional and often the game-changing ingredient in our business dealings. Everyone needs Milenia on their team."
Jeffrey Robinson, Managing Partner, MJ Globus LLC

***

Business Links
https://www.milenia.us/about-me

https://www.linkedin.com/in/milenianazaret/

Dr. Preeti Kachroo Bhagat
BollyOne Singapore
Singapore
preetikach@gmail.com

Chapter 2

A Zeal to Transform Challenges to Opportunities

Dr. Preeti Kachroo Bhagat is an Ayurvedic Physician, Yogini, TM Teacher, and Researcher for more than two decades working closely to bring healthcare to the consumers. She is a philanthropist, Beauty Queen, and passionate community worker. She works as an ERG lead in GSK. In Singapore she is the LOANI Chair, working closely to bring the inclusive mindset in Society.

Mission and Vision

My mission is to bring the community together regardless of race or ethnicity and create a world of equal opportunity for all to give the opportunity "by people and for people of the community", and to connect globally with like-minded people who want to build the harmonious community together.

Starting from Scratch

Singapore has been a city of dreams. My move here was ecstatic. However, as it was the first time settling into a new culture with a different language to become part of the society or to even be an entrepreneur, it was not a cakewalk. To engage with the community and be part of their culture, I started volunteering with a grass root organization and non-profit organizations like the Breast Cancer Foundation where I could use my health skills as well as my passion to network with more people. BollyOne company was born out of a desire to give a platform to the people residing in the community, to participate in cultural events, and to inculcate an inclusive mindset. BollyOne started with Dance and Yoga classes and has its recognition among various age groups-including students from schools. I found a foothold with common Language like English to connect with people and by emceeing in the Community center events started building my network. While eagerness to support each other bonded all, the non- English speakers also joined hands as I made space for each one of them by learning a few words of mandarin and other languages, using them in my daily conversations.

Big Why
You can Do It

A zeal to convert the challenges into opportunities and getting inspiration from leaders and people around me to name a few–Mr. Lim Biow Chuan, Tin Pei Ling, and Caroline Makaka-motivated me. These amazing leaders from politics to philanthropy each one had a lesson to share. Remember to believe and trust in yourself; it will help you to bounce back from any challenge of life. A spirit of #Youcandoit is something that I tell myself and also people around me.

If you desire earnestly, it will surely come true. If you take that initial step with the zeal of "I can do it",it will not only help you to move forward but also act as a north star to people around you.

Aha Moment Epiphany
Hand in Hand

I started volunteering in my Condominium functions for Diwali celebrations. An opportunity fell straight in hands for a women's international dance competition. BollyOne Company was born with my vested interest in Bollywood and went on the stage with friends in Singapore, and then there was no looking back. From 'yoga' which started as a passion for good health for kids around me, it developed into community Yoga classes with BollyOne. If you find that 'Aha' moment in life, chase your dreams. Take those risks on your belief and plan for your business moment. Have a mentor who can guide you through that moment to achieve your vision.

Secret Formula
World is Oasis

My secret formula is networking and mobilizing people towards their goals in life. In my success story that took shape in the community center, people got connected to BollyOne through Community participation. Different dance performances from

children to adults within the community became part of BollyOne to bring the performances 'for the community, by the community'. BollyOne spread its wings outreaching students from various schools who trained for the dance competitions. The words spread like fire with more and more people getting engaged and inspired to be part of BollyOne. Remember to identify what your hidden strength builds on and work on your blind spots. Once you have decided on what you are most passionate about and charted out a plan for your future endeavors, time will add wind to your wings.

Steps to Build Success from Scratch

Brick by brick BollyOne was built from the Community lens by giving free classes to the residents of the community and slowly moving to minimal competition and lesson fees. Using various communication and social platforms like 'Radio Masti- A radio station', other TV channels, and making a partnership with other event makers – got the BollyOne into business.

Step 1: Get yourself registered as a business of your interest.
Step 2: Explore the competitive landscape on what are the best service providers of similar nature.
Step 3: Have a clear objective in mind what, why, and how you want to achieve
Step 4: Learn it from the masters or have an experienced mentor who can guide you to establish the nascent steps.
Step 5: Use digital, social, and event platforms for networking, and communication with your focus, availability, and commitment to providing quality work.
Step 6: Embrace your failures and share your success.
Step 7: Patience pays off.

With the above mantras of success steps, you certainly made a mark in your choice of work

First Sign of Success

The mantra of success remains to believe in yourself and work hard to achieve and partner or network with the right people. Don't shy away from communicating the benefits of your business while keeping it human.

When you are in business, it is important when you share the success mantra, and

keep the good company. While it was great to see that my business inspired friends around me to venture into similar business proposals, it also gave a glimpse of the few right people who owned your success, encouraged, and acknowledged the part you played in their success. These are the people whom you should keep close to and make part of your journey to a longer road to success. As the saying goes, "Alone we can do so little; together we can do so much". Events like Kids Charity Fiesta conducted by BollyOne-created a new platform 'For kids, by kids which attracted hundreds of children and parents attending and performing in the event. The event was graced by guests of honor from various fields – Politics, Education, and Philanthropist. As a beauty pageant winner, Preeti took BollyOne to a wider platform for outreach. Remember success is a journey, not a milestone or destination. Celebrate every learning as it is a true mark of success!

Ultimate Solution

My solution is to find more people through Community Center Events Participation with additional training and leadership preparing myself to give the best quality

solutions for the consumers. I keep an eye on the ongoing events to get visibility on the nature of business by participating or collaborating on the same. I developed my skills in public speaking by joining the toastmaster clubs and workplace events. With my role as a Grass

Root leader, every day has been a learning journey with people from every race who volunteer their precious time and effort above their day jobs to connect and engage in building a safe place to live. You have to decide how are you going to invest your time in developing the soft skills while nurturing your business acumen along the journey.

Free Gift

Here comes your free gift to turn your business into a success, the "gift of learning". Learn from your every mistake; don't get disheartened by your failures or others' success. Listen to success stories around you, celebrate failures, and take risks to explore the unknown. There is no problem, which doesn't have a solution. You are the only one who can discover and unravel the solutions to your every challenge while discussing, sharing, and taking action on it with the right set of friends and family.

Accolades and Achievements

Action speaks louder than words; my work towards women empowerment, and mentoring students, clients, and friends help me to be established as a better human being. I have been fortunate to have received the accolades such as Most Inspiring Women on Earth 2022, Sunshine of India 2022, and Best humanitarian 2021. While breaking the biases and experimenting to be better version of myself, I explored the unknown world of pageantry to win awards like Ms Personality 2013, Ms Courageous-Mrs. India Universe 2017, and Wonder
Woman 2018, paving the way to give a voice to the upliftment of minorities and women in various fields. This learning journey has just started, 'miles to go and illuminate the lives of
Many'!

See What They Are Saying...

"Thanks for your support, I am able to find my right path."
"Your guidance helped me to join a company of my choice."
"I owe my success to you."

Media Links

Preeti Kachroo. Age-based versus weight-based dosing or oral liquid paracetamol, potential for dosing errors in pediatric patients, "Asia Pacific Journal of Pediatrics and Child Health".

Link: http://www.apjpch.com/?page=apcp2018abstract&abstractnumber=1238
Preeti kachroo Bhagat. Practical Challenges—Use of Paracetamol in Children and Youth
Who are Overweight or Obese: A Narrative Review. Pediatric Drugs. Link:-
https://link.springer.com/article/10.1007/s40272-020-00417-z"
Preeti Kachroo Bhagat- Author, Speaker, Coach (facebook.com)
https://linktr.ee/preetikachroo

Cheryl Thibault
Mirage Spa Education, Inc.
Cobble Hill, British Columbia, Canada

Chapter 3
Beating Betrayal while Building Beauty

Cheryl Thibault is a true visionary, entrepreneur, educator, influencer, award-winning and best-selling author, and game-changer in the beauty industry. An assertive and uncompromising beauty professional for over 40 years.

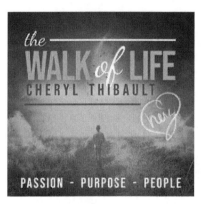

Cheryl's podcast called "THE WALK OF LIFE – Passion, Purpose, People" showcases not only her student's success stories but many amazing people as well - from all Walks Of Life.

Mission and Vision

Cheryl's mission is to foster a positive community of beauty professionals who aim high and strive to achieve a higher personal purpose and to help create a positive difference in the lives of others. Her vision is not only to help individuals visualize and achieve their dream but improve industry standards, as well as the public's perception of this very rewarding career. This is
what inspired her to write her Award Winning and #1 Best Selling book CAREER IN THE BEAUTY INDUSTRY - DISCOVER IF IT'S FOR YOU.

Starting from Scratch
Thieves are too often trusted – Betrayal is the worst form of Theft

I recognized the need for Esthetic Training in my city, so as a young and inexperienced single mom of two, I took it upon myself to create a school to offer this career choice to others. I had the only Esthetics school, it was as though it was an overnight success, and it didn't take long for enrollment to reach full capacity. I had a 3-year wait list. I needed help! I hired a makeup artist who would also act as my administrative assistant. During this same time, I was also preparing to relocate the school to a beautiful new location.

Beating Betrayal while Building Beauty

I came to learn that my assistant secretly met with the students and had convinced them to believe neither I nor my school was credible and persuaded them to quit my school and follow her to her new school. I discovered she had been secretly photocopying all my clients as well as my current and future student's files. Her goal was to open a school of her own with the intent to bankrupt me. She and all my students walked out, and the students demanded a full tuition refund.

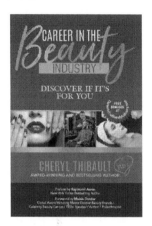

A massive loss of this degree was certain to set me back significantly. She did partially succeed in her covert takeover; she did open a competitive school. Somehow, she also managed to secretly acquire my future location. I had an amazing realtor; he found me a better location than the one I had lost.

My students soon caught onto the deceit and underhandedness of her scheme, and they all returned to my new location to complete their course.

It was an enormous setback, and at the time I questioned whether I should continue. I want to share that what I was living through was one of the most difficult times of my life. Not only did I almost lose my business, I was also in a terribly abusive personal relationship and my daughter was hit head-on by a truck while crossing the street. She had broken bones in her neck and lost several teeth, we were not sure if she would walk again as she was suffering from internal damage. With endless faith and support, she was blessed with a miracle and fully recovered - only a few minor scars remain.

I honestly did not know how I was going to make it through. The stress seemed unbearable. Nevertheless, I persisted. I kept my faith and drew from the strength of my higher power. I believed if I was given the dream, it was mine, and no one could take it, and that my daughter would be fine. I got busy contacting my clients and future students. Fighting to survive - I put on my warrior clothes and went to battle offering incentives and whatever I could to build back the business. Pushing through the sheer exhaustion of each day. The business continued to grow. I did succeed once again.

That experience was traumatic and life changing. I was scarred so deeply that I was unable to trust anyone or put them in an authoritative role in my life for over 35 years. I built my companies single-handedly because of this mistrust.

I buried the memories to dull the pain and never wanted to face it again. It wasn't until I entered my 60s that I came to realize these pressed down and hidden emotions were only working against me. I am thrilled to now stand tall and feel proud of my accomplishments. I have a very loyal team working alongside me and together we face the future.

My company has grown from near bankruptcy to International. We have students all over the world taking our courses.

ONLY because no matter what… I didn't give up on my dream.

I DID NOT QUIT!

My BIG WHY.
Quitting was NOT an option!

Being bruised but not broken, I persevered through all this chaos when others would have quit. I had made an obligation to others; they depended on me to provide them with an education so they could attain their career and fulfill their dream. Additionally, I had two children to feed and bills to pay. Quitting was NOT an option.

I pressed on. It was ingrained in me from my parents that when you give your word, you keep your word NO MATTER WHAT!

Aha Moment Epiphany
See the BIG Picture: You CAN do it!

Let's go back to how this all began. There was no Professional Trade School in the beauty industry where I lived so I had no option but to leave my children with my parents and move to another province 400 miles away to attend school. Relocating was one of the toughest decisions I'd ever had to make at that time of my life. I knew in the grand scheme of things, it would, in time, not seem so traumatic. I never wanted another parent to experience the heartache of leaving their children and their support system so they could attain their careers. I put the wheels in motion to solve this problem and opened the FIRST Professional Esthetics School in my province.

Secret Formula
Never Stop Working Towards Your Dream – Make the Changes as Needed

Mirage Spa Education Inc. is the First and Only 100% Fully Registered totally Online Beauty School in the industry that I know of to date. It operated as a regular brick-and-mortar school with a physical address. The students performed Esthetic Services on clients. The business was very successful; we had won Best in the City three times.

Then, I was in a tragic motorcycle accident. Being confined to a wheelchair for almost a full year resulted in the loss of my largest location. Remembering the pain from decades earlier I knew I would make it through, I just needed a new game plan.

Realizing the advancements in technology, with the introduction of the internet, and needing to save what business remained, I knew it was time to reinvent my business and it was necessary to create a new delivery system that was accessible to all, everywhere. I launched the school on an online platform, and today we are an international company that continues to grow and help others achieve their dreams. Our students can access their training anywhere in the world. I have fallen and crawled back up again so many times, not only in business but in my personal life as well.

I have coined the phrase "Life is an Endless Beginning - so live with Passion and Purpose" Every day we start again.

Steps to Build Success from Scratch

1. Find your passion. It is imperative to truly know in your heart what your goal, desire, or purpose is. If you love what you do, you will never work a day in your life. Your motivation will pull you toward your goal. If you are not passionate about your dream, nothing will be enough to help you achieve it.
2. Find a personal mentor/coach or join a support group to encourage you through the hurdles you will face. You will also need a business mentor who can help with legal and professional advice.
3. GRATITUDE. Always be grateful for what you have, even the smallest things. Recognition of others goes a long way as well.
4. MOST important of all.... NEVER GIVE UP ON YOUR DREAM

First Sign of Success

My first sign of success was opening day. Everything was perfect and ready to open the doors to receive my first students. My family and friends were there to support and celebrate with me. I have been blessed with amazing friends who have stuck by me through every win and every setback. Their love, support, encouragement, and belief in me kept me strong even when I thought there was no hope. I realized I was making a difference when I could see the positive changes in the lives of the students and their families. This is still what motivates me to this day.

Ultimate Solution

I realized early on that I needed the assistance of professionals. I joined networking groups and attended business events where I put myself in the presence of the professionals I sought. Was I nervous? You bet I was. I was also smart enough to know we don't know everything about everything – it is imperative to find mentors.

Free Gift

In my 41 years as director of a school, I have come to realize the concerns potential students face when deciding on a career path. The choices are many. I have written a FREE e-book called "From Setback to Success; Is a career in the Beauty Industry your answer to Safety, Sustainability, and Job Security?"

This book summarizes the many jobs in the beauty industry and will guide you on your best career choice.

I invite you to go to MissCheryl.com to get your copy today.

Accolades and Achievements

My business achievements include a TV documentary entitled "Making Your Dreams Come True" and I was featured on a book cover "Starting a Business in Saskatchewan". In 2022 I was nominated for the Small Business BC Award and for Teacher of the Year. I am a Recipient of the 2022-100 Successful Women in Business Award. I have received the award for "Impact and Innovation in the Beauty Industry" for writing my #1 Best Selling Book "CAREER IN THE BEAUTY INDUSTRY - DISCOVER IF IT'S FOR YOU." I am a featured guest on many podcasts and shows, and I invite you to my personal website MissCheryl.com to access all the issues.

See What They Are Saying...

Problem: A single mom struggling her entire life as a victim of unfortunate circumstances, desperately wanting to create a better life for herself and her son.

Solution: Mirage Spa Education Inc. offered a professional career course providing the opportunity and support to encourage her and help change her life through mentorship and friendship.

Result: For the first time in her life, she believed in herself and found a sense of accomplishment and self-worth, having become a successful working woman who was able to put her son through college.

Alicia M. - Canada

***

Problem: An educated woman is being held back in her career due to physical disability, and no option to attend a regular school due to financial constraints.

Solution: Was able to study from home through Mirage Spa Education Inc. at her own pace while maintaining her current job.

Result: Graduated with confidence, recognized diploma in hand and was able to make money to help her family while working from home.

Nancy M. - Canada

***

Problem: No accredited school in her area and no ability to leave home to study due to family obligations.

Solution: Mirage Spa Education Inc's online platform offered convenience and flexibility to study when time allowed.

Result: Self-employed and loves her new career. So grateful to have found this course.

Danielle F. Canada

***

"I learned that courage was not the absence of fear, but the triumph over it. The brave man is not he who does not feel afraid, but he who conquers that fear." –

Nelson Mandela

Media Links

https://www.flipsnack.com/yoursuccessmagazine/november-21-your-success-magazine/full-view.html?fbclid=IwAR1IeIg_kij3N7D-X2BLPMRJLhpnZT81QDZo1TiXUeMCEmyuUDrStCC4jCl
"

"Life is an endless beginning, live with Passion and Purpose - Keep Creating."
- Cheryl Thibault

www.misscheryl.com
https://www.instagram.com/cherylthibault1/
https://www.facebook.com/cheryltbo

www.miragespa.ca
https://www.instagram.com/miragespaeducation/
https://www.facebook.com/miragespaonlineeducation

Mimi Mala
Peace on the Streets Radio
Orlando, Florida, USA
Peaceonthestreetsradio@aol.com

Chapter 4
Become the Voice of Women

Mimi Mala is an American broadcaster and Owner of the music radio show "Peace on The Streets Radio" on WOKB which provides others a platform of opportunities. She's able to stay focused on assisting nonprofit organizations, and local, and small business / independent talents. She has been honored as "Best Host," "Most Influential Women of Orlando," and "100 Successful Women in Business" ---three Stellar Awards in a row and is currently nominated for her fourth. She has ownership of her broadcasting and media productions radio show remaining independent on a mainstream broadcasting station, Peace on The Streets Radio. Tune in every Wednesday 9pm-12am EST on radio 1680am/109.7fm or website WOKBRADIO.COM Mimimala.com

Mission and Vision

Mimi's mission is to create a movement for women who are working and have children who need to reinvent themselves by creating a business and to help them become empowered in the media.

Finding my Purpose

Are you employed in the corporate world and feel stuck? Do you have children and can't seem to balance work and family? About 9.8 million working women experience burnout in the U.S. because they have to juggle child-care, doctor appointments, and work. Burnout happens because of the lack of support. It is not your fault that you feel like this.

I was in corporate since I was 18 years old. I witnessed how women have been harassed, abused, and misunderstood. Many employers don't seem to understand mothers or mothers-to-be. It was very discouraging when I was pregnant with my twins. As a working woman being pregnant, I faced burnout and professional impact. Working moms face challenges in terms of feeling pressured not to miss work when having to schedule doctor appointments. It is extremely difficult to return to work especially after having children. We are forced to take a break after giving birth. Because of the lack of flexibility, many women try to negotiate flexible work arrangements with their employees.

Starting from Scratch and Big Why
Motherhood Matters

I was one of those women who struggled in the workplace because I was pregnant with twins. I ended up being hospitalized because of a c-section to have my twins. My employer didn't care what the doctors recommended. I had to reinvent myself. I set up my own business. I stayed home because the reality of motherhood kicked in. I know other women are experiencing burnout and coping to be a working mom.

I was expected to go back to work even if I was in intensive care at the hospital (NICU). I was let go from my job. I ended up suing them for the mistreatment and ended up winning the lawsuit. I have now become the voice for women and working moms. It is a movement to help moms release working-mom guilt. Stop beating yourself up. You have the right to be a woman and a mom and choose to be there for your children when they need you. During COVID-19 69% remained at home to become full-time caregivers, and only 39% decided to return to work within 12 months. If you are one of those women who decided to stay home and to start a business from scratch, you are not alone! I was able to stay home for three years without getting paid, but I was helping other women.

Aha Moment Epiphany
From Struggle in the Workplace to Finding My Voice

My aha moment took place when I had my twins. I had to reevaluate my priorities. One day I was coming back from a doctor's appointment; my manager came directly to my car and knocked on the car window and said, "Come in now". This was a horrible experience with lots of pressure that many mothers and I have to deal with.

Starting my business and staying home with my twins was the best thing that ever happened to me! I made it into something larger than myself and successful. I never said, "Why me?". I've always said, "I'm ready!" I love facing a challenge and making a change. I created my own business so I could control our atmosphere. Don't get me wrong; my job helped me gain and shape me into who I am now. I was promoted so many times and have never been disciplined as much as when I was pregnant. At the time, I couldn't believe this was happening to me. It does happen. I felt America didn't support pregnant women and families. We are supposed to make our kids stronger so now I have a movement for pregnant women.

Corporate would not cater to families with being threatened to come back to work in two weeks or you lose it isn't your job! I thought that was insane, going against doctors' orders. I did not return in their two-week frame, so I was fired. I ended up having a case and pursued legal charges and won for my family and me!

35

Secret Formula
Become the Voice

First, I serve God and women to help them find their voice so they can stand up for their motherhood rights. I not only help women but those individuals looking for their voice. I reinvented a workplace for mothers. I give people a voice by giving them a platform. My desire is for women to be empowered to impact their families. We have 80,000 listeners, so big definitely retaining more clientele. A few people have been published due to being on the radio. A couple of people have been investors, sponsors, and clientele published. It's all about exposing their work. There are so many connections out there, so they are going to gain something when they come on the radio show. Even our interns can benefit by gaining clientele because of working with these professional people and guests and getting hired by these people.

God has given you a gift; no one can take that from you!

I have created a workplace for women where the feedback I receive from women is that they feel safe and secure in a peaceful environment. I work with interns from the ages of /18 to adults in broadcasting. The people are very thankful. I serve the people on the show to give them a voice, so they have been able to broadcast freely. Whatever their gift is, they're empowering themselves and their family.

If they want to advertise their work? Of course, Apple pays for that. That's an advertisement for casting to Google ads. If they want to go on a live interview, those things are paid. If they want to work like they have to pay for that then the PCs like everybody else does. as right as they want to work for us that we hire. So, we get paid to work because we're independent. We're independent of LLC, so we're all owned companies. So, anybody that we've worked with, we've worked so we get paid, traveling gigs on the way, and tons, of course, are freaking that coming from college. Okay, so I started my business ever since I started so it was a production company. And I just started networking, collaborating, and going to events and doing it myself by casting, sneaking, interviewing, and doing a lot of highlights in the city and that's what I get recognized for by producing and doing highlights in the city for different events, nonprofit organizations.

Finally, we suggest networking, respecting others, and never being afraid to collaborate.

Steps to Build Success from Scratch
Reinvent Yourself and your workplace

You can find a career or job that is flexible with you raising your kids or you can create your own business. Make sure you take your power back. Working full-time and being a mom is not easy, but it is such a blessing. I highly recommend that you take time for personal growth. You are an inspiration even if you have to hold a job or own a business, manage family life, and raise a family. How do you do it all with only 24 hours in a day?

- Love what you do
- Find a support network
- Know your limits
- Reinvent your own workplace
- Be authentic
- Find a mentor (someone stronger and more successful than yourself)
- Enjoy your children and create special moments with them

First Sign of Success

Winning my 3rd Stellar Award
Our ratings, social media accounts, and audience have risen to
over 80,000 listeners "I knew that I had something special in me when I was
winning awards on a Spanish station that was an internet station, when we went on
to get an FM station, and when I started winning awards for producing.

Ultimate Solution

When you have children, your world may seem to change. You might feel stressed
and experience burnout. I give women an ultimate solution by giving them a
platform to shine. I help my clients to turn their message into profit. With
broadcasting, you literally have a direct line straight into people's ears. You can
grab their attention through this medium by creating authority. I put women on my
platform to help them build equity in their brand and
attract new followers. Each person that comes to me is different. I listen to the
needs and create a unique package for each person so he/she can shine on my
broadcasting platform. I help create the buzz needed for the business.

My advice is to surround yourself with individuals like yourself or platforms larger
than yourself.

Free Offer

Collaborate with me. I will expose your brand, idea, mission, your change! We give
out free consultations for 30 minutes.

We discuss whatever you want to expose. Everybody is different, and every gift is
unique. I want to know who you're trying to target, and then we can make it happen
for you. I open up these side gigs that help you survive and get paid, and it
consists beyond the broadcast.

Accolades and Achievements

I love what I do and love my family. The passion and courage to stand up for what I
want and believe have led me to several awards and recognitions. I am proud to be
me and honored to be a mother which is the biggest award and accomplishment of
my life which is motherhood. The following awards are also a blessing:
☐3X Stellar Award Winner
☐100 successful women in business
☐Most Influential
☐Best host

☐Best radio show
☐Cover of Latin Connection Magazine
☐Published 9X
☐Title winner Ms. Teen
☐Title winner Ms. Pre-Teen
☐Ambassador
☐Published Model
☐IMDb credited Actress
☐Cover and spread on VIBEONE Magazine
☐ Running for Crown Title Ms. International World / Ms. Latina International -
Puerto Rico ☐☐
Own Muriel display in the City of Orlando

My future goal is to own my own broadcasting station. I am the Brand Ambassador
for Genius, a common movement.   - Bruce George Co-founder of Def poetry jam
on HBO
   • Chief Officer of Media Content and Broadcasting for Radio & TV
Entertainment

Owner Of "Peace On The Streets Radio on WOKB, Orlando 1680am / 100.7 Fm
Kissimmee. Fl.
Broadcasting and Media Productions
Airs every Wednesday 9-12 am Est
WOKBRADIO.COM

- Registered Bilingual Reporter" I have helped other women in business receive
more clientele. "Cover and spread on VIBEONE Magazine

See What They Are Saying...

Glenn Allgood
Mimi "...can expand her mind and cannot hold her down.

DJ Prince of the South
Mimi is a gem of light that you can feel her energy immediately.

Ms. Angela Posillico
CEO Miss International World
Mimi is a firecracker.

Learn more at

https://www.facebook.com/MimiMala4
**https://www.linkedin.com/in/mimi-mala-%F0%9F%8E%A7%F0%9F%8E%A4-
09b1a110b/**

Madeleine P. Wober
America's Scottish Sparkle/ Intuitive Healer
Austin, TX
maddiewober@gmail.com

Chapter 5
Believe It Before You See It

Have you ever dreamed of reaching a goal but felt like it would take a miracle to make it happen!? Despite all my health adversities, I knew deep down inside that I could live a fulfilling and beautiful life if I could just rewire my brain to truly believe it! But how do we do that?

Madeleine P Wober (aka Maddie Sparkles, America's Scottish Sparkle) delivers sage wisdom with childlike enthusiasm connecting people to their Internal Light (& Guardian Angels). After 3 decades of medical setbacks including severe anxiety, depression, and panic attacks in her 20's, Ovarian Cancer in her 30's and diagnosed with MS in her 40's, she helps others to release their fears and step into their power so they can live a truly magical life by seeing the silver linings around every seeming obstacle.

Mission and Vision

My mission and vision is to help people release their fears and step into their power so they can live a truly magical life by seeing the silver linings around every seeming obstacle.

Beginning from Scratch ...

Growing up in Glasgow, Scotland, watching Charlie's Angels, Magnum PI, and Fantasy Island on TV as a child, I always dreamed of living in the USA. I didn't realize it, but I was manifesting my future dream from the age of 10!

With a colorful career, I began as a Beauty Therapist working in all the top Hotels & Spas in London, as an aesthetician to celebrities. Later I worked in a private family photography studio selling high ticket packages to many international HNWI's including royalty and sports personalities. I landed many sales and marketing jobs over the years due to my love of building meaningful rapport with people. I traveled all over the world and became a life coach - always truly wanting to help inspire and uplift others.

The Wake-Up Call

I was on top of the world. Life was great. I had gotten myself into a University in Manchester, England, and I was just beginning my new life! Then out of the blue, I had a huge panic attack and fell to the ground in an uncontrollable body spasm. I had no idea why this had happened, but shortly after I realized that it was a giant wake-up call for me to get very honest with myself and what I truly wanted to be doing with my life, rather than what I thought everyone else wanted for me. This struggle became a blessing - because over the years it made me truly listen to what my heart and soul desired and know the right path to take based on what my body was telling me. I was always drawn to helping others and this early incident in my 20's led me years later to create the business I am in today! During this period in my 20's, I had to pay attention to every thought, and challenge it so I could learn to rewire my brain from chronic fear of anxiety and irrational thinking to living a life of freedom. In other words, the traumatic experiences I encountered with my health, beginning in my 20's and stretching over the next two decades including Ovarian Cancer in my 30's and MS in my 40's took me on a path of immense gratitude for my body that I had completely overlooked in my teenage years and during my 20's. I began to tune in, and really listen, using my body as an internal compass and direct connection to my feelings about my life and the things I was participating in, at any given moment. I learned that although my body is temporary, it is the body I have been gifted with this lifetime, and if I treat it well and with loving kindness, it can give me the strength, courage, and invincibility I will always need to get me through any situation. Combining my intuition and healing abilities through voice with spirituality became my superpower.

Big Why
The Intuitive Healer Calling

I found myself working in the video game industry for the five years leading up to the Pandemic, and now, at age 50, I am an Intuitive Healer (working with the angels & spirit guides), Voice Actor, Inspirational Poet, & Transformational Empowerment Coach. My extensive background in Sales and Marketing has been an immense help for my business since almost every business works on relationships, referrals, and repeat business, but it wasn't always easy

DESIRE, IMAGINE, EXPECT has been my mantra for a very long time. No matter what the situation, I knew intrinsically I could master it with enough determination, belief in myself, and then
letting go of any attachment to the outcome. Trusting in what is for me won't go by me. You too must listen to your intuition to help you make better decisions in life.

Aha Moments
EXCITEMENT, JOY, AND FREEDOM

I wanted to live a life of Freedom and Adventure! I wanted to travel the world, and I wasn't about to let my physical body, or my limiting mindset stop me from experiencing life to the max. If I could overcome my crippling fear of heights by bungee jumping in New Zealand and Skydiving in Australia, I would go above and beyond to prove to myself I could do anything I set my mind to.

PURPOSE, PERMISSION AND TRUST
During the Pandemic. I wanted to find a way to share positive energy, and help others feel more uplifted and less alone. I asked myself, "What can I do with the innate gifts and skills that I have, to make a real difference in people's lives at this time?" Following your purpose, giving yourself permission to live a life of freedom

and adventure is your choice, and you must trust your intuitive guiding system. I did! Now, I am helping many with Intuitive coaching and Angel Readings combined.

Secret Formula
Messages from My Guardian Angel

The answer came from my Guardian Angel. My Guardian Angel told me, "Combine all your skills from Coaching and Corporate relations, with your love of Spirituality, and offer Angel readings for people". For many years I had been connecting with and guided by the angels, although I didn't discuss this with anyone.

The messages that come through during the Angel/Oracle card readings are always spot on. My global clients are constantly sharing wonderful, humbling testimonials online, which has led to the MADDIE SPARKLES brand, and website, having a much bigger platform than I ever thought possible. I keep introducing new Oracle decks into my readings. I started with 2 decks of cards and now I have 43! Due to the numerous podcasts, television interviews, magazine articles, and my online presence on Facebook and Instagram, I have been extremely fortunate to attract an incredible international clientele, many of whom are now regulars. My online course "Guardian Angel At Your Service" has helped many people feel more connected to a power higher than themselves and the feedback has been from many that it has changed their life for the better, knowing they are divinely guided and never have to feel alone.

Steps to Success
PASSION, FAITH, AND COMMITMENT

Here are the 4 steps I took to build my business from scratch:
1. Being my authentic self
2. Doing the things, I love to do with sincere Gratitude
3. Walk the talk
4. Being of service

It is extremely important to ask for help or get a mentor for 3 reasons:
1. Two minds are better than one
2. It is truly humbling asking another human being for help, in addition, this gives them a gift
3. We each have a Guardian Angel who only wants our highest good and will always support and guide us, but only if we ask it to.

First Signs of Success

Success is having a positive outlook no matter what cards you have been dealt. It is about seeing the silver linings in every seeming obstacle and bringing good energy to everyone who crosses your path.

My dream manifested. I was sponsored by a promotional company as VP of International & Domestic New Business Development where I secured numerous multi-million-dollar projects within the Video Game industry. This earned me my green card. I stayed for 5 years and left a month before the Pandemic began. With all of my corporate experience in a fast-paced, booming industry, I developed the innate wisdom of what true rapport with others looks like in the business world.

When I pivoted from the corporate world to my own spiritual path, the first sign of success was the response from my post on Facebook, offering my Angel readings. It was a true risk at the
time, not knowing if I could do this with complete strangers, but as the requests came in, the risk I had taken putting myself out there was a dream come true and immense relief. I felt that I was truly living my purpose and everything I had experienced in my life up until that point, the good, the bad, and the ugly, was illuminated and everything felt right. I knew I was exactly where I was meant to be. When my first client shared with me what immense support they felt and how much clearer they were in their mind and heart about their own purpose, this brought tears to my eyes. I was able to help others doing what felt 100% natural to me.

Ultimate Solution

My path to finding the ultimate solution for myself and my clients was life itself. I was constantly asking, what is life trying to teach me right now? My angels guided me to find the solution, and this was facilitated by my own dedication to my morning meditation practice. I always had a life and/or business coach, and was always embarking on some sort of training, workshop, retreat, watching ted talks, and learning from the masters like Tony Robbins - all throughout my life and continue to do so today. 'Abraham Hicks' is also a big resource for me.

Free Offer
LOVE, LEARN, AND LIVE

My free gift to you, my dear reader, is to experience a 30-minute Angel reading for yourself!

This will reveal many truths for you with gentle guidance and loving care from your healing team of angels, so you can connect with your internal light, feel divinely guided, and live a more
magical life of manifestation and abundance. Take action now - this offer is valid until December 31, 2022. Visit www.maddiesparkles.com for more information and sign up for my online course "Guardian Angel At Your Service" to deepen your experience of your true Self.
https://bit.ly/maddieangelcourse

Accolades and Achievements

I have loved being interviewed on ABC, NBC, and FOX and being able to share my own angel experiences, as well as what it felt like to pivot from the classic corporate world into the heart space of healing and helping others in a profound spiritual way during the Pandemic.

I also thoroughly enjoyed being an Executive Contributor for "Brainz Magazine" and writing articles for "Authority Magazine" and "Thrive Global". This led me to collaborate on various podcasts with other thought leaders and spiritual activists in making the world a better place for us all It was an honor to be awarded a number of times through WOHA in 2021 (Woman of Heart Award) for Diversity and Inclusion and being of service to women globally, helping to lift their spirits and create possibilities for them to believe in their own self-worth.

See What They Are Saying...

"If anyone is even slightly curious about Maddie Sparkles Angel Readings - book in for one now!! I've never done anything like it before, so didn't know what to expect but came with an open mind and heart, but if I'm honest, I secretly hoped that I'd get a little nod for something I've been wanting for such a long time. All I can say is wow wow wow! My cheeks hurt from smiling so much and I'm so excited about what's to come! Hearing Madeleine pass on messages from the angels, acknowledging what is in my heart, and then hearing particular keywords that no-one else would know about, truly resonated with me (and gave me goosebumps). It was both calming and uplifting, and I'm taking it as more proof I'm on the right journey. I will definitely be looking through the photos of the cards and listening to the recording again, to make sure I take on board ALL the messages I received today"
(Tracy, LA, USA)
***

"Thank you, Maddie Sparkles, for your card reading yesterday. You helped me in such a loving way to get clarity on a specific issue, lifted my focus to a much higher level and your wisdom and intuition helped me see my path from here. You truly have a gift to heal the world. Love to you from Malue, Denmark, Europe"
***

"Maddie is simply amazing. I have had several angel readings with her now over the past year, and the guidance I receive from these always leaves me feeling uplifted, inspired, loved, and ready for the next phase. How she reads the cards is unlike anyone else I know. Her insight and intuition are off the charts and listening to her offer her wisdom as it relates to my personal situation truly feels magical. The way she describes the cards, and then how she describes what she sees, and the guiding questions she asks, brings me to the understanding I was seeking and the encouragement to expand my spiritual growth. She leaves me feeling positive and surer of myself and the path I'm on. - If you are seeking encouragement, guidance, more magic, or light in your life, I would highly recommend scheduling time with Maddie. You will be so glad you did. ~ Thank you again, Maddie. I feel blessed to have met you, and can't wait for the next time I can do another reading with you" (Kelly, CA)
***

Dr. Randi D. Ward
Randi D. Ward, Author, Coach, Editor
Lawrenceville, Georgia, USA
randiteach@yahoo.com

Chapter 6
Believe! Don't Dream Big; Dream BIGGER!

Dr. Randi D. Ward is an Educator, Book Coach/Master Editor, Editor of 3 magazines, International Speaker, Best-Selling Author, Student Mentor, World Traveler, Multi-Award Recipient, World Peace Forest (Africa) Honorary President, and ANC USA Director.

Mission and Vision

As a Book Coach and Master Editor, her Mission for her clients is to help people write their inspirational stories and then edit them to make them as appealing and grammatically correct as possible. Her Vision for her company is to provide excellent services for her clients and build a solid and large client base over the next five years that includes numerous best-selling books and successful authors.

Starting from Scratch
Success, Grief/Loss, Rejuvenation

For the first 37+ years of my career, I was an American/Egyptian Language Arts and ESOL educator. After retiring from teaching in 2012, I became an author with my first memoir on my life in Egypt as a teacher during the 2011-12 revolution. I now write in all genres, except drama. Life was great. I had experienced two successful careers.

However, after the sudden, tragic death of my husband in December 2019, my grief temporarily severely affected my writing. Then COVID-19 shut down our world. Now totally alone and even more devastated, I needed to find a way out of my "slump" and depression. A Teleconference Call with a Coach on WPN became my God-given answer. From April thru July 1, I became certified in 4 coaching categories.

I then decided to begin Career #3 and start a new business at the age of 71 years. Since I had taught writing to many students, I chose to become a Visionary Book Writing Coach and a Master Editor. I began researching how to form my business and attract clients---things that were not part of my expertise. My life was rejuvenated. I love to keep reinventing myself.

Believe! Don't Dream Big; Dream BIGGER!

Big Why
Stories Inspire Others

Being a writer/storyteller, I believe everyone possesses his/her own unique stories that can inspire, teach, and help others facing similar situations. However, most people do not know how to write them. My dream/desire was to help them find their voices and give them the confidence to be open/genuine in telling their stories. COVID has been so devastating. I felt helping people write their stories could be therapeutic as it helped me once I started writing again.

Aha Moment Epiphany
Editor Book Rescue

My editing career was not an instant success even though I advertised. Patience was needed. However, my first job involved a brilliant lady---Dr. Sofie Nubani. We met on Facebook. Sofie had completed her 400+ page book entitled "Optimize Your Creative Mindset". She was stressed because she had a publishing deadline and had not received the final edited copy. I immediately agreed to help her and was able to edit her manuscript in the next intense 18 nonstop hours. She met her deadline. Her book became an Amazon International Best-Seller and got me the recognition I needed for future books.

Have you experienced your Aha Moment yet? If not, do not give up. It will happen. If you have, how did you feel? Did it make you work harder? I made a wise decision to offer this business service. My business is now soaring.

Secret Formula
Share Your Skills

Having taught writing and having evaluated thousands of student compositions, teaching writing skills and editing are easy processes for me. I encourage others to use the skills they possess and enjoy when creating their businesses. If you love what you do, success is easier to achieve and less stressful. Being active on social media and many business groups, my clients come from these groups and by word-of-mouth. I have created a YouTube Video on how to write a Short Story and have written several writing hints on my website www.randidward.com. I keep busy editing anthologies and books of individual authors. Two anthologies have become International Best-Sellers. Some men and women in the anthologies had never written their stories before. I guided them through this process via coaching techniques and my creativity for successful results.

Believe! Don't Dream Big; Dream BIGGER!

We need to think outside the box in our competitive business world. What creative techniques can you develop to bring that extra special attention needed to attract new clients and keep your current ones satisfied? Use technology. If technology is not your area of expertise, find people skilled in this area. No man is an island even in the business world. Sharing our skills is beneficial to everyone.

Steps to Build Success from Scratch

As an educator, the business world became a new adventure. I knew how to do these services but creating a business was the challenge. I had to change my mindset from working with teenagers/students to working with professional adults. Thus, my research began. My steps are unique to my Editing/Coaching Profession but possibly can be adapted to other businesses. They involve doing research, acquiring the needed knowledge, finding the correct mentors, advertising, and providing excellent client/customer service to ensure returning clients/customers. Make a PLAN and complete each step to the best of your ability.

1. Research the different editing options available and decide which ones to offer and learn from successful, established editors.
2. Check out advertisements posted by established editors and create your own.
3. Speak about your Coaching/Editing Business on appropriate platforms.
4. Ask for testimonials from satisfied clients to use for promotion.
5. Offer reasonable rates. Consider the client's financial situation.
6. Complete each manuscript in a timely manner but with complete concentration to every detail, offering needed suggestions. 100% Client Satisfaction is essential.

First Sign of Success
Believe! Dream BIGGER!

Dr. Sofie Nubani's book's success was a huge moment for my business followed by the other Best-Sellers. I will forever be grateful for the writers/publishers who entrusted me with their books. However, I realized additional success when I became the Editor-in-Chief of 100 *Successful Women in Business, Inspirations for Better Living, and Morocco Pens.* In the next few months, I will proudly be the Co-Owner and Editor-in-Chief of a new magazine *CMR Unlimited* with my partners Dr. Caroline Makaka and Chaudhry Masood Mahmood Bhalli. Also, my fiancé and I are creating a new business entitled RM Infinite---One Stop Possibilities.

My son Markus, the Art Director for *Readers Digest* in Germany, has always been my biggest supporter. My close friends and new business associates also are impressed with my skills, my work ethic, and my desire to help others. Client referrals have originated from them.

Believe! Don't Dream Big; Dream BIGGER!

Ultimate Solution
Reach for the Stars

When I start anything, I give it 100%. I believe in myself, dream bigger, work hard, and never give up unless I have no other option. My mother was my role model who taught me these life values. Also, my husband helped me to believe in myself. Sadly, my husband Bill and my mother are deceased, but I can still hear them "cheering" me in my head. I do not have a current mentor. I have become a mentor to others though and recommend using them to guide and encourage people in their personal and business journeys. We learn from the experts to help us from making avoidable mistakes. My life philosophy/copyrighted quote: "Believe! Don't dream big; dream BIGGER! The Sky is the Limit so reach for the Stars!"

Do you have a quote that inspires or directs your life as I do? In those rare frustrating moments, I refer to mine, and my soul and spirit are renewed. I once again BELIEVE anything is possible.

Free Gift

If you cannot start your story, I can help. You must share your incredible UNIQUE story. Readers NEED to get to know you—to be inspired by YOU!

Contact me at randiteach@yahoo.com for a 30-minute complimentary consultation phone/Zoom chat to get you started and visit my Social Media Platforms for inspiration.

Accolades and Achievements

I have received seven IAOTP awards: Top Inspirational Entrepreneur, Lifetime Achievement Award, Educator of the Decade, and Female Visionary of the Year. She was featured on the Reuters Times Square NYC billboard. She received Top 100 Registry Woman of the Year in Writing and Language Arts. She received a GIA Honorary Doctorate in Humanitarianism; a Nelson Mandela Medal of Honor; USA Presidential Lifetime Volunteer Service Achievement Award; two Beautiful Survivor Awards; Global Change Maker (LOANI); WAW Hall of Fame Award; 2020 "She Inspires Me" and 2022 SIMA Special Love Award; 2021 100 Most Successful Women; 2021 GSFE Humanitarian and 2021 Vision Builder Awards; Hoinser Inspirational Leader of Excellence; WOHA Selfless Servant; World Record of the Earth Inspirational Woman; Hoinser Top 20 Inspirational Women; HERA Award; World Records of the Universe Most Influential/Inspiring/Iconic Woman of the Universe.

Believe! Don't Dream Big; Dream BIGGER!

See What They Are Saying...

Thank you so much, Randi! The manuscript is so well edited. Again, I appreciate your hard work and will recommend you to others.
Teresa Palmer --- Finding Sanctuary in the Pandemic Age,
August 8, 2020
***

My Editor failed me. Then Randi, an earth angel, showed up to assist in the birthing of OYCM book one. What a blessing it is to have such a character and genuine soul like Randi. Thank You Randi for the bright light that you are☐
Dr. Sophie Nubani --- Optimizing Your Creative Mindset
(July 2020)
***

Randi D. Ward edited my first book. She uses her God given talents to guide you as she goes through your writings with a fine-tooth comb. She is dedicated and precise. I highly recommend her.
Stephanie L. Dolce, The *Ledger* (August 20, 2020)

Believe! Don't Dream Big; Dream BIGGER!

Books and Media

My other books include anthologies *Quarentina (2020)*; 2021 *Global Achievers, Vol. 1*; *Finding Joy in the Journey, Vol. 2*; *The Red Blazers*; *2021 Hoinser Queens Book; Hoinser 2022 Book; Expert World Leaders Book* plus numerous magazine articles. Featured with Co-Authors of *Finding Joy in the Journey,* she was once again on a Times Square NYC Billboard as well as one in Atlanta, GA.

Please visit my website.

Vaneese Johnson
The Boldness Coach
San Francisco, CA, USA
vaneese@theboldnesscoach.com

Chapter 7
Bold, Big & Bad

Vaneese Johnson, The Boldness Coach™, is a Global Leadership Coach, Keynote Speaker, Brand Strategist, and Author. She teaches, empowers, and challenges professional women to step into their Bold, Big & Bad ™ and up-level their career choices and successes with intention, ownership, and self-direction.

Mission and Vision

Her mission is to help women around the world develop the courage to live a life that is bold, big & bad (tm) with no permission needed.

Starting from Scratch
Heart-breaking, Disappointing, Life-changing

I was on top of the world before I got divorced. My business, my career, and life were great! Then one day, my then-husband said he wanted a divorce and I agreed. Out of the blue, I had to figure out what my life was going to look like after the divorce. How was I going to go from a two-income household in one of the most expensive places, the San Francisco Bay Area, to live in the United States. Imagine a sudden change in your lifestyle that you had no control over. The burning questions became "What am I going to do?" "How was I going to get over this major roadblock?" Just imagine for a moment what you loved the most, no longer loved you back. The rejection cuts deepest when it is someone intimately close to you. I had two choices; either, let this happen to me or for me. I chose to let this happen for me! This struggle became a blessing as out of this emotional and financial turmoil, I created The Boldness Coach ™. It's okay to start over.

My Big Why
Determination, Tenacity, and Resilience

It's interesting what a setback from rejection will do to your spirit. In that season of my life, I felt like I had to get my mind right as I needed to make a major shift in my life. My "WHY" became my need to set things right in my life, career, and my spirit. Determination became my energetic fuel for me to tap into my tenacity as I was about to embark on a major life journey. A sense of boldness developed in me as I had to be audacious and take a stand for who I was, what my talents were, and what I was capable of becoming. Resilience was needed as I was willing to withstand any future obstacles that arose from this one time period in my life. When you get clarity on your "Why" nothing can stop you from pressing forward.

Aha Moment
Clarity, Courage, and Creativity

I have been a full-time entrepreneur for more than 26 years. It has been a roller coaster ride, to say the least. Sometimes I focused on the bad times more than I did on the good ones. There were a lot of times of self-doubt, insecurity, and worry. But somehow, I always seemed to make it through what I thought was one of the worst instances. One day I  had just finished a session with my business coach, and she told me that I needed to give myself credit for being smart and intelligent. Smartness is practical with solutions (trying solutions out to see what works) and intelligence is a theory (using technical solutions, research, and tools to identify solutions). I always created, identified, or discovered a solution to my problems with little to minimal help. My "Aha Moment" was when I acknowledged my abilities to apply practical solutions supported by theory; then I became unstoppable with achieving my goals and solving problems. This led me to three words that I use whenever I feel like I am struggling to find a solution to my life's or business problems.

Clarity gives me the opportunity to be introspective and reflective to remind myself of what I am capable of achieving based on past experiences.

Courage allows me to rise above difficulty by tapping into my smartness and intelligence.

Creativity is where I get to use my imagination, experiences, and my story to design solutions, resources, and tools that will help to solve problems for me and the women I serve.

***

Secret Formula-
BOLD, BIG & BAD

It's a true statement that "you already have everything that you need inside of you." Another way to interpret this statement is that we all have a "Secret Formula" that is unique to our individual DNA. When used properly, it can change our lives and perhaps the lives of the people around us for the better. I discovered my "secret formula" over lunch one day with a friend and colleague. As I was unpacking how I had lost myself, crippled my business, and was suffering from low self-esteem (because of my divorce), she asked me who I would need to become to shift out of this state of being to create a new reality for myself.

Bold, Big & Bad

After mulling over her question, having moments of silence, and really digging deep for the right answer for me, I stated, " I need to be bold, big, and bad to live the life I truly felt like I deserved to live. Even though my "secret formula" sounds like a catchphrase, it has deep meaning. Becoming Out Loud Daily (BOLD) means owning the evolution of you every day in every way. We are in a

constant state of self-discovery and growth. When I owned that about myself, I brought fluidity to my life. It's important for me and you to give ourselves some grace on our growth journey. We were not designed to stay the same our entire lives. Building In Your Genius (BIG) is about me recognizing that I was born with at least one talent in me. If I identified and tapped into it to maximize it, then I could create exponential financial growth and change my life while bringing a positive impact to the lives of others. Blessed And Deserving (BAD) is recognizing that I was born to live a blessed life full of abundance. When I acknowledged my truth of being BAD, it put me in a state of gratitude for what's to come in my life. Being bold, big, and bad gave me a greater sense of purpose and excitement for the next phase in the journey of my life. Living in my bold, big, and bad helps me to tap into my resilience when necessary. In addition to living bold, big, and bad, I have three value foundational phrases that kick me into overdrive whenever doubt rears its head: Be unapologetic, be audacious, and trust the process!

Being **unapologetic** is understanding what level of boldness was required of me to overcome life's obstacles and not apologizing as I press forward, past negative people and old situations.

Being **audacious** is about showing a willingness to take surprisingly bold risks.

Trusting the process is knowing from the depth of my soul that everything, outside of my innate talents, God will provide for me as long as I just get started and keep going.

I am blessed to serve women in the 50+ age who are going through a life re-invention. I find clients through referrals, networking events, women empowerment events, speaking from stages, and social media. My coaching services help women to take a courageous stance in their lives to go after their dreams and live life on their own terms!

Steps to Build Success from Scratch
Self-Awareness Self-trust Self-Love Self-Direction

Becoming successful is less about technical abilities and more about willingness to self-examine to identify your mindset and personal values. When I started my first business at the tender age of 27, I had no formal entrepreneurial training, no college degree, and very little resources. I could have easily found excuses and reasons to never show up for my dreams. However, I took a simple

approach to get me mentally ready for boldly stepping into my dreams and building my success from scratch. *I am confident my simple steps to success will empower you to move boldly toward your dreams:*

Steps to Build Success from Scratch

1. Self-awareness-Take an account of what's happening in your life. Be honest with yourself that you are not living the life that you imagine for yourself.
2. Self-trust-Develop a sense of what is right and true for you. Accept and believe that you know what you know, and you can survive whatever comes your way.
3. Self-love-Develop a deep sense of this by creating healthy daily practices, showing respect for your well-being, and taking responsibility for your own happiness. Embrace all your past, present, and future self.
4. Self-direction-Develop a strong internal radar to determine what, when, and how certain things will unfold in your life. The unfolding would be through your internal spiritual connection and not from external influence.

Realizing, accepting, and knowing that success starts with me. I stood in my courage and took a stance in my boldness to live my dreams out loud!

First Sign of Success

My first sign of success was after I spoke at an event and sold out all of my products. I knew then I had knowledge and content that could help women. My spirit was so relieved as it felt like a confirmation that I was on the right track. I then successfully started producing women-empowerment events. I was supported by family, close friends, and a sisterhood community of other successful women entrepreneurs. It hasn't always been smooth sailing but remembering my first sign of success reminds me to keep going. Girl, keep going! Signs of success are waiting for you.

Ultimate Solution- 4 Critical Beliefs That Hold You Back From Living the Life You Deserve-eBook.
Mindset Shift-Checking Your Beliefs

Have you ever had a moment in your life when something major happened and it shook your confidence to the core? My divorce was that "incident" for me. It caused me to question everything I believed about me deserving and having an abundant life. Changing my mindset would be the key to moving forward.

I was able to achieve this by identifying critical beliefs that were holding me back! I thought to myself, what could be available to women around the world if I shared my "Ultimate Solution"? The answer is that women could change their lives and make a positive impact around the globe. My solution identified four critical beliefs that were holding me back and perhaps, most women, from living a life they deserve. I simplified my solution into an action eBook so you can jumpstart your success journey now. Download this FREE action eBook "4-Critical Beliefs That Hold Your Back from Living the Life You Deserve.

This eBook addresses the impact beliefs have on holding us back from achieving our goals. Unbeknownst to most of us, we are operating from belief systems in our lives that have been ingrained in us from cultural standards, "what is right" in other's eyes and what family says "we should be doing"; these beliefs could very well be the saboteurs that are keeping us from having increased joy, success, and fulfillment in areas of our life. This e-book will start you on a thought-provoking journey with questions and activities to support you into a journey of discovering what adopted beliefs may be negatively impacting your life.

Accolades and Achievements
My Glow Up is my Grow Up

Two of my greatest professional achievements have been to grow into this incredibly successful global businesswoman and to help women around the world become bold, big, and bad! My audience consistently teaches me and challenges me to become better at my craft of entrepreneurship through their growth and successes. The more they grow, the more I grow. My direct impact on the women I serve has been realized by them starting and scaling their businesses, supporting their families, and inspiring other emerging women entrepreneurs.

My efforts and contributions to women's success have been recognized as a recipient of numerous awards and certifications. I have been a two-time Global Awardee-Women of Excellence Award for creating and executing my self-funded global book release tour to four countries in eight weeks. I received the Madame CJ Walker-Entrepreneur of the Year award for my outstanding accomplishments as a black woman-owned business. My Supplier of the Year-Woman-Owned Business of the Year was awarded to my business for being an outstanding service provider to corporate companies.

My certifications as a Diversity, Equity, and Inclusion Consultant (DEI Consultant) confirm that I am certified to consult with businesses on developing and executing cultural inclusive programs for their workforce. As a Certified 360 Administrator and Facilitator, I use this assessment tool to help existing and emerging leaders to identify opportunities to evaluate performance and leadership readiness. Being a Certified Crucial Conversation Facilitator allows me to facilitate a discussion between two or more people where the stakes are high, opinions vary, and emotions run strong.

See What They Are Saying...

Vaneese is an inspirational resource for becoming the professional I wish to be. She offered valuable advice, easily implemented it, and encouraged me to be bold in my plan and action. This is helping me to take the important next steps to reach my goals! Thank you Vaneese! *Sue A.*

***

What I really appreciated about Vaneese and our session was not only did she take me step by step through a plan but I was given very actionable items that I could implement right away. After our session, I felt relieved because I had much more clarity about my career path. *Lisa L.*

***

She helped me create a vision plan, a mission statement and helped me develop my business brand. Most importantly, she kept me motivated and accountable throughout this intensive "teamwork". Vaneese has a gift for coaching. *Paula B.*

***

Bold, Big & Bad

Published Book: Boldisms-Disruptive Thoughts to Help You Live Bold, Big & Bad, 2018, The Brag Media Company-Logo, New York, London.

Contributor to Published Book: I Bared My Chest-21 Unstoppable Women Get NAKED! Chapter 8: Journey Into Boldness by Vaneese Johnson (pages 291-316), 2017, The Brag Media Company.

https://voices.berkeley.edu/extension/vaneese-johnson-has-your-back

Business Links
Learn more at
Linktr.ee/theboldnesscoach

Be sure to collect your FREE giveaway

Dr. Amber Ann Lyons
From Pain to Purpose, Inc.
Stone Mountain, Georgia, USA
alyons.frompain2purpose@gmail.co

Chapter 8
Building from Ground Zero, There's Nowhere But Up

Dr. Amber Ann Lyons is the CEO & Founder of From Pain To Purpose, Inc. She has become known for her authentic, loving spirit "*Queen of Smooches*", vibrant personality, and her fiery passion as a transformational speaker, domestic violence/teen dating violence, author, podcast host/producer, and global youth leader.

She diligently works with her Healing Pain Through The Arts Youth Program to help rebuild the village of support for our youth and create collaborative opportunities for them that will position them for leadership success.

Mission and Vision
Mission: To provide the resources, tools, and support in order to assist adults and youth with life transformation from past pain to living in their true purpose through Healing from the Inside Out!

Vision: To mobilize a global community of women, men, and youth who will work together and re-build the village, which is vital to the success of OUR upcoming generation of youth leaders by empowering their voices to impact this world positively.

Starting from Scratch
God Woke Me Up... It Was God!

From Pain To Purpose, Inc. is all GOD! Just because I was a woman of God serving in ministry for so many years and raising my children while doing my best to be a good wife, that didn't stop me from having to suffer many years in silence. Finally, after God Woke Me Up to realize that I needed to be Free to Stop the Scars that not only I was sustaining, but my children were... I GOT UP and had to go through the shame and embarrassment of being the talk of the church because of a failed marriage. After seeking help, getting counseling for a year and an additional year and a half with my son. What was my next step? Volunteering to help others and from my spirit of humility to serve; the assignment of becoming a Domestic Violence Advocate was presented to me and That's when I knew that God had BIGGER PLANS... AHA! He birthed my Non-Profit Organization within me.

Big Why
When Your Why is Not Just About You

They Suffered Enough! My Why that kept me moving forward in the midst of chaos and many life challenges were my 3 Children: NaQwanna, Janelle, and Emmanuel. They had seen me suffer for so many years in an unhealthy marriage, and they suffered as well. I had to somehow begin the healing process for myself and my children. Although my oldest daughter had been away for college and then remained in Atlanta after graduating, they were my motivation! Many times, we cannot do what we need to do for ourselves, so if that is you, do it for your children… but, ultimately, it should be for YOU! You must heal and forgive those who hurt you or caused you pain… BEFORE YOU CAN EMBRACE YOUR WHY!

So, let me ask you… Have you found your WHY? Do you know Why you were called or assigned to do whatever it is that you know within your soul is the reason that God put you on this earth for? If not, What is Stopping You? Begin to seek, pray, and move forward to find out your WHY! When you find your Why, contact me and let me know… I will be waiting to hear all about your journey! If you do already know your WHY… let me ask you… Are you walking in it? Are you fulfilling your purpose? If not, What or Who is standing in your way? Tomorrow is Not Promised, so LET'S GO!!!

Aha Moment Epiphany
From Victim to Survivor to THRIVER

It Was God! From Pain To Purpose, Inc. is all GOD! After Volunteering to help others and from my spirit of humility to serve; the assignment of becoming a Domestic Violence Advocate was presented to me and that's when I knew that God had BIGGER PLANS… AHA! He birthed my Non-Profit Organization within me. I can literally remember the exact moment when I was on a plane coming back to New York and God showed me in the spirit that I needed to WAKE UP! I was allowing my relationship with God to keep me bound in an unhealthy marriage because I did not want to be divorced… for the 2nd

time. I really wanted my marriage to work, but there is a saying: God is trying to break you away from what you are trying to hold on to. God knew that I was dying inside, and my children were suffering as well. But, most of all, God had a plan to take me From Pain To Purpose and use what I experienced to help so many others. God took me from victim to survivor to THRIVER! What I went through was never about me, but those to whom God assigned me to minister.

Secret Formula
Lead with Love!

The Queen of Smooches is all about spreading the Love of God to everyone who crosses my path and most especially those people who have been clients, and those who I have partnered and collaborated in business with. I have a saying "People don't care how much you know, until they know how much you care." It is with the love of God shown through you that allows people to know that they can trust you as a leader in business or life PERIOD!

Building from Ground Zero, There's Nowhere But Up

Being a Domestic Violence & Teen Dating Violence Advocate and Global Youth Leader, I serve Women, Men, Youth, & Young Adults. Many of my clients have been referred to me pre-pandemic, and now many are connected via the global world-wide-web (i.e., social media) Lol! The focus

of assisting people to transform and transition from their years of pain and trauma through various programs, workshops, speaking engagements, etc., has blessed me to be able to impact people positively as they continue their life journey and walk in healing and embrace life's purpose. What is your secret formula, your secret sauce? What makes you stand out from the rest? I bet it is connected to your journey. How have you been able to help others with what tried to block or hinder you from being successful in business?

I have been blessed to build partnerships that are a blessing to others, especially our youth. Dr. Angelica Benavides and I have launched a Youthpreneurs Tribe, where we Ignite, Inspire and Impact young business owners to go to the next level in business.

We have provided a platform to interview them on B-Global Power Talk Show, which helps provide exposure and collaboration opportunities. We are also planning our first Youthpreneur ThinkTank, which will be a powerful networking event. Connect with our community via Facebook:

Steps to Build Success from Scratch
Put the Oxygen Mask on Yourself

First of all, Always Put God First! We cannot do anything without having faith from a higher source that continues to strengthen us during our weak moments.

Second, believe in yourself even when others don't. Trust me, I have been there many times!

Third, build a strong support system to rally around you and in turn support others as well.

Fourth, FORGIVE & HEAL! Forgive Others & Yourself to remain FREE from past pain.

Fifth, make sure you take care of yourself (self-care)! Put the oxygen mask on yourself before you try to help others

Lastly, don't forget to enjoy life and do the things that bring you joy, laughter, and happiness while making time for what truly matters, family and friends

First Sign of Success
Don't Ever Despise Small Beginnings!

My first sign of success was I was able to share some of my stories during my Domestic Violence Advocacy 4 Day Training in San Antonio, Tx. I was there to learn and be trained, however, the moment of me speaking before so many other professionals was Liberating and Sealed my Purpose to help others as an Advocate. Success also is that I have been blessed to receive the support of my wonderful children and family, friends, and colleagues as well during all of it—the good, the bad, and the ugly times. As a new Domestic Violence Advocate so many years ago, I was honored at a Gala with Celebrities and so many people for my story and beginning work as a Domestic Violence Advocate. One of my first clients who helped me realize that I was on the right path was a mother whom we blessed with a Makeover with Wardrobe and an interview to share her story.

Ultimate Solution
Leaders Bleed Up!

Everyone needs a Mentor! If a leader, especially a spiritual leader (which I am) bleeds down onto the people you are serving, then you can do more harm than good. So, always remember to release or vent up to someone who can lift you up. Many times, that can come from anyone; a smile, laugh a good word, or a hug. However, mentors need mentors, too. I am blessed with spiritual mentors and business mentors.

Our Healing Pain Through The Arts (HPTTA) Youth Program has provided mentorship for so many youths locally, nationally, and globally through our HPTTA Youth Spotlight Awards, Youth Speak Out Podcast and other programs.

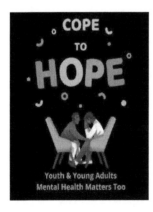

Youth & Young Adults
Mental Health Matters Too

Currently, we are working on a newly added program since May 2022 called **COPE To HOPE (Youth & Young Adults Mental Health Matters Too)** has been our focus during such critical times of high mental health awareness, gun violence, mass shooting, and violence that we are experiencing at such rapid rates, not to mention the increase in depression and suicide. We are seeking to help de-stigmatize the discussion of this critical topic that is plaguing so many within our youth and young adult community, create a safe space and provide resources needed for them. We are excited to be hosting our 1st In Person Check-In Event, where we will have a Therapist, Youth Mental Health Advocate, Youth Transformational Coach, Speakers, Performing Artists, and a Panel Session to let OUR youth & young adults know that we are here to support them.

Additionally, it has been an honor to serve as the Global Youth Leader of the World Women's Conference & Awards organization for the past 2 years, under the amazing leadership of Founder, Ragne Sinikas. I was proud to be named as the Women of VISION Awards Youth Leadership Winner!

When you look back over my life of building a business from broken pieces and re-building my life from Ground Zero; please remember that no matter where you find yourself or how far down you feel life has knocked you; just know that there is **Nowhere to Go, But Up!** Remember to take one step at a time and go at your own pace. As long as you are moving forward with the help of God, you will accomplish your goal. **See You at the Top!**

Free Gift
FREE 30 Minutes Consultation Session available via https://linktr.ee/alyons63

Accolades and Achievements

My most recent life milestone and accomplishment were to receive an Honorary Doctorate (Honoris Causa) as a Doctor of Philosophy in the specified area of Humanitarianism and Conflict Response from Theophany University and validated by Charles Walter's Society for Innovation & Research (Dr. Abhishek Pandey). I am also blessed to be the recipient of many awards, the magazine featured articles, and being interviewed on numerous televisions, radio, and podcasts in addition to speaking at global summits, conferences, and panels. I am a 3rd-time author with this being my 4th Book Collaboration, for which I am grateful. Every time the Lord allows me to share a small part of my story to bless others is my purpose being fulfilled.

See What They Are Saying...

Amber! You continue to be an inspiration in troubling times!! -L.Stellar

***

Congratulations Dr. Amber Ann Lyons!! This is such an honor; you have put in the time and service! -Michele Patton Johnson

What an awesome honor. Your hard work and devotion is being outwardly recognized. You deserve this moment so bask in it. -Angela Dunn

Congratulations to you for your dedication to the work the Lord assigns you to do. Blessings to you on your next Assignment. You always give God the honor and glory.
-Gloria Catten

***

As a mother of 3 Adult Children and Grandmother of 4, I am by nature a nurturer as most women are. I have prayed, supported, financially supported, encouraged, and verbally counseled many women, men, and youth. They have been able to gain a new perspective regarding their life or present situations that they were dealing with, which helped them through some difficult and challenging times and life's decisions. I have provided various resources and affirmations to help them, and even scriptures to provide a source of added strength. God has also allowed me to be used to help assist with helping others to be given a renewed HOPE after they were contemplating suicide!

My God is Awesome!

Vee Escarment
Generational Wealth through Real Estate &
Generational Wealth through Homeownership Inc.
Lauderhill, Florida, USA
veeescarment@gmail.com

Chapter 9
Champion: From Trials to Triumph

Vee Escarment is an Entrepreneur, SAG AFTRA Actress, Empowerment Coach, Speaker, Host, HUD Certified Counselor, Certified Real Estate Developer, Licensed Insurance Professional, and a Notary. She is the President and CEO of Generational Wealth through Homeownership, Inc. a 501c3 nonprofit housing counseling agency and she is the President & CEO of Generational Wealth through Real Estate LLC. She is the Vice President of the South Florida Board of Realtists Foundation and a Trustee Member of the Minority Builders Coalition.

Mission and Vision

My mission is the following: To acquire underperforming properties throughout Florida and transition them into primary residences for its citizens to build and impact communities one property at a time empowering communities, changing lives one person at a time, and educating individuals to create generational wealth.

Starting from Scratch
From Adversity to Wisdom

The business was going exceptionally well, and I went through a season where business slowed down. Every bad experience has served as a learning lesson for me. Some bad experiences happened when I paid for mentorship. My mentor took the money and never rendered the mentorship coaching sessions. I paid for 3 websites and was hosting them on the web developer platform; when I no longer wanted to do business with him, he took my websites hostage. I had to create the websites from scratch. Through all these circumstances, God brought me through it! When I thought it was over God said to me, "Don't let what you see make you forget what I said!"

The most valuable lessons I have learned on this journey are growth, wisdom, and patience. These lessons have tremendously added to my character. I had to learn to have patience and know that everything will happen at the right time. I had to learn that as long as you don't give up and continue working hard you will accomplish your goal. It will all work out! No weapon formed against me shall prosper and I know that all things work together for my good! "I never lose. Either I win or I learn"- Nelson Mandela

Big Why
Legacy

My "Big Why" for moving forward in the midst of chaos and challenges in my life is God. God has placed me here to encourage, empower, and impact lives. The world is waiting on my gifts, skills, and talents. My purpose is greater than my pain. My story will impact millions of lives. My story is connected to a bunch of other people's dreams. If you knew the power in your story, you wouldn't be sitting on it. Everybody talks about the fear of FAILURE. But one of the most underrated fears people have is the fear of SUCCESS. This is my TIME! I will make an impact and leave my mark!

Aha Moment Epiphany
Elevation Requires Separation

The epiphany happened when I stepped out in faith and started taking steps to create the business—from registering the business, creating the business plan, getting an EIN number, getting a business license, reading books about starting businesses, researching, and taking business development courses. At the time, I was working a full-time job and doing all of these things in the evenings and the weekends.

The circumstances are nothing more than distractions. Life is full of distractions and being able to separate yourself from these distractions is key to elevating yourself one step closer to your dreams. We separate from the things we are no longer in alignment with. Don't allow your past or present condition to control you. It's just a process that you're going through to get you to the next level.

Transformation is a process and as life happens there are tons of ups and downs. It's a journey of discovery; there are moments on mountaintops and moments on deep valleys of despair.

Excellence requires discomfort. Every season has its peaks and its valleys. Growth happens in the valleys. You learn in the valleys so you can earn in the peaks. The valley serves a purpose; that's where fruit grows. There is no place to look but up. Even if you

can't see what God is doing, know that just like fruit, He is growing you, He is maturing you, and He is strengthening you in that
valley. Without valleys, you can't appreciate mountaintops. A setback is a setup for a comeback. You face your greatest opposition when you're close to your biggest miracle!

Secret Formula
My Secret Sauce

They can steal your recipe… but the sauce won't taste the same. My secret formula is *Each one, reach one. Each one, teach one!* I educate, encourage, and empower! We service the low to moderate-income families in the Tri-County areas of Miami Dade County, Broward County, and Palm Beach County. We service the South Florida Community and beyond in homeownership, credit counseling, post-purchase counseling, and financial literacy. By
adopting the National Industry Standards for homeownership, GWTH utilizes best practices to assist its clients in achieving Homeownership. We are focused on educating and empowering the community on these various topics through our Workshops. I provide eBooks that the client can purchase on these various topics. Clients find me through social media such as Facebook, Instagram, or the company website. I attract clients by marketing and advertising on Facebook, Instagram, and the company website, and speaking on podcasts, shows, and conferences. I also receive clients through referrals and word of mouth. I have been able to help 1,000 clients over nine years become first-time home buyers. Being a life changer, I have helped clients to begin their legacy for their families and create generational wealth for their families. I have dedicated the last nine years to assisting the low to moderate-income communities in becoming knowledgeable so that they can take necessary steps toward building generational wealth through financial literacy and homeownership.

Generational Wealth through Real Estate LLC particular specialty is developing affordable housing for low to moderate-income residents in the Tri-County areas of Miami Dade County, Broward County, and Palm Beach County. Our focus is on affordable rental properties and affordable housing.

Steps to Build Success from Scratch
Playbook to Success

On my journey from being an employee to becoming an entrepreneur, I had to seek wisdom from God and have God order my steps! I had to be intentional and make changes in my life. I had to form new ways of thinking, new habits, and a new way of life. I had to be very specific and write a plan with steps to help me reach my destination in life.

Below are the steps that I took:

1. Prayer/Brainstorm- Write the vision and make it a plan! Write out your ideas! Pray to God so that he can give you clarity and show you what steps to take.
2. Research- the field you are in and your competitors, and what makes you stand out from your competitors.
3. Create a business plan- It is a road map and direction to how your business will operate.
4. Business development courses/cohorts- earn how to run and operate a business.
5. Funding/Sponsorship/Grant writing- Schedule meetings, form partnerships, and get access to capital, funding, sponsorship, grants, and government contracts.
6. Internship/Mentorship- Find an entrepreneur you can intern for and learn the ins and outs of running a company in your field of interest.

First Sign of Success

The first sign of success is when I was able to change a person's life by helping them improve their credit, increase their savings, bring down their debts, and qualify to purchase a home with down payment assistance and they were able to refer a family member or friend. Then I had companies from all over contacting me to present workshops for their organization, being a speaker at conferences, and being interviewed on shows, podcasts, and magazines. My Pastor Karen Felton and my close friend Valerie Gardner have supported me through good times, bad times, and ugly times. I have a few friends who are prayer warriors that have prayed with me through it all.

Ultimate Solution Expert:

My path to finding the ultimate solution for myself and my clients came from years of experience in the industry. I had a Score Mentor that guided me to find the solution. It is important to ask for help because in order to grow and scale your business you will need the right team and board members. Also, by asking for help you can become aware of the various resources out there and know what options you have. Mentorship is vital to success! Connecting with a mentor in the same field of business can help you learn how to operate the business and what pitfalls to avoid.

Free Gift

I offer free financial literacy workshops. Potential clients can purchase coaching sessions with me through my EMPOWER HER PROGRAM where women will learn to increase their income and gain financial stability. Each client becomes empowered by working with an empowerment coach and receiving guidance on how to earn more, keep more of what she earns, and grow what she earns to build savings and assets.

An Empowerment Coach is someone who instructs and works with their clients to prepare and guide them in achieving their short-term and long-term goals. I also have eBooks available to purchase. veeescarment@gmail.com

Accolades and Achievements

I have received considerable recognition such as I was awarded the 2019 Woman of Empowerment Award from the Professional Organization of Women of Excellence Recognized (P.O.W.E.R.), CEO Today USA Awards Winner for 2020 and 2021, Legacy South Florida Most Influential and Prominent Black Women in Business and Industry for 2020, Legacy South Florida's 40 Under 40 Black Leaders of Today and Tomorrow of 2021, Legacy South Florida Magazine's Most Influential

and Powerful Black Professionals of 2022, and the Haitian American Chamber of Commerce of Florida Top 20 under 40 Young Professional of 2022. I have been featured in many publications such as the Top 100 Magazine, FOX News, Passion Vista Magazine, VIP Global Magazine, Exeleon Magazine, CEO Today Magazine, Legacy South Florida Magazine, Shoutout Miami Magazine, Voyage MIA Magazine, NBC, CBS, Yahoo! Finance, and Black Enterprise. I have been interviewed on the Lunch with Legacy Leaders Show, HOT 105 Community Spotlight with Rodney Baltimore, and the "Dunn Wisdom Morning Show".

See What They Are Saying...

Vee goes the extra mile!

"I am so grateful to you Ms Vee. I pray for you often because you helped me a lot with the process. You're so patient and willing to go the extra mile to help your clients. You are such a wonderful person. You really made a difference in my life Ms. Vee! May God bless you and your family."

Marie Brunine David
***

Vee offers an awesome experience!

I was led to this website after praying. God told me to go and get my house and that is what I am doing. In faith, I am taking this leap. The course was very thorough and detailed. After every module, there was a small quiz to take. It was an awesome experience. Thank you for this wonderful opportunity."

Schadita Miller
***

Vee offers resources!

"I am happy I attended the class. I did not know all these resources were out there and available to us. It was really informative. Vee and her group are great. I actually want to find out more about the services they offer. I want to know even more. I plan to use some of the presenters in my quest to get home."

Sashane McDonald
***

Learn more at
https://linktr.ee/Veeescarment

Be sure to collect your FREE giveaway!

Rodeline Robinson
Meer Consulting Group, LLC
Broward County FL
rodeliner88@gmail.com

Chapter 10
Creating a Purposeful Seamless Business

Born and raised in Broward County FL, No High school diploma to MBA Graduate, Angel Investor, Entrepreneur, Mother, Wife, Business and Career Coach

Mission and Vision

My vision is to help first time home buyers and small business owners build their credit for loan approvals and help small businesses diversify assets.

Starting from Scratch
Grit. Resilience | Resilience. Faith.

Growing to the top of the world. I came from very little. I am the First of my 7 siblings to Graduate College with an MBA. I dropped out of High School because I had to work to support myself. After becoming homeless, I decided going back to school would allow me to achieve a high-paying career. During the pandemic, I learned I don't like to be told what to do. I want the ability to be creative, implement new ideas, and make decisions. I chose to start a business to support small businesses with Starting. I'm passionate about Problem Solving and Evolving, and I chose to make it purposeful assisting with a need that most founders seem to have in common, credit and working capital. Engage your high school dropout readers or readers who felt like giving up tell them to get grit, gain resilience and faith is important

BIG Why

I can name 4, Melody, Elias, Eian, and King! My children and my God Son. They are who motivate me to Lead by example and create standards they can be proud to follow.

Aha Moment Epiphany

With so many business ideas I trusted the one that was seamless, favors that I was already doing for free to help family and friends advance. I decided to make it a business by becoming an angel investor, business, and career coach assisting with credit, financial literacy, and diversifying assets. I must teach my community to diversify so we don't rely on one income avenue. The pandemic has shown us how important it is to diversify revenue streams for operational needs. Engage the reader ask them questions or guidance on investments

Secret Formula
Word of Mouth.

Why is word of mouth important as a secret formula? How will it help the readers to use this strategy? How do you use it and when did you decide to use it?

I work closely with my community building relationships and empowering them to create a big picture goal while planning the small details. My clients believe we are breaking generational, and we are contributing to our world. Engage the reader

Steps to Build Success from Scratch?
Faith. Start. Keep going. Don't stop.
Faith. Keep God First. Some days no one is going to believe you can make it happen. But it is God within you who gives you the Will to know you WILL! Stay prayed up.

Start. No one may come to help in the beginning. You start. No excuses. God will send the believers you need.

Keep going. It may feel like a weight at first and that's ok. When it gets heavy, you keep pushing.

Don't stop. Allow yourself to rest. But don't you dare STOP!

First Sign of Success?

When I graduated with my associate degree, I knew that was the beginning to no end. When earning my bachelor's and MBA. My husband and children encouraged me through hard nights and long days. My first client is an old friend needing assistance with building business credit and support as she grew her skincare line. I knew I was on the right path when she told me I inspired her because I always told her she had beautiful skin. Fast forward I'm consulting and coaching her through her skincare line. Engage the reader and remind them that they should celebrate small wins, find support, community, or mentors

Ultimate Solution

It's important to **seek mentorship** to help eliminate distractions, specific risks, and mistakes. A leader is also a student. **Practice wisdom** and **continue to learn.** I learned from my professors, managers, and Directors, directly and indirectly.

Accolades and Achievements

I earned an Associate's Degree in Human Service Management after dropping out of high school in hopes of becoming a philanthropist, a Bachelor of Applied Science in Supervision and Management while developing a team of 20 people to be empowered in providing customer service, and a Master of Business Administration while working for Government Human Resources.

See What They Are Saying...

I've assisted women to pass their state board exam by empowering them and building their confidence. Angel Investor assisted women-owned businesses with working capital and assisted women with building their credit and increasing their ability to purchase all free services. I recently started receiving profit.

***

Business link

MEERMOTIVATION3

Scan QR code

Shamila Mooloo
Techademy | Techknowledgy beyond the classroom
Pretoria, Gauteng, South Africa
shamsmooloo@vodamail.co.za

Chapter 11
Dynamic without a Degree!

I would like to think of myself as an EDvocate because I am a mum, a Ph.D. student, researcher, educator, lecturer, directress, and facilitator who is currently involved in women empowerment projects, particularly in the field of early childhood teacher development. I am a mentor to undergraduates trying to achieve their high school certificate and am an entrepreneur of a home school and teacher development academy. My passion is uplifting those around me by educating them to be successful women who not only contribute positively to society but develop a sense of pride and joy. I believe that acquiring a good education or nurturing a skill can be a life game changer. I have an open mind and a compassionate heart and believe we are defined by our character.

Mission and Vision

Techademy, a social innovator, built on the foundation of empowering women Early Childhood Development (ECD) teachers and aims to provide access to ECD resources.

My company's mission is to upskill these women thus creating a connected learning community by using social media applications. Techademy strives to develop women by turning their caregiving talents into their livelihood thus contributing to the spirit of "Ubuntu" (an eternal African philosophy of unity and respect).

Success is the result of persevering in the face of failure
Starting from Scratch

I used one of the most cathartic and depressing points of my life as the catalyst to define my take on success. It came when I was at my lowest when I lost my younger sister. This tragedy led me through the different stages of grief and as a result, I developed a sense of resilience. I immediately began to recognize, acknowledge, and even accept the reality of my situation. Rewind two years prior when I ventured on my own business project. I had all the ideas, the plan, and the name, and even the registration of the company was on point. This ordeal directed me to revisit my project, and I channeled all these mixed emotions into something positive. I needed something to help me cope, and my business became my survival kit. I was consumed by working on it day and night. My mind was flooded with new ideas for perfecting my business model, but more importantly, I possessed a new quest and drive to make my business a success. I had a thought that resonated in my mind, that *success is the result of persevering in the face of failure*. I had to persist.

Big Why
My mum
The Power of Hope

My mum, a strong uneducated woman, with four children, had left her married life of abuse. Penniless she headed into the unknown with the hope for a better life. Armed with her courage, she boarded a train uncertain about what her future held. She took her love for hairstyling and immersed herself in the hair industry eventually becoming not only a professional hairstylist but a successful businesswoman. Her story made me realize that life's struggles somehow give birth to growth. I always

felt my purpose was to be instrumental in the lives of others by uplifting them to greater heights. I initially started my business in the midst of the pandemic and wanted to offer teacher development because I felt that I had so much to offer to young aspiring teachers. I truly believe that by following your passion, you inspire and awaken the hearts and souls of others. I knew I could make a big impact on little minds by training teachers.

However, during my planning stages, I lost my sister, which left me devastated. All my hard work of compiling programs and resources was suddenly replaced by deep grief. Work ceased and failure lurked. My response to this emotion was my complete lack of motivation. For a year, I just existed. Then I looked at my mum and realized the battles she had fought and still held on. Why? Because there exists a certain power in losses and failure, and that is the power of HOPE. This newfound hope to rise above my possible self, led me back to the drawing board to map out my life.

I haven't reached the peak of the mountain yet. I'm climbing, slowly and steadily,

it's not easy; there are obstacles along the way, but I stop to deal with them and am keeping the momentum by moving nowhere else but *up* to new heights.

Aha Moment Epiphany
If you believe, you can….

In my first few years of teaching, a colleague commented in the staffroom that some girls in her class were not chosen to participate in her dance recital because they had two "left feet." My immediate thought was: "That is exactly what our job is as teachers-to teach children that despite our setbacks we can achieve anything if we believe we can!"

Dynamic without a Degree!

This was why teachers needed trainers like me, I thought. This spurred me to register for my master's research where I explored the social media teaching concept to train and develop teachers. Little did I know that this concept would form the cornerstone of my business. All my business skills, teaching experience, and academic knowledge were merged into Techademy. My mum was the epitome of hope and a product of what hard work could accomplish. That is why I wanted to empower women and awaken their sense of pride and determination to succeed. By training ECD teachers, my philosophies will have a ripple effect on young children, too, because teaching was a profession that molded minds and carved characters.

Secret Formula
Enthusiasm, Education, and Evolve

My formula for success is to do some self-searching and tap into your skills and your passion. My mum was a strong woman who picked up the pieces to build a strong and thriving business with her talent which she didn't know she even possessed. It emanated from her job that she loved immensely. My enthusiasm for training and developing teachers and empowering women was my business ideals. I empower single mums, school dropouts, teachers, and the unemployed by teaching and upskilling them to eventually become economically independent. I am also a freelance facilitator for women from disadvantaged backgrounds and am involved in a toy run annually to provide the poor pre-schools these women operate with toys around Christmas time. I attract clients from early childhood centers by advertising on social media, arranging conferences, and coaching current ECD owners by assisting them to grow their centers and advance their skills through mentorship. My formula is to discover things in your life you are enthusiastic about, educate yourself in that field, and evolve by learning and improving yourself. The key is to persevere through all the obstacles.

Steps to Build Success from Scratch
Acquire, Enquire and Aspire

Remember success is not a destination; it's a journey to the peak of your potential. Ensure every day you are happy and celebrate little milestones you achieve along the way. My certificates, my job titles, my children, and my health are all achievements in my life. My mum buying her own home, getting her driver's license, obtaining an occupational certificate, and opening her own business were all little accomplishments that led to her being a businesswoman whose expertise was well respected. Build your success.

Dynamic without a Degree!

Take a moment. Close your eyes. Imagine your life the way you would like it to be.

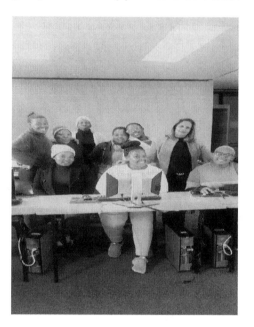

- Write down things you enjoy doing or what you good at
- Write down all the milestones you want to achieve in your life. Circle the milestones that define your character and the skills you possess.
- Work out a program to achieve your milestones and set date deadlines.
- Create opportunities to start changing your life.
- Start learning all you can about the field of work you would like to venture in. Attend workshops, conferences, and expos in your field of interest to build a network of like-minded people and professionals. -educate yourself
- Acquire and sharpen the skills you require.
- Make a bold social media presence.
- Most importantly pray, keep positive, and have an open mind and heart. Aspire for greatness!
-

Find your own version of success and rock it!
First Sign of Success

 achieved first prize for my master's research and was whisked away to Mumbai to present my research at the University of Mumbai, I knew then that I was destined for greatness; that this is what I wanted to do with my life—to be a key player, a game changer, and an influential leader in the educational and training field. My greatest fan was my mum who always believed in me; she was instrumental in ensuring I pursue my studies further. My research on using social media as a training tool proved to be successful because I proved practically that it was indeed a powerful communication tool. I used it wisely to start assisting ECD teachers who were grateful for my guidance, knowledge, and experience. I used this platform to send information, files, links, etc. to these teachers and was awarded a special recognition award for my contribution and involvement. That stamp was all the reassurance I needed to fuel my passion. If I ask myself what it was that made me successful, it would be my mum's old recipe of hard work eventually pays off.

Ultimate Solution

My mentor had to be my mum, her hardships, and her continuous striving to learn to become a professional in her field were what motivated me. She started as a shampoo lady in a salon and ended up a shopkeeper. She progressed from a train passenger to driving her own Mercedes Benz, it was not only a rags-to-riches story but rather a mission to gain independence, economic freedom, and above all respect. She was not defined by education. Many of us chase career titles, money, or social status — and yet we don't feel successful when we get those things. That's because you can only measure success in your life when you define what drives your happiness and helps you find purpose. Success for my mum was giving back to women by making them feel beautiful and giving them the confidence to take on the world. They left negativity and despair at her salon and walked out with positive vibes. Success for her was a sense of giving back to the world. This became my mantra. This is what humanity is all about!

Free Gift (Advice)

I offer to mentor Early Childhood teachers and assist them with advice on how to grow their education business. I also provide them with teaching resources and workshops to develop their professional skills. As a lecturer, I am able to train and supervise students aspiring to become teachers. I am writing a book revolving around the idea of reaching an EPIPHANY WITHOUT AN EDUCATION. Where ordinary women have become successful without degrees but with a drive to succeed and have done so by looking deep within themselves to find their talents, nurturing it to become their lifestyle. I would be happy to share some advice, consult or provide a free online workshop for ECD teachers.

Accolades and Achievements

My greatest achievement will have to be my children who have grown up to be good, dedicated individuals because I was able to provide them with a good upbringing. Being a mother always kept me grounded and taught me the art of compassion and empowerment. Their achievements will always resonate with me. Although I have received awards for my research, have obtained cum laude in my degrees, and have held leadership positions in various entities, I am grateful for the entrepreneurial, corporate, and academic skills I have acquired that are the steppingstones to my success. I am currently a doctorate student, developing an early education curriculum and writing a book on

Dynamic without a Degree!

ACHIEVING WITHOUT ACHIEVEMENTS, all in the name of improving and changing lives. My greatest honor would have to be the lives I have touched and made a positive impact on from my preschool learners to the adult learners I taught. Therefore, amongst all my titles of teacher, researcher, facilitator, lecturer, and directress my best title will always be EDVOCATE. Enlightening minds, transforming lives, and shaping characters through education.

See What They Are Saying...

When you see someone who seems to have it all, you don't see the full picture. People project their best accomplishments and rarely expose their hardships and failures. In other words, you see the highlights — a glamorous montage of triumphs, successes, distinctions, and talents.

*The **testimonials** below are what motivate me to do what I do best.*

Since you gave me the concept of making my early learning center an inclusive education center assisting learners with learning disabilities, my services are indeed a need in the community. My school roll grew from 6 to 45. I am now educating myself in inclusive education teaching methods. Thank you! I am making a difference in these young lives.

***

Your expertise has made me a better preschool teacher. Now I have a structured program and my preschool is even recommended by the primary school teachers because my learners are ready for school. I feel so honored that they have acknowledged my work.

***

Thank you for the toys and easter eggs you provided for my kids. Your generosity will never go unnoticed.

Dynamic without a Degree!

Be sure to collect your FREE giveaway!

www.linkedin.com/in/shamila-mooloo-24295b127

www.techademy.co.za

Rose Marok
AGLP Enterprises, Ltd
Solihull, West Midlands, UK
rosemarok@gmail.com

Chapter 12
E³ (Engage, Encourage, Empower)

Rose is an entrepreneur, Director of Miss India UK, Mrs. Asia GB and Mrs. Asia India, trademark properties of AGLP Enterprises Ltd. Winner of Mrs. India UK 2019, and director of Mrs. India UK 2020. She also runs a dental practice with her husband in Solihull, UK, as well as raising 2 children. She has successfully proven that working in partnership with her husband, family, and work-life balance can be successful and at the same time achieve her dreams. She is also a CIPD qualified HR professional and certified mental health awareness worker and is currently working towards a master's in psychology at Coventry University.

Mission and Vision
Engage, Encourage, and Empower

These are my missions and my personal mantra in life.

Women empowerment comes to my mind, and we can achieve this by engaging and encouraging each other. More and more women should support each other. This is my mission, and I have created my business as a platform to encourage what I believe in and to turn this vision into reality.

Starting from Scratch

Life is a big teacher, and it teaches us something every day. With all our successes, failures, happy moments, sad ones, and all the people that we meet, we need to embrace them all.

I am who I am today because I have learned from each and every step of my life. Coming from a lower-middle-class family, I saw the struggle, but I also learned to find happiness even in the smallest thing. My dreams were very big, and these dreams of mine kept me going. My parents may not have given us a luxurious life, but they gave us the best education and dare to dream. I am always thankful for this.

Challenge
Rediscovering Myself

Moving from India to the UK changed everything for me. I left everything behind but gained a life partner who became my backbone and stood by me in all my good and bad times. Throughout all the challenges in life, my husband Dr. Marok gave me the courage to stand tall and keep going.

In 2019 when I came across a platform where I went on a journey to rediscover myself, my husband Dr. Marok, and my kids were my biggest cheerleaders. After coming back from an international competition, where I represented the UK, I realized how much of an impact one person can have on the community.

This is where I decided that I was going to create this platform to help others around the world to come together and do something different and go on a journey to rediscover themselves. I strongly believe that Life is a journey, not a destination and we all have to keep going. It will be a bit bumpy at times but remember it is a phase and it will pass. We will have to keep going. Remember choice is an illusion because you already know what you must do and that is to keep going.

Big Why

My Big Why was to "be the change that I want to see in this world". This 'Why' of mine I came across while I was in an all-girl's boarding school in India. There were many things that I complained about but never did anything myself to solve those problems. But as soon as I realized that in order to solve those problems, I can at least initiate by looking for solutions, this is when I knew that we can complain as much as we want, but in order to bring any change, we will have to make the start. This" big why "of mine has always kept me going all my life. I have always believed in "walk the walk and talk the talk". So, for me, if there is anything that we want to change, we need to start that by being that change ourselves.

Just remember if and when you find your 'why', follow it with all your heart. Trust the process, and if you don't succeed, remember there is no failure in life. We either succeed or we learn. You only lose when you give up and admit defeat.

Aha Moment Epiphany

My big Aha moment for my current business was during my pageant months when I went on to represent the UK internationally and saw all the wonderful women from around the world working passionately towards their goals to make this world a better place for future generations. I have had this epiphany that I want to create a platform that can be a launching pad for all the women who have the same dreams and aspirations and where I could put all my experience into practice and my vision became my mission.

Apart from my current business, I have had many Aha Moments in my life, which encouraged me to create different dreams. With my very first business, my "Aha" moment came while I was talking to a friend who wanted to start a business but was struggling financially. I saw her vision and offered the investment because I felt this was the opportunity to help and to create something good. With this business, we helped and employed many students from India and the UK and gave them skills that will help them in the future.

We all have many of these moments in our life, and it is very important to pay attention to these and see where they can lead us. Most successful people around the globe started with this. Also, remember to be present in the current moment as this is the moment that you are living right now. We do not control the future, and we cannot change the past so live in the present and learn from the past, and the future will be brighter.

Secret Formula

"We may not have it all together but together we have it all".

There are no secret formulas to success, but I am a people person and I believe in teamwork. This helps bring people together and create beautiful things. My winning formula has always been people around me, my team, and my "not to give up" attitude.

I do believe that you are as good as your team is, so surround yourself with good people, and if you happen to come across some not-so-good people, just learn from them and move on.

With my platform, I wish to gather people who understand my vision to give this launching pad for all the women around the world to provide them with a platform to fly and achieve their personal dreams and to make this world a little better place for our future generations.

Together we can bring change, be it environmental challenges, education, domestic violence, mental health awareness, or any other.

Our business will be a one-stop shop to provide mentoring and coaching for women around the globe. We are working on creating an institute that will produce community queens to lead their communities because when we gather people who are passionate about their goals, then it becomes their duty to achieve those goals, especially when the goal is to serve the community. Within our institute, we will help these passionate women to find their goals and to give them all the tools they require and navigate them through different pathways to achieve those goals. During the last few years, the journey of many of the ladies that we have mentored has resonated with my belief and my platform. They became people who didn't like going out or wearing nice clothes to now being on the TedEx stage as one of their speakers.

Steps to Build Success from Scratch

So now that you have had your 'AHA' moment and you want to take the next step to make it a reality. Start with your homework, which can be background research, and then progress. With each project, I have made sure to do my background research before I commit myself to anything.

Then, just give your all in.

Remember If you want something really badly, concentrate and give your best effort. But if at the end you didn't get what you set out to achieve, don't dwell on it; let it go. God has better plans for you.

In our business, we offer a journey to all our clients that starts with them being themselves but at the end having a totally different view, a new and better version of themselves. All our clients are ladies aged between 16-55 from around the world, and together they all have created many platforms and helped many.

First Sign of Success

My first sign of success was when I could pay my staff without any support from anyone. I felt elated because at that point I knew that I had reached a breakthrough and now I needed to keep this going. In my good or bad times, my husband has been my rock; he has supported me through all my good or bad decisions. My friends and my family are my big moral support; they lift my spirit every day, but my biggest learning has been to celebrate all my wins "small or big" and to surround myself with people who will support me and celebrate with me.

My biggest success in my life is all these people who have lifted me, celebrated all my wins with me, and were there for me when I was not so successful.

So, remember it is very important to always celebrate every win, every success, no matter how big or small it is and to have good people around you.

***

Ultimate Solution

The ultimate solution is to work together and not give up. You just must give your best, believe in yourself, and trust the process. If things don't work out the way you imagined, just find a way to make it better but don't waste your energy or time on what's already done; learn from it and move on. It's always good to learn from people around you. Trust me there are very good life coaches. Hence, it is very important to surround yourself with people who inspire you. We will equip you with all the tools you require for your ultimate success by providing you with the best coaching and mentoring by people who are passionate about their work and by surrounding you with like-minded people.

Free Gift/Offer

I feel by sharing my experience, and my vision with you all in this book, I have hopefully provided you with the free gift of something that will stay with you forever such as "not to stop dreaming" and to "surround yourself with good people".

If after reading this chapter you think you would also like to be part of our journey, then please do join us and mention the book in your registration form.

Remember your life is yours, and you are the only one that controls it.

Accolades and Achievements

My life has been full of blessings, and many great things have come my way over the years. Being a special guest at many prestigious events to meeting many inspiring people in life are a few of my many achievements. My story was featured on BBC WM and BBC Asian.
I have been the host for many movie premiers in Birmingham and featured on many Asian TV channels.

Winning Mrs. India UK 2019 and then representing the UK at the International competition as Mrs. UK International has been one of my biggest achievements. I have had the privilege to meet many good people and learn from them. During the lockdown, I took part as a guest speaker at Women Millionaire Summit 2020. Also, I was actively involved in debates and discussion panels during India's farmers' protest.

In 2022 I was awarded Inspirational Woman of the Year at Vietnam International Awards by LOANI (Ladies of All Nations International). I have also had the privilege of being a jury member for Mrs. Euro Philippines Universe held in the Netherlands.

See What They Are Saying...

"Rose is a Strong, determined, focused, and talented individual. She is extremely passionate and has been an excellent support to me during Mrs. India UK and Mrs. Universe pageants. She has always motivated me, and I really appreciate her positive approach and can-do attitude. She has been a fantastic support throughout my journey in providing guidance. She is a classic example of beauty with brains and has played an integral role in motivating women and mentoring them. I am very proud to be associated with her and would be happy to recommend her."

Mrs. Kanchan Jawale
Data product Development Manager
Lloyds of London

"Having known Rose for over a decade, she is always there for me. Especially in the hard and good times. She's always so thoughtful and listens to all my problems. "

Manisha Patel
Homemaker

"Rose has been such a wonderful director and mentor throughout my journey to the Mrs. International pageant. She helped me be something which I was not before, helped me build on my strengths and improve on my weaknesses, and prepared me fully for the international stage. An inspiring woman who has been helping many other girls believe in what they are capable of. Very proud to have worked with Rose and one of the inspiring women doing more and more in the pageant industry. Thank you for everything and for making me a family member of her Pageant world."

Radhika Murthy
Data Engineer
Amazon

"In my hard times, even when my family disowned me. Rose stood by me. She gave me shelter in her own house when my ex-in-laws kicked me out of their house. She gave me courage and strength when I gave up on life. She even went all the way with me to the immigration office and sponsored my ILR (indefinite leave to remain) when my Ex-husband refused. I am the owner of a business which was again with the help of Rose. With her help, I got out of an abusive relationship and now I'm living a happy life."

Lovely Kaur
Business owner

***

Business Links
https://www.100swb.com/?playlist=c3071f3&video=2e810dd
Global Trade Chamber"

https://linktr.ee/rosemarok

Merete Stangeland
The Power House - Mental Training and Coaching
Larvik, Norway
merete@kraftrommet.no

Chapter 13
Expanding Your Awareness

Merete is a strong, powerful woman leader here to wake people up and realize that their time is now. She is a person who will tell people how powerful they are and show them that there is an opportunity that exists now that was never there before. She is a Power House, offers Mental training, and believes Mindset matters. She is a voice for professional women in a male-dominated world and industry. By using her own experience from long work life, combined with the tools she uses as a Certified Proctor Gallagher Consultant, she inspires personal growth and transformation by expanding her client's awareness. She shifts how you see yourself and realize how dramatically it can change the world when you step into your true power.

Mission and Vision

My mission is to create a significant change in society. We must change, find new ways of thinking, and innovate. Women are needed to stand together with men to create a high-performance team culture. My legacy and vision are to leave the world a better place!

Starting from scratch

I started from scratch again and turned away from my safe, well-paid, and respectable job. I left a company that for many years had taught me so much and given me the opportunity to grow into a confident woman. It was time for a change. I knew that it was my time to make an impact, so I prepared myself to do so.

We are in a time where the world needs good leaders, people with the will to use their imagination, be creative, and dare to dream big. I equipped myself with a mentor, teamed up with another lady, and started my own business. Today, we have built a nice reputation and have satisfied clients taking quantum leaps in their personal and professional lives.

Big Why
Shame Up to My Neck

As a child, I was extremely open and curious, a chatterbox, an animal lover, athletic, nature lover, and piano player. I was born with this amazing attitude of always being a positive person and a go-getter. I grew up with adults having addictions with behavior patterns that were trigging people in our society. My parents divorced, and several of my family members passed away. I found myself suddenly alone. Excluded from social interaction, I was bullied at school, name called, stared at, and physically and psychologically abused. Inside I began to feel insecure and afraid of being abandoned again, As a teenager, I had several challenging relationships. I often attracted people with great personal problems, so I headed straight into rapes, sexual harassment, and gaslighting. These experiences gave me a bad taste in my mouth.

Have you ever felt this ugly wave of emotion going through your body? That was SHAME... and it filled me up to my neck!

Aha Moment Epiphany

I was still wonderfully naïve, presenting my heart in my outstretched hand. I never gave up, no matter the circumstances. My attitude started serving me like a magnet towards some wonderful people, who always came into my life when the time was right.

The statistics often tell a story about how likely it is that we walk down the same path as our parents. It is believed that if your parents are on social security, you stand a great chance of the same, or if your parents are successful, you will stand a better chance of success!

I guess that can be true, but it certainly was not like that for me.

What we are experiencing early on in life is not defining who we are or what we can become in the future; it only defines something that has happened in the past! I realized that I had an amazing inner drive, a desire stronger than anything else.

Merete Stangeland

I was always able to attract something positive in life. An unexpected experience would occur, and good people would just turn up in my life providing exactly what I needed at the right time. Some people might say it was fortunate circumstances, a stroke of luck as we often say, but I know better. It suddenly dawned on me that I was not depending on other people, all I needed was to turn my attention within and I found what I was looking for in life. Namely my freedom.

Secret Formula

It had all to do with me and how I chose to react towards any situation. I understood this, but I didn't really understand how it really worked out for me. I Invested time and money in myself.

After over 35 years of corporate work, I was puzzled why people who I believed to be more than competent did not dare to speak their mind when they were met by injustice.

I am giving back to people what I have so fortunately learned and passing on the knowledge to others so they can prosper and have success in life and business. Everything that had worked for me in life, despite everything that was going on around me, really had made me think. How did I make it? What did I do right?

Steps to Build Success from Scratch

I knew that my purpose was to be a mental trainer, a coach that could help other people reach their purpose and dream. I am a Proctor Gallagher Consultant, a transformational life coach. I run a Norwegian company called "Kraftrommet" and the
English-speaking division of it is "The Power House". We teach in person and online via our social media channels and zoom.

We do one-on-one coaching for leaders, groups, teams, and companies as clients.

Our office is in Larvik, Norway, but the world is our workplace.

You will see me as a public speaker at events all over the world. At the Women's Star Conference in 2022, I was fortunate to share my story on international Women's Day. Last year I also published a book together with other life coaches. I have studied several life-changing programs and educated myself for many years.

Ultimate Solution

When I decided to become a life coach, I started planning carefully, updated myself on social media, and started to build trust. My strong belief is that trust is the key word when you want to attract clients.

For me being a mental trainer is not only a job, it is a lifestyle and a calling. Even my family is included in the process. Our clients are included in a strong, safe network and are guided through the process step-by-step all the way towards their success.

First Sign of Success

My first sign of success was when I understood that I had to make a clear decision. I needed to have a clear goal and nurture the desire toward my destination. When I jumped into the new, everything changed! I had to change my environment completely; many so-called friends had to be left behind. New relationships developed and grew into strong connections.

When one of my first clients met up on my door with flowers and a letter, telling the story of how much I had changed her life, I knew that I definitely was on the right path.

Surprisingly, my family, apart from my children and my husband, gave me the hardest time. I met up with other people's fears so many times, and so many people had an opinion about me and what I was going to do. I had to lock everything out and turn my attention inside myself.

I had to work on my belief system and strengthen my self-image. Finally, it was the Proctor Gallagher Institute and the solid Bob Proctor himself who made me realize what I was destined to do. From that moment I never looked back, and the distance that I have gone since then is unexplainable.

Free Gift or Offer

Today I have several mentors and guides, as well as amazing people working with me towards our common goal. Without a mentor, I would never have landed where I am today!

I will offer 2 free discovery calls for those who want to find out what I can do for them.

When having the first call you will receive a little workbook that we will discuss in the second call. Our high-ticket coaching program "Thinking Into Results" will take you exactly where you want to go if you choose to join our 6-month transformational program.

The 6 months includes 10 one-on-one coaching calls of 1 hour each, group coaching every week (Mondays), visualizing and meditations every week (Wednesday), and free access to all future webinars and networking with like-minded people in a safe environment.

If you take action now before December 1st, 2022, I will give you an amazing price!

If you are a group, team or a business, we will agree upon a price that you will be happy with."

Proctor Gallagher Consultant, Star Conference public speaker, Global panel speaker, Author, Technical engineering, Ship Operations, HR work, QA safety work.

Accolades and Achievements

You will find me as a public speaker at events all over the world.

At the Women's Star Conference in 2022, I was fortunate to share my story on International Women's Day. Last year I also published a book together with other life coaches: "Find yourself handbook" is The guide on how to practice self-love, boost your self-confidence, find your voice and use it authentically.

I have studied several life-changing programs for many years. Silva Life System, Silva Intuition System, Thinking Into Results, and ended up as a Certified Proctor Gallagher Consultant, trained by Bob Proctor and his team at the Proctor Gallagher Institute.

See What They Are Saying...

"I never would have thought how much that could happen in only 3 weeks." *Gro Raugland*

***

"You inspired me to get into balance so that my life again has been filled with joy." *Bente Seljestad*

***

"Merete has a heart filled with care for others. She inspires you to use your thoughts for change that will influence your results." *Tonje Udnes Gyttrup*

***

Business card

https://blinq.me/61BLYmVUkD2J

99

Ines Pardo
Career Coach /Altos Ejecutivos
Bogota, Colombia
ines.pardo@altosejecutivos.com
linkedin.com/in/ines-pardo-0201b

Chapter 14
Finding a Life Purpose

I was born in Bogota, Colombia. I obtained a degree as a psychologist at The Universidad de Los Andes. I have attended several institutions for Coaching Certifications and Leadership programs, such as Rice University in Texas and Latam Business School in London.

I started my own company in 1992, attending Fortune 500 companies, first recruiting talents for High Tech industries and years later developing and coaching Top executives in Colombia to improve their careers, helping them to find opportunities to have a better work-life balance.

Mission and Vision

My mission is to have a high-quality consultancy firm, working with clear values in order to support top executives in Latam to encourage them to lead with empathy, generosity, and courage while being highly effective at the same time, promoting excellence, values, and a purpose beyond money in their companies and team.

My motivation to start a business was having a career and a family at the same time, which was a real challenge for women at that time, believe me!!

Starting from Scratch
Hope, Faith, and Perseverance to Go Ahead.

My life could be divided into many chapters: When I was 33 years old, I had a university degree, a nice family, and two daughters, and I started my own business. Then it was a long journey working for Fortune 500 companies and struggling to keep balance with work. After some happy years, the most painful and sad part of my life came; my youngest daughter had cancer and died. For years I was working and living on "automatic pilot". Simultaneously I got several certifications as a Coach and joined international associations—maybe being successful in corporate terms again.

Then another chapter for good, HAPPIER THAN EVER began; it included— traveling, feeling free to decide and enjoy life, continuing to help top executives in their Outplacement process, helping them to reconstruct their lives, maybe as I had to reconstruct many several times mine, and letting know they were valuable, despite not having a job, a social recognition, status, any income, helping them to find how valuable they were besides a better job, and allowing them to feel they were "successful" again.

During this happy time, I had health issues, but I decided to continue ahead achieving dreams and goals.

Big Why
Share, Serve Others

Trying to find a life with purpose, I read a lot and learned that serving others is the best way to be happy and find your purpose
I believe that if you have any talent, you have to use it to serve and help. Recently I have been inspiring myself in THE BEST SELLER written two thousand years ago to translate messages to the corporate world. Through social media, I try to influence C-level executives to be humans with values and encourage their companies to do so.

My focus is to help executives in the corporate to spread principles and share prosperity. If they really serve, they will be happy and understand that Life is much more than money or
A job title!!

Aha Moment Epiphany

When in your life did you have the epiphany? Being 33 years old, I was forced by circumstances to start my own business as nobody was going to hire me half-time with flexible hours at my own pace.

Now I write articles, make posts, call colleagues to share ideas, and start projects. I learned to pray and to live in peace. I find happiness in listening, giving advice, and trying to be a relief for those who are struggling to be successful in the corporate world. Everyday things come to me. God's incidences and good outcomes happen. That encourages me to continue. Miracles occur every day; they are small happenings that we do not even notice and should be grateful for. Accepting that there are facts that science cannot explain is a relief. Understanding we are small creatures from the Universe, being humble to understand we are not so powerful, and knowing we need God and are vulnerable as human beings help us to do greater things.

Secret Formula

Have the purpose of sharing, serving, having a commitment, and giving added value at work to achieve professional success, but honestly, the KEY is not to tie earnings and money with success.
Strive to be useful, and in the end, money will come to help you to achieve the purpose you have.

Thanks to the pandemic, many things changed, for good again. My journey continues, and I am doing my own transition, trying to
leave a good legacy and continue to influence leaders in a positive way, especially reminding them about values, being humble, and not forgetting our spiritual and transcendent side.
It is unbelievable the big challenge it is for a successful high executive not to lose their essence, principles, and greater mission beyond having status, money, or titles.

The big challenge is being humble and effective servant leaders who have a mission, must be devoted to helping, and develop strong teams. The secret to building a business from scratch is to constantly grow, have a prosperity mindset, and be successful.

Steps to Build Success from Scratch
Free Access 24/ 7

It is wireless, no password, all languages available, all ages, is tax-free, global access

1. **Praying:** trusting God. Trying to give, help, and serve others are the main ingredients of my secret formula. I try to learn from THE book to follow the rules written thousands of years ago. In the morning, every day I hear priests and a few experts, who inspire me to translate messages to the corporate world.
2. Laugh at life. Do not lose your good sense of humor; do not be overwhelmed by circumstances. Smile; have a happy face and a positive attitude
3. Accept being vulnerable. When I have difficulties, I **ask for help** from friends and colleagues. I consult mentors and ask for advice. I try to be thankful for all the good things. I try to nurture myself with love, not fear. Do not lose hope and faith.
4. Use your gift networking. I use my Gift: I identify high potentials and promote **networking** among those talented people encouraging them to share and serve others to create synergies to accomplish bigger projects. Remember effective networking is a two-way give and receive.

First Sign of Success: Being hired by big multinationals was A Good Sign of success. First Signs of Success

Having my candidates promoted to international assignments was really a good reward and a better sign. Having a 30-year high-quality small Company with really Big clients and the best team of consultants, partners, and colleagues is a great satisfaction.

Having more than 15,000 followers on LinkedIn on my personal account and more than 10,000 on our corporate account is a great sign. We have been constantly persevering, always ready to help. But honestly, I think I could say we have been successful because I am at peace, happy, and grateful, and someone has always helped me. There has been a superior purpose in the team we had, giving added value and working with passion to help others to be better human beings.

My reward is learning to pray and having two granddaughters that I love. Being able to visit my mother, enjoying nature, and silence are great rewards.

Being nominated for this award, the best prize is the cherry! 🍒 on the cake! 🍰

Ultimate Solution
Hope, serve, create synergies, spaces to share and grow for free.

Honestly, I have not found the ultimate solution! I discovered advice from reading about history and people like Confucius, Budha, Jesus, Mohamed, Moses, and Abraham for whom we no longer listen! They are the masters. We complicate life. We could be happier if we followed the precepts and rules from these Masters that preceded us.

Now, we are reinventing wheels every day. We all want to be superstars!

In my case, maybe having huge corporate clients for years and more than 15,000 followers on LinkedIn could make me think that my success has happened because I have been perseverant, providing a high-quality service, good advice, and creating synergies among them, but the truth and the secret formula is that I trust God to help me and to help others, and I try to encourage talented executives to help each other and their teams.

I have reached many people to listen to their advice—friends, mentors, colleagues, and partners who permanently inspire me, give me feedback, and help me to overcome difficult times.
I have also participated in different workshops, webinars, several trainings, and cafe networking sessions to share experiences to learn from others how to construct better outcomes.

But the truth, honestly, is that I have tried to follow values and principles, and finally I am trying to understand the basics to translate those in the corporate world, sharing it with talents to encourage them to help each other to grow as human beings and leaders.

Free Gift

Are you trying to find a purpose in your life? Do you want to be successful and happy?

Be humble; understand there is a superior force. you cannot see it, but it exists to protect and love you. You are a very valuable creature despite your job, title, earnings, or income; ask for help
when you are in trouble; share: there is enough food, work, and shelter for everybody; pray every day. Be grateful.

Our free gift: Remind leaders to believe in miracles, be aware of God's incidences, and become servant leaders.
We as consultants are always trying to help others, give good advice connecting talents and people to help each other with a superior purpose

Another gift: in our web page and LinkedIn profile, there are two e-books published on Apple with beautiful testimonials and pictures from expatriates all over the globe and their stories during the pandemic.

The Best and Great Gift for free 24/7 will be available always, wireless, no links, no passwords needed: assist any church, pray, laugh, love, remind to be humble, read the Bible, give a hug, ask for help, smile, be grateful, be aware of God-incidences and enjoy nature and your family.

www.altosejecutivos.com.
www.linkedin.com/in/ines-pardo-0201b6
www.linkedin.com/in/altosejecutivos?original_refer

Accolades and Achievements

During the pandemic, I had to keep in a box several certifications, contracts with big companies, a few prizes, some nice pictures, and some mentions in magazines, and newspapers. I learned they were very small things compared with my best achievement: my two granddaughters and the legacy. We are trying to leave with my daughter in terms of values. Hugging my father while he was dying. Being able to visit my mother instead of any big client.

Those are the best achievements in my life, also volunteering activities, the other awards, prizes, certifications, and titles are nonsense compared with those intangible rewards.

Being invited to a world convention to receive an award on the 24th of August, coinciding on the day of my daughter's birthday, the one who had cancer and died, is THE AWARD for me, a proof of God's Incidence as many that had happened to me are priceless.

The best medal I won was for volunteering with veteran soldiers to become entrepreneurs. Being nominated for this women's award and learning that just to try to serve others is enough is the best recognition I have ever had in my life.

See What They Are Saying...

In general, my support has been helping many professional executives to recover their self-esteem because of losing their jobs and status and reminding them how valuable human beings they are at the end of finding a new job or developing skills to continue their professional life in a more human way.

***

*The Best testimony is from **Shajitha Ibrahim,** an outstanding lady from India, whom I really do admire, and is very generous with her words, which reminded me of what my mother always told me: I was a diamond in the rough...*
***

"Ines Pardo is one exceptional woman entrepreneur who has made an impeccable track record in everything that she has done. It's her heart as a leader that's intentional about touching every life with whom she comes in contact makes her who she is today and sets her apart. One of those rare gems to find."
***

Books and Business Links
"You are Unstoppable" Sherry Knight. Canada
"Networking" Jose Minarelli. Brazil
Emisora Minuto De Dios, Colombia
"Amen Comunicaciones" Padre Carlos Yepes Colombia
The Seven Habits. Stephen Covey
Leadership and Management Gustaykäser International

100 Most Successful Women Around the World: Build...

Tonya McNeal-Weary
Founder & Managing Director
IBS Global Consulting, Inc.
Detroit, Michigan, USA
tmcnealweary@gmail.com

Chapter 15
From Local to Global: How I Built an International Business from Scratch

Tonya McNeal-Weary is a multi-award-winning entrepreneur, international business expert, world traveler, author, and global champion for women's economic empowerment. She is the Founder and Managing Director of IBS Global Consulting, Inc., a global management consulting firm that specializes in helping Small and Medium Enterprises (SMEs) expand internationally.

For over a decade, Tonya has built an excellent reputation as a global thought leader with a passion for helping entrepreneurs and small businesses connect to international markets. She travels to countries around the globe, working with and advising entrepreneurs, CEOs, and owners of small businesses on how to "Think Global" and develop disruptive marketing strategies that set them apart from the competition.

Mission and Vision

My mission is to inspire and empower entrepreneurs to think global and create greater opportunities for women entrepreneurs to do business internationally. My vision is to create a company that attracts and brings the right people together to attain maximum results for our clients.

Starting from Scratch
Resilience. Determination. Patience.

Growing up as a young girl, I would go to work with my mother because she could not afford childcare. She worked for an insurance agency in Chicago, where I grew up. Eventually, I would work for the same insurance agency when I graduated from high school. My entrepreneurial journey began in 2001 when I decided to move from Chicago to Detroit. I always had an entrepreneurial spirit, so in 2002 after being fired from my job at a bank, I decided to take control of my destiny and start my own business. My first company was The McNeal Group Insurance Agency, LLC. I was so excited that my mother decided to also move to Detroit to help me run the business. Again, my mother and I would work together in an insurance agency, however, this time, it was our own. Everything was going great until it was not. The recession of 2008 severely impacted my business. That is when I knew I had to get clear - about my career and my future. Giving up on my dream to be my own boss was not an option. I knew I had to change my business direction and focus. So, I went back to school to further my education. This experience taught me the importance of resilience and staying strong through difficult times. My determination to succeed was greater than my willingness to fail. I learned to be patient and understand that success does not happen overnight, and the road to success is sometimes bumpy.

From Local to Global: How I Built an International Business from Scratch

Big Why
Purpose. Passion. Persistence.

I kept moving forward because I knew my life had a purpose – even if I did not know what that purpose was. My passion for creating a life of meaning and designing a business I loved grew even more. I was persistent and determined to keep pushing forward. When you face roadblocks in life, you have two choices – turn back and give up or find a new direction to reach your goals. I began studying finance at a prominent business college in Michigan. Although I didn't know the future direction of my insurance agency, I knew I wanted to continue being my own boss.

Aha Moment Epiphany
Experience. Mindset. Perception.

I knew I had to build a recession-proof business – a business that would be able to sustain economic changes. During my MBA studies, I had an opportunity to travel to China as part of a study abroad program on Doing Business in China. Besides Canada and the Caribbean, I have never traveled outside the country. Although I was terrified, I did not let my fear get in the way. This experience expanded my horizons and changed my mindset and my view of the world. The world and the opportunities in it seemed so much bigger. Immediately, I became interested in international business. So, I decided to change my major from finance to international business.

Secret Formula
Plan. Connect. Brand.

"If you fail to plan, you are planning to fail." – Benjamin Franklin. I carefully planned to launch my company after graduating with my MBA in International Business. I conducted the necessary research and took the time to learn and understand my industry. It's not always what you know, but who you know, so I spent time networking and connecting with the right people.

When I launched my company IBS Global Consulting in 2009, I needed to build a strong brand with a global footprint that would attract the type of clients I wanted to serve and the experts who could bring desired client results. By creating a strong brand, I built a global consulting company and a consulting team across four continents and attracted businesses from all over the world that wanted to expand their global footprint.

IBS Global Consulting participates in its first out-of-state trade event - Asian-US Business Summit, California USA - 2011

Steps to Build Success from Scratch

Everyone has a "why." I decided to build a business from scratch so that I could be in control of my life and build a legacy for my family. Here are four steps you can take to build your dream business from scratch.

1. **Vision**. It all starts with having a clear vision for what you want to achieve. I had a vision of what type of company I wanted to build and what it took to get there.
2. **Resources**. Make sure you have all the necessary resources and tools to run a successful business.
3. **Adaptability.** Everything will not always go as planned. You will face many challenges while building your business. So, being flexible and having the ability to adapt to changing circumstances is critical.
4. **Support.** You cannot do it alone. Trying to do this will only lead to burnout. It was important for me to surround myself with people of like minds who could support my goals and the growth of my business.

L to R: Manish Behl, IBS Global Consulting India (Mumbai), Gautam Khurana (New Delhi), Tonya McNeal-Weary, IBS Global Consulting USA (Michigan) and Deepti Vithal, Esp. (New York)

First Sign of Success

My first sign of success was when I realized that I could make money doing something I loved while making a difference to others. I had a tribe of like-minded and supportive people who wanted to see me succeed. It's one thing to make money but seeing the impact I had made on other people was the ultimate sign of my success. I found my purpose. I had built a global company from scratch connecting entrepreneurs and small businesses to international opportunities. I was inspiring other entrepreneurs to think global and build global enterprises. My company was helping small businesses grow their customer base and increase revenue by expanding into new markets.

Female-Focused Business Delegation to Bangkok, Thailand L to R: Nicole Parker, Tonya McNeal-Weary, Dr. Mary Segars, Elizabeth Chaney, Dr. Anita C. Powell

Ultimate Solution

My path to finding the ultimate solution for my business and my clients' businesses were forging valuable partnerships and leveraging these partnerships to enhance my company's capabilities and deliver added value to my clients. The combined capabilities of our consulting team and strategic partners gave us a competitive advantage in our industry. Success is not just about being better. Success is also about being different. To remain competitive, you must be open to trying new approaches and implementing innovative ideas. It's also about having the right mindset. Throughout my journey, I quickly learned that our attitude and way of thinking is a major factor in our own success or failure. We live in a global world, so to be successful and compete on a global level, we must establish a sense of global thinking in the way we operate.

Africa Trade & Investment Global Summit, Washington, DC USA 2018

From Local to Global: How I Built an International Business from Scratch

Free Offer

Receive a digital copy of my *Think Global Journal: 42 Affirmations to Inspire You to Think Global and Develop Good Habits to Boost Business Success*. In this journal, I share 42 affirmations not only to change the way you think but also to expand your mindset to think bigger! This journal will help you shift your mindset and take new approaches to take your business to the next level.

Accolades and Achievements

I am an Accredited Management Consultant and Certified Small Business Consultant with a passion for helping entrepreneurs and small businesses succeed globally. I've earned numerous awards and recognition for my work in the fields of international business and entrepreneurship, including the 100 Successful Women in Business, Exceptional Women of Excellence, and Entrepreneurs of Distinction, to name a few. I also received the Most Distinguished Award of Excellence from the Egyptian government under the auspices of H.E. President Abdelfattah El SISI.

In 2003, I founded Michigan Association for Female Entrepreneurs (MAFE), a nonprofit organization dedicated to supporting, promoting, and empowering female entrepreneurs in Michigan. Through my work with MAFE, I have helped thousands of women turn their entrepreneurial aspirations into realization.

In 2020, I launched the Women Going Global Initiative to help women entrepreneurs build their capacity to grow their businesses on a global scale through specialized training and coaching to address specific challenges and barriers women business owners face.

I have regularly served as a mentor to women around the world, providing advice, guidance, and support to help them reach their business goals. That included connecting women to helpful resources and relevant connections and supporting their leadership development.

See What They Are Saying...

"Tonya is a leader who is passionate about helping women entrepreneurs grow globally and is diligent about finding the right partners to help them prosper."

"Indeed, one can expand their global village and uncover opportunities by participating in a business delegation sojourn! I express my sincere gratitude to Tonya for further expanding my global shebiz footprint"

"Tonya is a businesswoman with a kind spirit and truthful intention of unifying people. She is a genuine, ethical leader who gets results."

***

Business Links
Learn more at
https://linktr.ee/tonyamcnealweary

Be sure to collect your FREE giveaway

Maria-Renee Davila, MBA
Global Trade Chamber
Fort Lauderdale, FL, USA
mariarenee@globaltradechamber.com

Chapter 16
From Modeling to Empowering

Maria-Renee Davila Macias, originally from Bolivia, is the founder and CEO of the Global Trade Chamber, an international chamber of commerce with headquarters in the US, helping companies to start, grow and connect worldwide. She produces and manages international business events around the globe.

Ms. Davila is the Founder of the 100 Successful Women in Business Network, a division of the Global Trade Chamber that empowers, connects, recognizes, and teaches women from many nations of all ages to start and grow a successful organization.

Maria Renee is also the publisher of the Women in Business Magazine and the Global Trade Chamber Magazine. She is the producer and host of several online streaming TV shows including Success Stories and Meets the Experts. In 2021 she launched the 100 Most Successful Women Around the World Book Volume I, which became a bestseller.

For over 12 years Maria Renee has been teaching business for higher education in several universities in the USA.

Mission and Vision

My vision is to be the leader in connecting entrepreneurs worldwide.
My mission is to connect entrepreneurs and provide them with tools to make them more productive and successful.

A New Beginning

At a very young age I decided to start my own company, a modeling agency, modeling academy, and after expanding to an event planning and video production company; I produced over 200 events including beauty pageants. With a lot of support from my mom, I was able to position my company as one of the best in the city.

I was doing great, then political instability started affecting my business, with almost everyday protests and strikes blocking the streets and bringing chaos. As a result, my clients started taking a very long time to pay me and costing delays in all areas of my business. As I became number one in my industry, due to the competition and the lack of loyalty and ethics from the models, it became very hard to compete in the market. Some of the competitors were not established companies with employees and offices like me. In the majority of the cases, they were working from home with no major overhead and staff, they provided services at low prices. In addition, some of the models were contacting the clients directly and offering their services for very low fees. I was getting very stressed and frustrated with the lack of professionalism and ethics in this business.

As a young woman some of the biggest challenges I faced, were discrimination and harassment. I was young and clients tried to take advantage of me and my models. We faced sexual harassment and lack of respect. This went as far as giving me a hard time when I tried to get paid for my services. I had to fight for my rights and what was due to me. Through all these challenges, I always maintained a high level of ethics and standards for my agency.

Exhaustion and discouragement got the best of me, I sold my company and decided to move to the USA for a new beginning.

Education is Key!

I came to the US; it was a new world to me not knowing the language, how to drive a car, and not being familiar with the culture. This was a cultural shock to me! Once again, I went through a very stressful and challenging time. I went back to my country, feeling down and confused. My dad advised me to study something in the US to further my education that will help me better understand the country, the market, the culture, and how business is conducted in America.

I got a Master of Business Administration Degree advancing my previous degree in Business Administration. My dad was right, and even though it was tough to study in a different language, it helped me to better understand the market, and learn the language, and the degree opened the door to teach at colleges, and to work as an independent licensed event planner traveling to other countries to produce events.

Connecting Entrepreneurs...

Shortly after I decided to explore opportunities to start a new venture. I spoke to many people, learned, and found a niche that had to be filled. As the world became more global, there was an opportunity to connect, educate and help entrepreneurs explore and penetrate new international markets. Producing international events in several countries opened my eyes to the need for a global organization to connect and empower businesses and entrepreneurs.

Big Wy
I Must Win!

I always had a burning desire to do my best and reach new heights. My mom and dad always encouraged me to keep going and never give up. The more people tell me that I can't do it, to quit, or to give up, the more they push me and motivate me to succeed.

I am a dreamer and a visionary and will pursue my dreams until they become a reality.

Aha Moment
Globalization is the present and future!

After exploring other cultures and countries, I realized the importance and need to connect and educate people on ways to do business around the world. That was the **aha moment** for me, to start a global business organization.

During this process of structuring and creating this project, I met my number one mentor in life Mr. Al Otero, who is a very respected and well-known leader in South Florida and other countries. Mr. Otero is an international speaker, chamber executive, and master networker. He always had a global vision like me, and we became partners. With the support of investors including my loving husband and my mother, in 2009 we started the Global Trade Chamber, since then we have been helping members and non-members connect worldwide, providing consulting, business referrals, and business tools to small businesses. We do trade missions, global conventions, and matchmaking appointments. We also have a trade center which is a business center that provides virtual offices, meeting rooms, and digital services, just to mention a few. Currently, we offer over 20 different programs to help companies to start, grow and expand in local and international markets.

Secret Formula
Empower, inspire, educate

Serving others is my secret formula.

I serve multicultural entrepreneurs and small and medium-sized businesses with all resources of the Global Trade Chamber that enable them to succeed in global markets.

Some of the resources available for the chamber:

DEVELOPING LEADERS
The Global Trade Chamber has a series of webinars, seminars, articles, TV Shows, and interviews presented by experts from many industries, organizations, demographics, and cultures designed to help entrepreneurs become skillful leaders.

SMALL AND MINORITY BUSINESS SERVICES
The international team of experienced professionals from various industries, agencies, and nations is here to help individuals start and grow successful enterprises in local and global markets. The Global Trade Chamber's services include an official business address, virtual offices, website development, promotion, e-marketing, mentoring, counseling, sponsorship and advertising, business events, and connections.

CHAMBER-TO-CHAMBER INITIATIVES
The Global Trade Chamber network of business organizations in the US and other countries provides companies with exclusive access to multicultural communities around the world. The Global Trade Chamber offers several initiatives to help companies explore doing business in, and with those communities including monthly bilateral matchmaking events.

SUCCESSFUL WOMEN GLOBAL NETWORK
The 100 Successful Women in Business Network (100SWB) is an exclusive multimedia platform that provides a vehicle for amazing women of all ages and cultures to come together. The objective is to build relationships, learn from the experts, be recognized, empowered, and inspired, share unique stories, help each other grow professionally, promote organizations, and make a positive impact in communities.

PUBLICATIONS AND COMMUNICATIONS
The Global Trade Chamber provides businesses with several vehicles to reach new clients and markets including two digital business magazines, online streaming channels and shows, social media management, email campaigns, bestselling books, webinars, and global events.

GTC TV CHANNEL

The Global Trade Chamber produces several online TV programs that teach, inform, and keep entrepreneurs updated on news from industries, sectors, and countries important to their trade. All shows are streamed on several global platforms such as Amazon Fire Stick, Roku TV, YouTube, Vimeo, Trovo Live, Twitch TV, Nimo TV, Picarto TV, DLive TV, Kakao TV, Naver TV, Afreeca TV, Tele 2, and more.

HAVE A PERSONAL WEEKLY 30-MINUTE SHOW

Having a TV program is a great way for entrepreneurs to be known, build an image, share information regarding different industries, and educate others.

SUCCESSFUL WOMEN IN BUSINESS WEEKLY DIGITAL MAGAZINE

The Successful Women in Business Weekly Magazines are filled with great articles from experts, success stories, and world news to help women entrepreneurs to grow their businesses and be inspired.

GLOBAL TRADE CHAMBER MONTHLY DIGITAL MAGAZINE

The Global Trade Chamber's monthly magazine is filled with great articles from experts, success stories, and world news to help entrepreneurs to grow their businesses and promote their companies in local and international markets.

100 MOST SUCCESSFUL WOMEN AROUND THE WORLD BOOK

The 100 Most Successful Women Around the World Book recognizes accomplished women from various nations and industries that have overcome great challenges and have achieved their dreams. This remarkable book empowers women in business, working mothers, students, coaches, mentors, organizations, and nonprofits, making an impact capable of changing women's lives.

DIGITAL MARKETING AND EMAIL CAMPAIGNS

The Global Trade Chamber promotes companies and events by implementing an e-marketing plan that includes email marketing, social media campaigns, multimedia, and other forms of outreach relevant to specific industries.

GLOBAL EVENTS

The Global Trade Chamber produces, co-produces, manages, promotes, and organizes business events throughout the year, online and in several cities and countries including business expos, conferences, seminars, and conventions.

INTERNATIONAL BILATERAL MATCHMAKING EVENTS

Monthly live, in-person, and online activities hosted by The Global Trade Chamber and presented by Chamber Executives from many nations, bringing together buyers and sellers from the US and other countries looking to exchange goods and services.

100 SUCCESSFUL WOMEN IN BUSINESS ANNUAL AWARDS AND CONVENTION
This annual event recognizes successful women from many sectors and countries making a positive impact in their communities and the world.

SUCCESSFUL WOMEN IN BUSINESS CONFERENCES ROADSHOW
The Global Trade Chamber and the 100 Successful Women in Business Network produce conferences in different cities, giving access for women to meet and connect to other women and explore opportunities in new markets.

WEBINARS
The Global Trade Chamber organizes, produces, and promotes webinars for companies and entrepreneurs to present information about their industries, company, or services that are informative and educational to the viewers.

THE TRADE CENTER
The Trade Center is a business center that provides cost-effective office space for short to medium-term durations. The Trade Center rents offices, rooms for meetings, events, etc.

WEBINAR STUDIO
Get your message across from our webinar studio. Our studio is designed to get your message across as professionally as possible. We will record, edit, and broadcast your webinar, promotional video, commercial, or podcast at a fraction of the cost of other studios.

Steps to Success from Scratch

1. Determine what you are good at and what you enjoy doing. You can find in the internet a skill assessment test to evaluate your skills.
2. Have a Vision: Define where you want to be, plan the future with imagination and wisdom.
3. Get an Education: take courses, certifications, licenses, degrees, any complimentary diploma that will make you an expert in your field.
4. Find your Niche: Look for a specific audience, clients that you want to serve.
5. Your Purpose in life: Determine what is your ultimate purpose in life.

6.   Plan to success: Create a business plan for your company that will guide you.

Sign of Success!

The first sign of success for me was when Fortune 500 companies were calling me to work with me when National TV channels started calling me to be a contributor in their programs. When clients started recognizing me and the name of my company.

When the competition sees you as a threat is when you know you are succeeding in business.

Being an entrepreneur is not an easy job, but you have to be able to deal with the ups and downs of your business, it can take years before it gets better. During my journey, I always counted on the support of my family and friends. People that love me and appreciate me.

Entrepreneurs are born not made!

You are born with specific skills that you need to discover, what are they?

Some people are visionaries and leaders by nature, some others not. Some people are very creative and come up with amazing ideas for products or services that will help many people and change the world. Some people can build global organizations from just an idea. Some people are driven to go beyond their limits.

Entrepreneurs are born not made because they have the spirit, they are risk takers, they have a burning desire to innovate and execute their ideas. These skills are not taught at school. However, you can learn at school all the necessary tools to run a business successfully.

Ultimate Solution
Get a mentor

Learn from the mentor, their experience, wisdom, and expertise.
No matter where you are in life, you can always learn and grow from the experiences of others.

The ultimate solution is building long-term relationships based on trust.

Achievements, awards
Some of the Awards she received.

Hispanic Leaders Award from the
city of North Miami 2018

50 Most Powerful Global Trade
Advocate by the US Department
of Commerce and the MBDA
Export Center 2019

100 Successful Women in
Business Award -2019

Where People Need People –
Unity in Service 2019

Ladies of All Nations Global Award -2020

Recognition for helping women around the world by Miss International World
Organization 2020

Mandela Medal - World Peace Award 2021

Lifetime Achievement Award from President Biden 2021

Offer

Visit my website to get a FREE
membership and connect with amazing
women.

See What They Are Saying...

Maria Renee is very active and well known in the community and has accumulated many years of experience and expertise in the business and public relations areas. Maria Renee, very often, goes above and beyond the expectations of her peers to achieve her objectives. Her positive, professional approach, as well as her outgoing character has earned her a great reputation. Should you need to contact me for additional information regarding Maria Renee, please call me at 954- 741-2234 or via email at ofacey@crmfirm.com

Sincerely,
Dr. Owen Facey
President, Clarocision Research & Marketing
E: ofacey@crmfirm.com 7207 W Oakland Park Blvd, Lauderhill, FL. 33313/Phone: 954-741-2234/www.crmfirm.com

***

At Ana G. Mendez University, we are happy to count with professionals like you that do their job so well. We encourage you to continue contributing in such a positive manner to the teaching learning process of our students.

Regards,
Prof. Julie Carrion
Director of Faculty & Curriculum
E: jumily77@yahoo.com 954-278-5236

***

Dear Professor Davila:

I want to say hello and wish you well and much success in the future. Let me tell you that this course and subject has become a fundamental pillar for me because I am applying it with my clients to help the sales department to function better. Your classes are excellent, thank you for all the positive feedback that helps us to grow.

Sincerely, Jose

***

From Modeling to Empowering

Learn more about this author

Please visit our websites:

www.100swb.com

www.globaltradechamber.com

Follow us on:

https://bling.me/QHAzXnuIbc56

Kandee G
Kandee G Enterprises, Big Sexy Stables
kandeeg@kandeeg.com
Ocala, Florida, USA

Chapter 17
From Peanut Butter to Private Jets

Kandee G - Creator of the Vision Program, Author, Speaker, Radio Personality, Magazine Publisher, International Leader in Corporate and Personal Development, TEDx Speaker, Equine assisted Therapist. Les Brown, the world's leading motivational speaker says that "Kandee G has been gifted with the ability to help people change their lives." Les Brown also states, "Kandee G is recognized as being among the top in the industry."

Mission and Vision

My mission is to help others create their vision. I feel that the true path to having the life that you want begins with having a strong, clear vision—a positive productive clear Vision where you can feel it with all of the sensory vividness of reality.

Anyone can start a business. Many people have the belief that they can't create their own success. It starts with giving up that belief that it can't be done. Make the decision to believe in yourself and your dreams, and never give that up.

Starting from Scratch
The One Peanut Butter Jar

Loss, struggle, commitment.

Over 29 years ago, my life circumstances took a dramatic dow nturn. Everything I had worked so hard for retirement accounts, savings accounts, investment accounts, and my home were abruptly gone. I was alone taking care of my 4-month-old baby. With no family to turn to, I was horrified to get to the point where only one jar of peanut butter was left in my refrigerator. At that moment, I made the decision that I was not going to be a victim of life circumstances. I would be a victor. Don't get stuck on having one peanut butter jar! You can have much more than that. Train yourself instead to get stuck in powerful thoughts, feelings, and images of what you want your life to be.

From Peanut Butter to Private Jets

Big Why
Commitment, Faith. Determination.

Since that time, I have built four very successful businesses. I've been recognized as being among the top in my industries. I have been interviewed by major publications, television, and radio for my success. I would travel to most places by private jet; hence my story's been called "From Peanut Butter to Private Jets." I am living proof that life circumstances represent the intersection of mediocrity and personal prosperity. "Love, Compassion, Belief. My beautiful baby girl, now an extraordinary young lady, became my reason and persistent determination to make life work; wholly, fully, and happily. My success and subsequently my current work were born out of my search for my own path to personal and professional empowerment. I came to understand that there are timeless universal principles that underlie those things that we create. Reality is bound by these just as surely as the principles of math, chemistry, and physics.

Aha Moment Epiphany
Personal Responsibility, Creation, Manifestation.

I came to understand that thoughts are things and that you can re-engineer your thoughts so that you can redesign your life consciously and deliberately. Your thoughts, as well as your feelings, power your vision and your creativity- your ability to create-to manifest."

Secret Formula
Gratitude, Attraction, Surrender

I've brought my expertise to thousands through speaking events, TED talks, coaching, training, my own radio show called Nothing but Good News for 10 years, my own magazine that I published for 10 years also called Nothing but Good News, my online presence, and my signature Vision Program. With the understanding of the tools, people all over the world are enhancing and living the lives they have

been dreaming about. I am a published author of a book, "Now Boarding: Next Stop, Your Remarkable Life"

I continue to envision and create. I have a real passion for horses, natural horsemanship, and equine-assisted work. Natural horsemanship teaches you how to work with and train your horse utilizing the philosophy of working with them based on the horse's

natural instincts and methods of communication. Horses have a natural, mindful way of teaching us to stay singularly focused on the outcome in a safe, simple way. They teach us the extraordinary power of vision and so much more. I like to say we are playing with magic. These incredible, soulful creatures have a unique way of helping you learn some key lessons to make life work. Working with them teaches us how to use thought and feeling to communicate. I also do mini Ted-like talks from a horse and carriage called Conversations from the Carriage.

Steps to Build Success from Scratch

Understand your subconscious mind. Find out your real passion and purpose. Take the time to discover yourself. Thought-provoking questions are a great way to discover you. Learn to meditate; it is a pathway to your inner self. You are here for a reason. Make it your mission to uncover that. Then, create a system to keep your conscious and non-conscious systems on track. Make that what you do every day. Do not get sidetracked by distractions

First Sign of Success

I utilized my tools and systems to create a very successful sales team. I realized what I had created for myself, and my daughter was teachable. I could help other folks to do what I did. So, I set on a journey to do just that. My support came from my great good God that always showed me the way when I got stuck. I surrendered to his wisdom and continued to put one foot in front of the other. I have helped and taught thousands of folks around the world. I have brought companies back from bankruptcy. I knew early on with my own success that this was my path, my assignment, what I was put here on this earth to do.

Ultimate Solution

Just what are you feeling? It is vital to understand that emotion is just as creative as thought because our thoughts and emotions are so intimately linked. Our emotions mold our thoughts, and our thoughts likewise shape our emotions. How often are you experiencing positive emotions? How often do you feel good? George Bernard Shaw says that "Life isn't measured by the number of breaths we take, but by the moments that take our breath away." How often do you have those moments? Learn to look in on yourself and observe what kinds of thoughts and feelings you allow to occupy your mind. Remember that these internal raw materials build your exterior reality. You can learn to rewrite and regulate your creative thought process. When you learn to re-engineer your thoughts and feelings, you can change your life, consciously and deliberately, and build a highway straight to your dreams. You truly can design your own destiny. Your key is to find someone that has been there. Having a mentor or a coach is your quickest path to your personal prosperity.

Free Gift

I am willing to offer a free 30-minute coaching session to the first 20 people that respond.

Reach out to me at kandeeg@kandeeg.com

Accolades and Achievements

One of my most endearing achievements is that for five years in a row I was named as one of the 100 Outstanding Women in Broward County. These awards were received due to my ten years on the radio and my ten years publishing a magazine, both called" Nothing But Good News". In addition, I emceed many charity events. I also worked with many companies to help them change their internal culture.   I have received close to 200 special awards and acknowledgments.

See What They Are Saying...

"It is invaluable to me to have Kandee G as my CEO concierge coach as it gets me centered; it centers me back to what is important. It reminds me of our vision and right values that can be lost so easily with distractions and day-to-day decision-making. It is so important to have that one place where I can go to help to shift the chatter in my head. It has been vital to me to have Kandee G as my CC Coach in these economic times because there is always a solution, but you can't always see it. To have someone there to help me stay clearly focused on the right direction has been not only our edge over the competition; but the key to our continued growth."
CC Coach Client

***

"To the best Coach, Trainer, Motivator and friend in the world. Thanks for all you've done."
Ricky and Liz J.

***

"Kandee G is living proof that you can live your dreams. I have had the honor of watching her bring her deepest desires to fruition through her devotion to her spirituality and her absolute belief in the power of the self and the Universe. She is truly living her passion and her greatest joy is in helping others do the same." *Vision Program Graduate*

***

Book and Business Link
"Now Boarding: Next Stop Your Remarkable Life
Brown Books Publishing Group
Publish date 2005 Kandee G"

www.kandeeg.com. www.bigsexystables.com

Karin Cristela Rodriguez
Signo Plast S.A.
La Tablada, Buenos Aires, Argentina
krodriguez@signoplast.com.ar

Chapter 18
Fundamental Messages of Life

Karin C. Rodriguez studied journalism at the University of Salvador and the Development and Management of the Pymes University of Buenos Aires. At the age of 15, she started working in the company her father founded, Signo Plast S.A. She has been a Partner and Director of Administration and Finance for 23 years. She is a graduate of the MED program, Women in Decision of Fundación FLOR. Karin carried out the virtual training for businesswomen and entrepreneurs from Latin America and the Caribbean known as the Win-Win program.

Mission and Vision

Karin's mission is dedicated to two passions: her industrial company and women's empowerment to ensure they gain personal, economic growth, achieve global recognition, and success.

Her greatest pride is being an example of struggle, effort, overcoming, and gratitude, for her 3 boys whom she loves more than anything in the world.

Build a Business from Scratch
Commitment, Taking Risks, Sorority

The key principle I live by is to give yourself 100% to what you do, and to others. I believe that my greatest value is to show myself as I am, to be transparent, and above all be humble. I am very proud of all my achievements, but I am aware that life can change from one day to the next, and I must be the same.

I think that you must be affectionate and warm with others, it is very important that whoever is on the other side feels our empathy and feels the same as us. Join a group of women with common interests for fellowship.

My coach says that I am a true mentor because of the way I generously support others. You should not be afraid of challenges and hard work. I know that I will always find the strength to achieve my purpose and you can too.

Trust in your ability and in what others see in you... there are opportunities in which someone proposes us to do something for which they saw us capable before we ourselves knew that we were.

Big Why
Love, Belonging, Pride... Desire Overcoming

When you love your company so much as a brother because you both grew together, you get the strength to keep fighting in the face of adversity. This love is what all entrepreneurs need to feel to undertake their projects.

I LOVE being a businesswoman. I am proud to be known to the world as the FCO of the company my wise father founded. For me, it is very important to help other women to achieve success in their businesses and in their lives. For this reason, with a group of businesswomen from the UIA, Union Industrial

Argentina, we founded Red MIA - Mujeres de la Industria Argentina.

Our great motive is for women to take their power, dare to be great, and own their position in a male-dominated industry. As a woman, she must be seen as a leader and capable of running a male-dominated business. RED MIA is an organization where we promote equal opportunities and enhance the role of women in the fabric of production.

Aha Moment
From Argentina to Egypt, My Great Challenge and the Beginning of Everything

In 2018, I attended a program on Corporate Governance with a Gender Perspective at Fundacion FLOR (**F**undaciòn **L**iderazgos y **O**rganizaciones **R**esponsables), of which today I am an ambassador. This was a pivotal moment in my personal and professional life. I understood that I had a lot to share with other women about my experiences. I began to participate in the Business Guild, representing other companies in UIPMA, Unión Industrial del Partido de la Matanza, from there go to UIPBA, Unión Industrial de la Provincia de Buenos Aires.

In March 2020 I was encouraged to travel to Egypt. Until that moment I had never left my children and my husband to travel alone; it was quite a challenge. This decision changed my life to participate in the Women Economic Forum there.

I met a universe of wonderful women, powerful, generous, and strong, who inspired me to continue growing and helping others. The forum was led by an incredible woman, born in India, Dr. Harbeen Arora. In this meeting, I felt the strength of women united by a purpose from different countries, professions, and ages, but all with the same goal: To provide thought leadership on what needs to be done for inclusivity, safety, economic and social empowerment of women globally, addressing gender gaps, and achieving gender parity within this decade. At that

moment, I decided that all my activities were going to be guided by these principles and with this objective. I also partnered with my dear Karen Bruges, from Mujeres Violeta, in Colombia, to contribute to achieving gender equality in different spaces through training and empowerment.

Later, during the pandemic, from the UIA, Union Industrial Argentina, we created Red MIA | Women of the Argentine industry to promote equal opportunities and strengthen the female role in the productive fabric. We are capable of empowering, inspiring, and becoming the change required to give birth to leaders with a bigger vision and purpose.

Thanks to my participation in these organizations, I was invited to be the Argentine Chair of Public Relations of the G100, Director of the Women Economic Forum Colombia 2022, Argentine Chair of Creative Women Platform, and other organizations.

Secret Formula
Fundamental Messages of Life

"**L**earn from all experiences, even the most negative", that was my father's advice. My dad, a self-taught but extremely WISE man, who founded our company more than 50 years ago told me this, while we were facing a big lawsuit brought by a former employee, that to obtain an economic benefit he was lying with his claim. Dad told me, "I prefer to be the one who is harmed by the lie and not the one who is lying". This is engraved on me forever, and it is a fundamental message in my life and one of my core values.

The most valuable lesson and principles from this are for you to speak the truth and be transparent with who you are and what you stand for in life. Be honest, loyal, and respectful with all you do.

The rest will be the seeds that you pass to others from generations.

Every time I felt that I couldn't, that I wasn't going to live up to expectations, I sought help. Do not be afraid to admit that you have weaknesses, look for those who can add knowledge, and experiences, but do not stop believing in your capacity. If you decide to start a business, if you start a project, seek support from other women who will guide you thanks to their experience. Fortunately, thanks to technology, there are countless tools today. We can study, and train at all levels with free tutorials that are available to listen to while we cook, do physical activity and drive.

Steps to Build Success from Scratch

It is important to share your success with others and above all to be grateful to those who opened doors for you, never forget who helped you when you needed it and in the same way, help those who need it. It is wonderful to mentor other women and guide them on their paths.

I am a grateful woman who lives with joy and love.

I highly encourage all women to join, network, participate, and commit to organizations that have a common interest, vision, and mission. The focus should be on growing and sharing your knowledge to support, inspire and motivate others to commit to their higher purpose. This will make them stronger, and in giving they will find their fullness. Make sure to do the following:

1. Commitment, risk, sorority
2. Dream, believe, be grateful, and share
3. Dream, don't be afraid, and don't limit yourself
4. Believe in yourself and in what you do
5. Do not limit yourself, and do not fear error
6. Learn from your mistakes.
7. Ask for help it doesn't make you weak
8. Share with others your process and your good fortune
9. Inspired others through your achievements
10. Be grateful
11. Open doors, just as the others opened them for you
12. Keep improving
13. Go after what you want
14. Keep networking and belonging to a foundation or association or several

First Sign of Success

The first sensation of success I had was when I was given the title of President of the Industrial Congress Pyme 2020 of UIPBA, the Industrial Union of the Province of Buenos Aires. At that moment I felt that my work on the executive committee was very valued. That sector of the industry is very male-oriented, and it was the first time that in this event a woman was a president.

Since then, I had a dynamic expansion into several sectors, and I was called to occupy other leadership positions in organizations that fight for gender equality. Experience has shown me that when you work with a goal, you commit to what you are doing, and the opportunities appear.

Ultimate Solution
Dare and Not Be Afraid

I propose to dare and not be afraid, be responsible, and learn to ask for help. Networking is very important even in our company. Brené Brown says, "The courage to be vulnerable is not about winning or losing, it's about the courage to show up when you can't predict or control the outcome" Do not fear challenges... They will make you grow and become a stronger woman day by day.

And about business, it's essential to show your integrity and trustworthiness. In my company, Signo Plast S.A., we manufacture signs for oil companies, banks, and other corporations. What our clients value in us is trust, quality, and seriousness. When your product is good, of quality, and reliable, with work and perseverance, success comes.

ALWAYS trust yourself... don't be afraid of challenges. Study, train. May each challenge in your life make you a better person. Day by day build your best version of yourself. Capitalize on all your experiences to become a wiser, stronger, more powerful woman... Marian Rojas Estapé, a psychiatrist I love to listen to, says that "Dream big; act small! Let your heart fly and make an action plan with a good strategy. If you have built a castle in the air, you have not wasted your time. Now get to building the foundation under it."

NEVER stop being yourself, be faithful to your principles, and take care of the greatest capital you have YOUR INTEGRAL AND TRUE BEING.

Free Gift (Advice)

Encourage yourself to lead your life, to believe in yourself. Get out of the comfort of your office and commit to participating in the representative spaces of companies and other organizations helping others. Be part of the change you think is necessary. Do networking and be reliable; don't change over time or with success. Never stop working for your dreams and try to be the best example you can give to your children and the world in general.

Accolades and Achievements

For my philanthropic activity, and permanent work to achieve the growth and empowerment of women in the world, I was honored with the following awards: *Leader of Excellence Award from, Global Women Economic Forum India, 2021; * WAW HONORARY AWARD 2021 from Woman Appreciating Women, * Breaking Barriers 2022 from Red de Sororidad Pacto entre ellas, Peru, * Mother Teresa Global Peace Award 2021 from Mother Teresa International Foundation.

Thanks, thanks, wonderful women who opened paths for me...

Andrea Grobocopatel, Lina Anllo, Irini Wentinck, Harbeen Arora, Viola Edward, Rosita, my mom...

See What They Are Saying...

Karen Bruges Zolano, Directora Women Economic Forum Colombia 2022, CEO Mujeres Violeta.

***

Karin Rodriguez is a light woman, Karin has strengthened my leadership not only as my partner in Mujeres Violeta but also by imprinting determination in my life; She, through her generous and loving heart, has made obstacles become learning moments, making everything possible.

***

She allows me to see when I am in moments of anxiety and connects me with the here and now.

***

Constanza Sena, President of La Matanza Industrial Union. "Knowing Karin is having the necessary support to achieve everything you set out to do. Her honesty, sincerity, and model of a business and industrial woman is the example that women need to know that we can break the glass ceiling. His simplicity and humility are admirable. I am so grateful to live for putting Karin in my path. It is like an angel that no matter what happens, you know that it will be there, to give you that advice, that hand, those words that will guide you to achieve the best solution".

***

Laila Wagner, Head of the SME, Secretariat ABAPRA, Association of Public and Private Banks Of Argentina. "Karin is my reference in the G100 women leaders. Wherever she has assumed leadership, she produces a strong impact, achieving tangible results in terms of inclusion, creativity, and development of human talent. A leader of leaders, who knows how to bring out the best in others to always go further".

Karin C. Rodriguez
Directora / Director at Signo Plast S.A

Buenos Aires, Argentina

Mobile: +541154259974
Work: krodriguez@signoplast.com.ar

Dr. Violet Howard
VIOLET L HOWARD, INC.
Boca Raton, Florida, USA
howardviolet@gmail.com

Chapter 19
Generational Poverty is not about Money but about Mindset

I was born and raised in the city of Chicago, Illinois, I had a very challenging childhood. My dad died when I was 9yrs old, so on a quest to provide for the family, my mom began trafficking drugs which led to her incarceration. As a child, I thought I had seen everything until upon her release, I subsequently witnessed her violent murder. Even though I was angry, feeling that life was not fair, and vowing to take a different path, I walked into the footsteps that had already been carved out for me. Sadly, I had allowed the ghosts from my mother's past to haunt me. I became her.

Mission and Vision

Dr. Violet's ultimate focus is to empower the disenfranchised to thrive by being the best version of themselves and believing their lives have value. Her mission is to create significant social change that strives toward mitigating and ultimately eradicating major issues associated with poverty.

Challenge
The Awakening to My New Brilliance

One day I found myself fighting for my life as my mom had many times, so I made a horrible decision to protect myself and was convicted for unlawful use of a handgun. Even though it was self-defense and I harmed no one, it was still a crime. The day I witnessed my mom's murder, and in that same day, I almost lost my life as well as changed my perspective on life it was like an awakening. I learned who Violet was and who she was not. I denoun ced that person. I knew within my heart that I deserved a better life. Besides, I was very smart; some called me a genius. I was a sought-after model and a great basketball player who was given a scholarship to Robert Morris University. Others saw in me that I couldn't see within myself. I was blinded by my surroundings and needed a horizontal shift in the right direction, so I decided to take my painful experiences and turn them into purposeful pursuits.

I left Chicago for a vacation to Chesapeake, VA, after my mom's funeral in 2011 and never returned. I wanted a new life, leaving everything I owned behind along with my mindset. I tapped into my brilliance and embraced a new outlook on life. I learned that my future was not predicated upon my past, there was nothing that could stop me from achieving my highest levels of success or enjoying life to its fullest potential, and what was designed to kill my dreams, caused me to triumph over my tragedies and failures. Always remember there's a light at the end of every dark tunnel as long as you keep walking forward the light will eventually shine upon your life.

Big Why
A shot to My True Reality (change subtitle if you desire)

When I decided not to return to Chicago after my mom's death, I felt free and filled with hope that I too can live a peaceful prosperous lifestyle. Being in a clean environment where you didn't hear gunshots outside your windows or being able to walk down the street being greeted by happy smiling people made me realize these are the experiences we are missing where I come from. I set out on a journey to learn their behavior traits and mannerism to lead a better life. Engage the reader in finding and going after their bigger why and how it will change their life. I have been taking care of myself since I was 10 years old due to my mom being in prison and my father died when I was 9 years old.. I've learned to survive … I learned to drive when I was tall enough to be behind the wheel. I learned not to let anything stop me from my purpose....

Aha Moment Epiphany
Rebuilding Your Credit

The moment I was exposed to a different world realizing we're not taught goal setting, working together, and dreaming beyond what we saw in our rundown impoverished communities. Also, we lack exposure to resources, information, and different profitable business-building strategies to better ourselves financially. I was inspired to create a consulting business so that I could further fuel my dreams into a profitable model designed to effect global change for generations to come. I wrote and implemented a curriculum to help individuals build more effective business models and create wealth through investing and leveraging affiliate programs. That gave me the passion to write a "D.I.Y. Credit Repair Book, 45

Days to Funding and Building Business Credit". I had overcome major adversity, so surely, I was paying it forward!

142

Secret Formula

I had to relearn what I know now. I had to learn about finances and how to rebuild

myself up. The only thing I knew was surviving. Now, I help women with the secret formula that I discovered which is ...My secret formula is being humble and providing solutions! I serve the underserved through my philanthropy work, social media, website, and eBooks by sharing information and strategies to develop more financially healthy situations. Most business owners fail in the first two years because they lack exposure to the proper information on how to do the basic things like building business credit, leveraging their social media accounts, professional websites, and affiliate products to generate multiple streams of income from one source. I know what it's like not being able to afford access to the proper information to excel further and having the only solution to "fail" in order to learn. I used to be a business owner attending all of the free networking events to learn bits of information to increase my network which helped me build my income and gave me the opportunity to pay for the more expensive events learning all of the techniques for building more profitable business models. Most people with access to this information are charging thousands to share the strategies and struggling business owners can't afford to risk thousands of dollars starting out.

Steps to Build Success from Scratch

There is no such thing as one key to success. There are multiple keys to multiple doors and multiple steps each one leading to the next.

Here are 6 steps that helped me grow.

1. Shifting my mindset by listening to motivational videos on YouTube daily
2. Reading all self-help books
3. Setting Goals and sticking to them
4. Giving 110% effort towards everything I do
5. Learning how to build personal and business credit
6. Leveraging affiliate programs for residual income

First Sign of Success

My first sign of success was when one of my ex-employees told me he started his forex academy, and another employee purchased her first home following my methods. I used to manage a call center where I hired a bunch of young adults to test my methods. I taught them marketing and sales and how to leverage their job to fund another business venture. They elevated from working entry-level jobs like McDonalds crew, earning almost $300 a week to averaging $1000 minimum per week. We must remember no matter how small the wins are that we celebrate them and consistently surround ourselves with others who inspire us to chase after our dreams.

Ultimate Solution

My ultimate solution is self-educating, and I have designed a website that provides business owners/aspiring business owners access to affordable techniques to build more efficient and profitable business models. Lead them to want what you have to offer and lead them to offer below

Free Gift (Advice)

My advice to other women would be to surround themselves with people who want to see them grow and win in life, get out of your own way, trust God, drown all negative thoughts and naysayers, and do what feels right for you and your family. Consistently seek collaboration with like-minded individuals, invest in yourself, and work hard. Support a local charity or non-profit organization with your time and money to show your local community through your actions how much you care. I designed an Executive training course to teach business owners how to get the most out of their employees, conflict resolution, and how to build more profitable business models—just to name a few. These areas are detrimental to a new business owner just starting out.

When you're loving, caring, generous, and supportive of others, life rewards you with everything you need.

In order to become the success that you desire, you must begin your own journey while being optimistic. You must believe in yourself, have a vision so big that it scares you, be willing to give it all you've got, and totally get lost in your purpose!

Website: violethoward.com

Generational Poverty is not about Money but about Mindset

Accolades and Achievements

In 2021, through God's grace, I received an Honorary Doctorate Degree in Humanitarianism from Global International Alliance, for many years of community outreach work. I also received the highest award in the country, the prestigious President Joe Biden Presidential Lifetime Achievement Award.

See What They Are Saying...

I have helped numerous single mothers build businesses online. I've also helped a former employee start her insurance consulting business. Also, I've helped one of my credit consulting customers build their business and personal credit to get access to funding for real-estate investing business.

***

Business Links

https://linktr.ee/drviolethoward

Hope Phillips Umansky, PhD, aka Dr. Hope
Innovations: Education Advocacy Group, Inc;
Hope, Health, & Healing
San Diego, California, USA
hope.umansky@gmail.com

Chapter 20
Grit, the Secret Roaring Underdog that Transcends the Shadow

Dr. Hope is a professor, psychology and educational consultant, author, and keynote speaker. Dr. Hope sees teaching and psychology as parallel professions. Her publications and presentations have been on NBC, CBS, ABC, and Fox affiliates, as well as being a featured interview in *The Washington Post*. Currently, Dr. Hope, when not writing or keynote speaking, teaches at the University of Massachusetts Global and other niche universities. She maintains a higher ed and integrative psychology consulting practice. She holds a BA in English literature, a Master of Arts in Liberal Studies in English literature, and a MA/PhD in clinical psychology with an emphasis on trauma, resilience, and the healing arts. Dr. Hope spends most of her time teaching, writing, working with people to find their literal and figurative voices, and being the mom to a daughter on fire to help the world. Dr. Hope is driven by a heart-centered fire to understand and help people.

Mission and Vision

In Dr. Hope's public role as a keynote speaker and author, she is often interviewed on the intersection of historical context and popular American culture with an emphasis on the complex human experience and transcending personal and collective trauma. Dr. Hope dives deep with a rogue and unconventional vision examining the edgy truths that make us who we are, influence our behavior, and inform our identity. Her integrative psychology consulting practice is both for individuals and organizations. She has been named the compassionate leader, for her unconventional ways of dealing with systemic issues with leaders and organizations.

Starting from Scratch

"You've always had the power, my dear, you just had to learn it for yourself." – the Wicked Witch, The Wizard of Oz, L. Frank Baum, 1900.

You hold all the power to begin your life anew at any time it requires. As professional women, especially if we are at or around the messy hallmark of life, we have been conditioned to see ourselves in a gaze that is not entirely ours. At the times when it seems the house of cards has fallen, we must remember we have the power; we just have to remember it is there. That was the witch's wisdom in Oz, and as we saw, there is no witch—just an illusion of one. Our conditioning that no longer serves us – we are too fat, too thin, too smart, too opinionated, too funny, too passionate, too "masculine," too decisive– can be shed at any time. It is an illusion like the witch melting. The power, wisdom, and intuition are what you can grab on to when all else falls away and something needs to be done, a business started from scratch with your particular passion. Jung, America's first spiritual or integrative psychologist, states there are two archetypes for women in our conditioned society – the victim, who takes on the identity of being helpless when tragedy strikes or we fail at something, which is entirely human; frankly, this is the jumping off place of brilliance. Choosing the latter archetype, the one of the woman who harnesses her power through the tragedy of disappointment, despite it, in fact, is always there deep inside us.

Challenge
Shock. Fear. Resilience.

Life is so full of surprises, tragedies, and triumphs, sometimes all at once. Sometimes they are all rolled in together. After leading one of the most progressive graduate schools as CEO and Academic Dean through a grueling accreditation process for a near decade, I missed the freedom to work with people and with students and to pursue my own passion for a kinder, more equitable world. When the position, while on the outside looks great, starts shrinking your heart, passion, and creativity, it is time to go. There is no title worth your essence. After experiencing my daughter surviving a rare tumor and losing an organ at age 11, and then caregiving, alongside my CEO and single mom role, my best friend, my mother, and my mentor to a two-year battle with stage IV pancreatic cancer, I knew I had to follow my heart and write the truth. The truth of the deep complexity of what it is to be called a female leader in this decade. If we are in the space to be called a female leader, without a doubt you are a warrior, a fighter, and can hold space for grief and happiness together. Thus, I
returned to teaching to pursue my consulting practice working with people as an integrative psychologist, consulting with psycho-education special projects, and writing/speaking to not lose the magic of this time of personal and collective transformation. The jumping-off places of life are scary and exhilarating. The skill is to learn to hold space for both. Hope always springs eternal.

Women, in positions of leadership, are often asked what is the worst thing that has happened to them and how did they get through it? What if, I were to say, it does not matter. I mean so much that can be considered tragic and violent but also so much beauty. What if we were to switch the narrative from what happened, to how will you transcend it. The story is interesting for sure, but we all know it – as women, statistically speaking, we have probably, most likely been sexually abused or assaulted at some point in our lives. What if the interesting part of the story is not the story, but how you source life and creativity from that to transcend it, where what happened is not the driving force? How I channel the rage into action – is a compelling story. That is the real hero's journey – transcending the disappointments and trauma to harness the great jumping-off point at ground zero of our lives.   Grit is the roaring underdog of resilience. We have to dig deep to find it, but it is there inside everyone. It is a universal truth that
everyone has the ability to transcend their story and make it something new.

The Big Why– Authenticity Compassion. Empathy.

There is no choice if we want to live. If your heart is open to humanity and knowing that everyone has a story, it is impossible to stop the impulse of speaking or writing about these universal and personal truths. It is my gesture of maybe making the world a kinder, more compassionate place through teaching, and allowing it to be ok that we are not ok and going on anyway. The secret underdog of resilience is grit. We all have it. Sometimes, we need some help finding it. When something we consider "bad" or "unexpected" or "tragic" happens, we have two archetypes and two choices. Sometimes they are not mutually exclusive. We have the choice to engage the victim archetype. Why did this happen to me? To which the mystics' reply is always, why not you? The other choice is the archetype of the powerful resilient spirit who can transmute tragedy into strength. The choice is ours, but we must wrestle with our fears, our shadow elements, in order to transcend them. Sometimes we might move between these two, but the critical point is it is our choice how we perceive what happens to us and the stories we tell ourselves about what now?

Look at what you would consider your deepest tragedy– what you would tell yourself is the worst thing that ever happened to you. Go deep. Feel it. It is in the past so it cannot hurt you now. There is always going to be trauma there. Some things cannot be unseen or undone. However, what inner strength can you pull on to shift the narrative into transcending tragedy to triumph– the place where you can find the tragedy and sit with it, while at the same time knowing you have the grit, everyone does, to keep going or see the narrative of self differently.

Aha Moment Epiphany
Creativity. Authenticity. A Full Heart.

My aha moment was knowing that although I had a CEO title, my passion and my creativity and the fire that got me to that position were not really welcomed in that C suite space once I got there. A bird in a gilded cage can be a beautiful sight to see. Using Maya Angelou's great metaphor of the bird in the cage which is the symbol of hope and resilience in her memoir, I began to ask myself the question, ok, I know why the bird sings while she is in the cage, but does she have to? I mean, in 2022, does she have to sing while in the cage? There are other options and when we feel our hearts start to close to life, we must make a change. The last 2 plus years of chaos have proven that it is always ok to reinvent who we are and what we seek. "Hope is the thing with feathers that perches in the soul" Emily Dickinson. Hope is the thing that is most important in all of history and the arts, the key element that keeps us going, that springs eternal. You do not have to look hard to find the AHA moment even if you are not sure it has happened to you yet. The key is not to overthink. What comes first to mind or bubbles up from the heart? Find that and harness its power.

Secret Formula

My secret formula is to not be ego or money driven. I do what I do because I am passionate about people finding a voice, figuratively and literally. When I write, speak, and teach, I do not hold on to whether it will "take off." There has always been a deep impulse inside of me to speak the truth of what I see and help people through the lens of my specialty as a psychology consultant and specialist in American culture so others can live authentically. In my work with organizations, I have often been called "the compassionate leader," because I am invested in our individual and collective voice and in helping humanity be a little more heart-centered. Whatever happens as a result of this passion, I will leave that up to life's great surprises. The secret formula is that there is no secret. There is no right or wrong or proper way to do things other than to be true to your True North. It is when we lose our way, we can always come back to this central place of heart-centered kindness and compassion for self and others that will right you along the way. True North is not defined by anything other than your heart and deepest desires for truth.

Steps to Success to Build from Scratch

To launch two consulting practices, one specializing in higher ed and one specializing as a psychology consultant and integrative psychologist, I had a vision that I did not want to give up one or the other. I am convinced that I will find the place of integration for them both. However, I went legal (got an Inc), made a logo and mission that spoke to me, had two websites built, and just started working. Connecting every day with those who connect with you. I do what sparks me up! I am always humbled and surprised by the success. Mission and Vision are the key to success, whether it is a project or an organization. Many business people begin with a business plan and do not put enough emphasis on creating the Mission and Vision. The Mission and Vision are the why to what we do. It may seem counterintuitive, but if the Mission and Vision are not strong reflecting your own deep values, the most robust business plan will fall flat. It is the Mission and Vision that energize the business. Then comes the how-to.

Articulate it through writing, narrative, and even keeping an oral journal using a voice to text feature can unlock a voice not used to uttering its own brilliance.

Grit, The Secret Roaring Underdog that Transcends the Shadow

First Sign of Success

After the jumping-off point when there is no other choice but to try something new, I became emboldened to tell the truth about what it means and really looks like to live your life as an authentic heart-centered woman at the sometimes-messy half point of life. Every day, there will be small wins and sometimes small or large disappointments. If we see the self as a kaleidoscope, a mosaic of experiences that are not good or bad but just human, this takes the sting out of the disappointments. Instead of buying into an outdated context of top/bottom, right/wrong, high/low, or wins/loses, and looking at things as a mosaic of experiences without labels, this frees the self-up from the self-limiting beliefs and judgments. It takes you to a place of neutrality. The experience just is. How will we adjust to either get more of what feels right and aligned with self and what does not? If you are clear in your intentions, this will come intuitively. There is no need to cling to an outdated binary structure of right and wrong or winning and losing. It is just all a part of the human continuum of experience.

Some days may be days we want to forget and crawl into bed and hide. To be sure, living a courageous life, paving your own way, there will be bad days. Practice radical self-love and acceptance. Practice radical self-care. Start anew the next day. We always have the opportunity to recalibrate. Celebrate even the smallest of wins! Keep track of them or have a group of strong like-minded women who will remind you of your wins when you cannot see them

***

Ultimate Solution

Each individual's solution is his/her own. Working with people as an integrative or psychology consultant, I am not the driver of the ship. You are. However, what I can promise is that we will work to find your authentic voice, literally, and figuratively, and enact real changes in your life to support your creative and innovative pioneering spirit. Our work together is its own partnership and develops its own consciousness. As a conduit for change, you will always walk away with new tools to remember that you have the power. My clients walk away with a light that shines brighter. I cannot concretize what will emerge in our work together as the answers are not mine to find. As a conduit, I will not stop working on healing and helping to assist you in integrating past traumas and disappointments or our current angst until your heart is full and you are sparked up again. (The truth is my clients do not really ever truly go away in the traditional sense; as their need shifts and changes, so, too, does our work together). I can promise you will walk away with a stronger voice, a deeper connection to your own wisdom, and a light that shines brighter.

Free Gift – A more full and authentic heart-filled, non-judgmental space

Dr. Hope offers a 30-minute free consultation. Please email her with the subject

line HOPE, and she will schedule your 30-minute Zoom or call, whatever you are most comfortable with and determine a path from there.
drhopeandhealing@gmail.com
https://drhopehealing.com/

Each journey is individual, but Dr. Hope assures you that your perspective will shift as a result of the work you do together, and you will come out the hero of your own story with a light that shines from the strength of rediscovering yourself. That is a light that never dims.

Accolades and Achievements

Although many would say that being appointed the rare lifetime achievement as a female CEO in higher ed is a career peak, I would say that whenever I have a new client with whom to work, a new publication that took off or am asked to speak and share my experience or wisdom with a group, that is all the applause that I need. If your motivation is to help and serve in whatever capacity– it has many different shapes and forms, that is the win. It is a win inside the heart that money cannot touch.

See What They Are Saying...

See what Dr. Hope's clients say about her work; maybe you can be one of them
https://drhopehealing.com/testimonials/

***

Grit, The Secret Roaring Underdog that Transcends the Shadow

Business Links

Hope Phillips Umansky, PhD aka Dr. Hope
drhopeandhealing@gmail.com

https://drhopehealing.com/

https://www.mediaambassadors.com/dr-hope-umansky51115575

https://innovationsadvocacy.com/about/ https://hopehealthandhealing.org/
https://www.mediaambassadors.com/dr-hope-umansky51115575

Hatice Ozalp
Aydin Life Pharmacy, Ltd
Cyprus
haticeozalp79@gmail.com

Chapter 21
Happily, Ever After

After graduating from Istanbul University Faculty of Pharmacy in 2002, Hatice opened her own pharmacy in her own place. After a short time, she moved to a bigger city where she could fit her dreams. She opened the island's first fully-fledged organic shop and a pharmacy next to it. Its message is that "if you pay attention to your diet and lifestyle, you will need less pharmacy. We will be serving you on both sides with love". She is the owner of two pharmacies and an organic shop—Aydin Life Pharmacy Ltd

Mission and Vision

As a healthcare professional, I realized that most of the problems experienced stemmed from the way of life, diet, and way of thinking. That's why we invite clients to get organic living and health coaching before they have a problem with their health. We are all unique, and our health and illness, and needs are also unique. It is our mission to raise awareness by expanding this perspective.

Starting from Scratch
Happily, Ever After

The stories we heard as children would end up saying "and they lived happily ever after". For me, I thought that when I graduated from university, the story would be like this. I opened my own pharmacy where 1000 people live. Neither the money in my safe nor my dreams were enough for me. However, as the last and only child of a family of 7 children who could be sent to the university, it would have been a nightmare for me to leave the job halfway and close the pharmacy. My father would be very upset, and I was a father-loving girl. At the end of 4 years, I decided to move when I was at the bottom of the material and spiritual. The coaching sessions I took at that time gave me strength, and I moved my pharmacy. I can't remember a time in my life when I was more scared. I was not only disappointed in everyone but also, I was on my way to the unknown.

First of all, I worried about my father, but after a very short time, my work and my life got back on track. I was nourished by new forms of treatment and awareness and bringing what I learned to the island. Now I appear in health-related programs on TV programs. I am a health consultant. Shortly before my father lost his life, he said, "It's a good thing you didn't stay in the village; they wouldn't appreciate it here." Life is a journey of self-discovery. Until we find ourselves on this journey, we may have been on paths that do not belong to us, or even that we will never be. At this point, there are two options that I find very valuable. Is this our destiny? Or is it a road waiting for us to decide on the route? In the environment where I live, people do not change houses, they usually build a house in the neighborhood they dig and live there. They also do not change, and life passes like that. While I was about to begin to think that what I experienced on my journey was my destiny, I was faced with a question during a coaching session I took. Where do you see yourself ten years from now, and is this place in the same direction as your dreams? My answer is "No, the place I see is not in the same direction as my dreams. Then this cannot be my destiny". When I looked at myself from this point of view, I realized that my options increased, and my dreams started to turn into plans. The courage to dream and my step to be truly honest with myself has supported and supports me.

Big Why
Behind the Why Find Yourself

I faced many personal questions, and you might have similar questions.

1. Why did this happen to me? What do I need to notice/learn from this?
2. Why not? What are the barriers for me to do?
3. If no one has thought of it until now, why shouldn't it come to my mind?

When I thought about this subject, I remembered a cartoon I saw years ago. A man sitting on a stone in the stone age said, "Life is so meaningless that they found everything; there is nothing left for me to do and discover." Behind the "why" question in life is an answer worth considering. When I found out that I was pregnant, I started to pay more attention to my life. I started eating as healthy and organic as possible. I live in the north of the island of Cyprus, and there were no organic shops where I live. I used to go to the south frequently and buy organic products during my pregnancy, and after I became a mother, every time I went, I met my acquaintances who had traveled for an hour for organic shopping like me. At that very moment, I said WHY shouldn't I open an organic shop? With this spark, our organic shop was opened. We brought different organic products from abroad; we bought organic products from domestic producers, and we still continue.

Aha Moment Epiphany
Sharing is Caring

When did you have your aha moment? I will start this question with the motto of my 8-year-old daughter, "sharing is caring". Since Cyprus is a small place, everyone is almost aware of each other. I think that the conversations I had with the clients at the pharmacy, the health coaching, the posts I made on my social media account, and the TV programs I participated in helped my journey. Engage the reader

Secret Formula

When we read how mystical and complex the secret formula seems. However, I think that simplicity lies behind most of the secret formulas. When I started to discover myself and my values, I did my job by focusing on the needs within the framework of my values. When a mother came, I approached her with my motherhood identity, and when a grieving person came, I approached her with my side who knew how to grieve. I asked myself the question of how I would feel if it were me, and I made a relationship considering the uniqueness of both myself and the other person. I made small celebrations when I realized that I was on the right track with the feedback I received. I let the kids be my role models most of the time. I brought the sound of my heart and inner voice to the same level as my brain. Both in our profession and in our private life, all roads pass through self-development and belief. When we love and believe in ourselves, we can love others, and where there is love, growth and healing are inevitable.

Steps to Build Success from Scratch

Success is a completely personal definition. First of all, one should realize this and start off. Therefore, the person needs to know himself, know what he wants, and define success. Secondly, he must imagine himself in what he calls success. While doing this, he should do it by thinking that everything is possible. and he

should be able to see all kinds of details while imagining. How do I feel when I am at this point of success, how do I look, what do I think of myself, what is my name, and AM I HAPPY? Do I feel successful? I should ask questions. If the answers are positive, the trumpet should stay in that mood and then start thinking. This point of success should always be in front of his eyes, and he should focus on the question of what would happen if I took a small step towards it. and it should determine the action steps in the framework of the realities it has. Believing in yourself and going step by step brings success. It is the key to success to remember the image that he created in the first place in this journey and to allow himself the flexibility to change the image if he wants.

First Sign of Success

Customers coming to pharmacies and organic shops say, "if Hatice says you don't need a certificate, you can trust them" and to observe that children who eat organic can grow up without using drugs. In the TV programs I participated in, I realized that my soul was one with the work I did when I stopped using the definition of organic with information and started saying "organic is a state of peace of mind" to the question of what is organic. In my good times, everyone supports me. In my bad times (depending on the bad situation) my husband and everyone I can call family. In any case, Viola Edward has a special place in my heart.

Ultimate Solution

I am here to remind you to trust your body and connect to nature. I focused on helping. It is very difficult to establish professional relations with clients. After a while, as the shares increase, the formation of an emotional bond is inevitable. When an emotional bond occurs, we may not be able to look at things objectively. At this point, we need a third point of view. I have more than one mentor in my personal and business life, the most precious one is

Viola Edward, I am grateful for her existence. The answer to all questions in life is in nature. Every time you are happy or unhappy, whenever an idea comes to your mind, or no new idea comes to your mind, look to nature. Look at how deep a tree can root its roots without looking at the tree next to it, or how high another tree's branches are soaring. How unique are they all? They don't blame each other; they don't get jealous; they don't block as long as they don't enter their field. We are all like trees with different branches and different fruits, unique and fertile. let our journey
begin with realizing which tree we are and thinking about what we can become

Offer

I am proud of myself to be a part of this organization. If my experiences have touched someone's heart in some way, it means we have a common path at some point in life. I will happily coach them about what they want from today to the future on this journey. If our path crosses with those who do not feel well-balanced at the point of health, I would be happy to coach them as well. This would be my gift to myself and to them. solution-oriented coaching; it is to accompany the person from today to the future on the path determined by himself, with the questions asked at the right time. In this friendship, the husband does not give any ideas, does not comment, listens and asks questions. Anyone who receives coaching from the right coach will definitely get closer to themselves and their dreams. In health coaching, the focus is on the person, not the disease. In the method that includes holistic treatment recommendations, the focus is always on the person and the goal is to bring the person mentally, emotionally, and physically into balance. I call these methods a journey because healing takes place in both the coach and the client together.

Accolades and Achievements

When I started doing the profession of pharmacy, at first I got a normal reaction because I did it with alternative approaches instead of a standard way. Now, I am going out as the speaker at the introductory meetings of the profession. I come home with a thank you award every time I go out. I was asked to prepare a course that will shed light on what they want in life for final year students from a university. I thank you for the message "Another point of view is possible" in the TV programs I participate in. Breastfeeding and first aid courses we organize for mothers, all of these are rewards for me.

Books and Business Contacts
HATICE OZALP "Tough Roads Creates Tough People"
JUNTAS ES MEJOR
QUERENTINA AND BEYOND"
https://linktr.ee/haticeozalp

SCAN ME

Daisy Gallagher
Gallagher & Gallagher Worldwide, Inc.
Washington, DC, USA
ceo@gallagherworldwide.com

Chapter 22
Have a Seat Around the Table or Bring Your Chair

Ms. Daisy Gallagher, AMA, CPM, CCH – Chairwoman, Gallagher & Gallagher Worldwide, Inc., Chief Global Strategy Officer, Senior Executive Advisor, Serial Entrepreneur, 20+ years Certified Military U.S. Federal Government Contractor, Global Executive Board Officer - Ambassador at Large, Co-Founder of SUSTAP LLC, TheraSyn Bio, Inc. and World Green Energy Symposium.

Mission and Vision

Gallagher & Gallagher Worldwide, Inc.'s mission is to be the best in the industry, we must continue to raise the bar, give our clients more than they paid for, more than they asked for; we must put their needs ahead of our own - we must realize that their success is our success." Daisy Gallagher, Founder, and CEO

Starting from Scratch
Persistence, Persistence, Persistence

After working in Corporate America for almost a decade, I decided to take a giant leap. I literally turned my back on a steady future and did something I had wanted to do since I could remember. Was I scared – you bet I was! I write this with more than three continuous decades as an entrepreneur. I started my first company in 1990, Gallagher & Gallagher, Inc, from my home. I really thought that it was as far as it would go. Never in my wildest dreams did I think it would grow as it did. After a few years of ups and downs as a start-up, the company grew from my home to my first office on Main Street, USA, and eventually to Washington DC. We then plunged into becoming a certified military U.S. Federal Contractor ultimately receiving top secret level clearance for contracts. I chose one of the most male-dominated industries, and to this day at times, I am still the only woman in the room. However, I am in the room! That is important, as women our responsibility is to have a seat around to the table, and if a seat is not available, "bring our own folding chair," as Shirley Chisholm has said. I have been a champion of equal pay and women's rights from the time I worked in Corporate America and have served on numerous leading women's organization boards over the years. In 2012, my book "How to Succeed in a Testosterone World without Losing Estrogen," came out. A tongue-in-cheek title, with powerful messaging inside the pages. It was written to guide women toward success and to encourage them to use their voices for change. If I were to surmise what it takes to be an entrepreneur and especially a woman entrepreneur, I would say "you have to be a risk taker - steadfast, fearless, persistent, thick-skinned, and unyielding in the pursuit of your goals."

Big Why
Work Ethic, Impact, Service

My work ethic and gratitude for this country come from my parents, especially my father who worked three jobs to put food on the table after leaving his country for a better future for me. He would always say how lucky we were to be living in such a beautiful and free country. They gave up their family and everything back home, and I always carry that with me. Every time I felt defeated, I pushed through and thought of what they gave up, how incredibly lucky I was to be able to be and do anything I wanted to, and how I always wanted to make them proud.

Although it may sound cliché, my husband and children have been the stabilizing force in my life. I have also been blessed with a supportive family, friends, and many colleagues who have stood by me cheered me on and inspired me throughout my long career. In particular, I would say I admire the many women, whom I have had the privilege of serving with or teamed with in business; their dedication, commitment, ethics, and professionalism have been extraordinary.

Aha Moment
Growing Without Limits

My Aha moment came when I plunged into government contracting and won our first major contract. I said, "Okay, now here is the opportunity where we may grow without limits if we choose to do so."
I never realized before that I could tap into the U.S. Federal Government market. It is the largest marketplace in the world, and every 30 seconds of every day the US government makes a purchase. I never thought I would be able to maneuver around the certification processes. It seemed so convoluted to me and out of my reach as a small business back then – nevertheless a small woman-owned business. I was under the impression only large corporations with a legal procurement and a contracting team could be successful at it.

We developed "The Government Contractor's Resource Guide" (GCRG) years later to help other small women and minority businesses navigate through the procurement process and show them that they too could do it with the support and guidelines they needed by providing them with the references to obtain the information they required to go through the process. The GCRG is now in its 6th printing and is used as a reference guide by contracting officers and university government classes.

Secret Formula
Strength, Courage, Confidence to I CAN Do This!

My secret formula is a combination: find a mentor, expand your outreach, continue learning, expand your network, and continuously implement the above, most of all never give up!

It has taken thirty years to get here, and it has been a lot of hard work, at times frustration, and failures along with celebrations, rewards, and success. Before I opened my doors to my first business, I studied the landscape, and competitors in the area, and most importantly I went to the Chamber of Commerce and asked for their membership book to see who the local competition was to ensure that my business concept was one that was not saturated. Today you do this online. I then went through the process of developing my business plan, and my marketing communications plan and hired an accountant and an attorney, since my background is in strategic marketing communications, I became my own agency representative.

I had to ensure that I had financing opportunities for my business, researched good locations for office space, and interviewed core employees. I then launched our Brand.

Steps to Success
Fail Towards Success

"It is not if you will fail. It is a matter of when you fail, what you do with those lessons which will dictate the future of your success in business." These steps to success are the steps I took. I had to follow a plan and implemented best practices:

Step One: Before opening your doors, study the landscape, and competitors in the area, and most importantly visit your local Chamber of Commerce. Today you can do all this online.

Step Two: Develop your business plan, and marketing communications plan, and retain an accountant, marketing strategist, and attorney.

Step Three: Ensure you have funds to finance your business, research a good location for office space, and interview core employees.

Step Four – Enhance your brand by networking, advertising, and publicity.

163

Step Five – Find a Mentor; this is KEY!

Step Six – Continue expanding your outreach, continue learning, and grow your network.

Step Seven – Continuously implement Step 1 through Step 7

First Sign of Success

My first signs of success resulted from volunteering and serving on committees, which was making connections. I strategically served on committees where I was able to work with representatives of several major corporations in the area. There were two specific early larger clientele that came on our roster as a result of those committees which I count as the jump start to the change of our company's recognition and growth. The first was the largest manufacturer of vaccines and they hired us to be their local public relations and community relations agency. The second was an Army Depot, which was our first government contract and the impetus for moving into the federal contracting arena and going through the process.

The whole idea of having your own business is to pursue your dream and do so to help change the landscape, create jobs, and provide important service in the field you are best in. You cannot be the one person in the room who does it all, surrounding yourself with talented professionals whose expertise is in areas not as strong makes you worry less.

The Ultimate Solution

A mentor is an important key to success! I cannot stress this enough if you are starting your business or are having any issues with your business, seek a mentor. I have had several mentors over the years. These are talented individuals who have already been successful – been there, done that and are happy to share their success and their lessons with you. They are experienced, filled with knowledge, and time to spare, and will help guide you through or prevent you from (many) pitfalls. I attribute my early success in large part to my mentor's guidance.

Special Free Offer

For any woman featured in this book who is interested in strategically expanding their customer base into the federal arena, I invite you to email me for an upcoming training class via zoom with the introductory steps which will highlight steps on becoming a government contractor at ceo@gallagherworldwide.com

Accolades and Achievements

During my long stance in business, my team and I are honored to have received more than 100 industry and community awards and recognitions.

I was privileged to be appointed to the US General Services Administration Industry Government Council Steering Committee and Industry Government Council, Washington DC and appointed by the then U.S. President to the Small Business Advisory Council. I had the privilege of being asked to testify before the U. S. Congress on pertinent issues impacting women and business. Other major honors and recognitions for myself and our company include being named One of the Top Women-Owned Businesses in the Nation (USA President's Award), Business Person of the Year (USA SBA), Rotarian of the Year, International Rotary Club Paul Harris Fellowship Award, The University of Scranton Woman Entrepreneur of the Year, Chamber of Commerce Citizen of the Year (served as Chairman of the GPCC Chamber of Commerce), United Way Gilford Volunteer of the Year (served as Chairman of United Way Campaign), Public Relations Society of America (PRSA) Overall Excellence Awards consecutive years, Women in Communications Sarah Award in Public Relations. The EAWC "Leadership Award" was presented in Congress by Congressional Members in 2012 and in October of 2017. I received numerous Citations from Congress (House & Senate) for Business and Community Service. In 2018-19, we were named "Integrated Marketing Agency of the Year, the U.S." and "Most Influential Woman in Brand Marketing of the Year," by AI, International, received EAWC Global Golden Artemis Leadership Award and honored as One of the Top Global Entrepreneurs of the Century both presented in Athens, Greece, the last by Member of Parliament. I was honored as co-Grand Marshall along with my husband, Professor Robert Gallagher, at the St. Patrick's Day Parade in Northeast Pennsylvania.

I have tried my best to be a lifelong learner, learning from others as well as books and my studies. In 2020, I earned a certificate of achievement for Harvard University's" Principles of "Adaptive Leadership." My educational background includes postgraduate Advanced Masters Project Management and master's Project Management certificate from Villanova University, and I am a board-certified Clinical Practitioner (CCH)

See What They Are Saying...

"Daisy's company provided me with outstanding support. Top qualities; Great Results, Personable, Good Value."
(Colonel M. Smith, *U. S. Department of Defense, U.S. Army)*

***

"Daisy Gallagher and her team are among the very best of the best. Gallagher is a world-class company capable of marshaling projects in the U.S. and Abroad. She is that rare professional who delivers more than is expected and achieves results no others could!!! She is Awesome!!!"
S. Pettit, *International Training Consortium, Inc.*

***

"Gallagher and her company have showcased astute first-hand past performance experience, expert level knowledge, and commitment to their customers. As the managing partner of a patent pending 100 million dollars sustainable technology company, I am abundantly pleased with the quality of work that I have been provided with by taking advantage of Gallagher's services."
(E. B. *Managing Partner - RRI)*

***

"Daisy Gallagher's business acumen is extraordinary. Her drive to succeed, exemplary. Still, the story does not end there. She has a razor-sharp mind and deep sensitivities toward serving and uplifting our human family. Only Daisy could write a book titled "How to Succeed in a Testosterone World Without Losing Estrogen" and keep business leaders, even government leaders riveted. I applaud Daisy Gallagher for all of her outstanding business achievements, as well as her stellar contributions to being one of the true "People of Distinction" in our world!"
A. Cole, *CBS Radio*

***

www.gallagherworldwide.com

www.gallagher-gallagher.us

www.linkedin/in/daisygallagher

Barbara A. Berg
Barbara A. Berg, Inc.,
Claremont, California
babsberg@earthlink.net

Chapter 23

Having Balance Between Your Personal and Public Life Provides the Best Groundwork for Success

Barbara Berg has focused her life on finding balance and stress management. She is a psychotherapist practicing with an L.C.S.W. license. She has written four books, two are about stress management and one is about positioning rings on your hands for more balance in your life, known as Ring Shui. My dreams were always about writing, speaking, and having work that "threw me into throngs of people and being a part of what was going on in the world." Looking back over my 68 years thus far, that happened but not in the way I initially thought. I ran my own child care center in a resort in Jackson Hole Wyoming, which later paved the way for me to direct one of the first onsite corporate childcare centers in the US for Zale Corporation in the early 1980s. I have been conducting psychotherapy for 30 years as a Licensed Clinical Social Worker; have done over 600 speeches, workshops, and "Ring Shui Events"; have been a guest on approximately 600 TV, radio, and internet-related shows; conducted 3 of my own internet radio shows; and had 4 books published- two based on Stress Management and two on "Ring Shui- Move Your Rings, Change Your Life", which have brought me great joy in connecting with people. What I "fell into" through my private practice was having done over 1052 Critical Incident Stress Debriefings at workplaces and landmark situations out in the world thus far.

Mission and Vision

Barbara A. Berg's mission involves supporting as many people as possible in having balance, structure, and a sense of hope and happiness in their lives, both locally and globally. She has been on over 600 radio/tv interviews and has conducted well over 650 workshops. I hope to do more podcasts and speeches. *Slogan- "When You Work with Who's Really Inside You, The Unique Best of You Will Appear."*
Starting from Scratch

Married to My Work

Are you married to your work? Work-life balance in marriage is not easy. I said I do 3 times. I found myself married to my work. You need to find a balance between work and marriage; otherwise, you will need to decide between work or marriage. Marriages with work-addicted spouses have a higher divorce rate. If you are a workaholic, it will just be a matter of time before your marriage starts deteriorating due to a lack of commitment to your family. I will share a few secrets on finding a balance and how I discovered a new passion in my career known as Ring Shui.

Challenge
Genuine Balance Work Life

My childhood was spent hearing my mother who went to the Julliard School of Music in New York City, tell me how she should have never left her wonderful music job in New York to get married and GIVE IT ALL UP. She always said, "A woman can have a career of her own OR be married, but she can't have both." I realize that times have changed, but I realize I grew up in a family where EVERYONE was out of balance including both my parents.

LET PEOPLE HELP. When I became an adult, I was determined to be happily married AND love my work life. My focus is to balance life and business. I found myself walking down the aisle with 3 men and saying, "I do", but I was really MARRIED to my 'career' and not to them. I did not more fully understand the importance of having some sort of GENUINE BALANCE with my work life and personal life until NOW. I've come to realize my LIFE is my CAREER and not just what I do for "Work". One supports the other. What I have learned from personal and professional accomplishments is to alter my course as possible when it is veering away from an overall balance. It also takes time-sometimes decades for it to all come together.

Big Why
GENUINELY BE YOU.

I had an ongoing drive within me to experience life, teach, when possible, support others, and live as fully as possible. What inspired me was seeing my mom give up in life and wither out of fear. I knew I couldn't do the same and was determined to play full out in life and not stand back and wonder what I might've done. This experience with my mom led me to find myself. You need to be you genuinely. Just be aware to balance your work life and marriage. You can do it all by balancing your life. Avoid the juggling act!

AHA Moment
Find Your Self Dignity

I was inspired when I saw how helpful and gracious our marriage counselor was. She gave me a sense of self and dignity. I was able to see the possibilities for myself. I became an L.C.S.W. and that put me in a position to help people who were mentally and emotionally distraught. I had mental and emotional trauma in my family as well which gave me a sense of wanting to help other families suffering from this.

What I have learned from personal and professional accomplishments is to alter my course as possible when it is veering away from an overall balance. It also takes time-sometimes decades for it to all come together. My grown daughter Brittany at 34 is an amazing joy, and I am also coming to so much more love and appreciate my (3rd) husband, George, and our life together. He truly makes it so much more possible for me to do all the things I do out in the world. I used to think I had to do it all myself-or it didn't count! One day, I discovered Ring Shui, which turned my life around and will make a big difference in your life, too.

As I began moving away from my long-term marriage in the late 1990s, I started wearing rings on my middle fingers, as was the trend at the time. A chiropractor who knew a lot about energy told me to take off my middle finger rings because I was attracting more conflict in my life, and I realized that was true! Following this advice, I surprisingly began to have more satisfaction and joy in her life and things began to flow more easily. My life became more balanced, hopeful, and rewarding for longer periods of time.

From there I became interested in the power of ring placement on hands and Ring Shui was born!

My Secret Formula
Inspiration Is the Key

My secret formula is to work with the subject matter and people with whom I feel I can be helpful and who appreciate what I do. I keep working with people in situations that inspire me and that I inspire so we can feel hopeful together. This helps me to keep growing, be involved, and be inspired so I don't get burned out or bogged down. I have written books and have been a speaker for many organizations and venues. I help those I work with feel joy and excitement and gain insights to help them move into a better tomorrow.

And my failures. - In reminding me that it is time again for me to now do a new yearly Vision Board, I believe my failures have mainly occurred when I wasn't fully conscious of my "frontline intentions" or I didn't take the time to realize what I needed to have as my team to support what I want to do and clearly ask for it until I got it. I am still in the process of learning that! Be intentional, make note of all your learning even when you fail, and enjoy every moment of work and life.

Having Balance Between Your Personal and Public Life Provides the Best Groundwork for Success

What I have learned from these mistakes is to have compassion for myself and appreciate what I have been doing and being. I am also learning to absolutely focus on what brings me and those I interact with the most joy!

Challenges I have gone through include finding out when I was 40, that I have a major case of Attention Deficit Hyperactivity Disorder. I took a TOVA test and found out I was in the 95th percentile! Even though I was "seemingly successful" out in the world and even at home at times, a psychotherapist pointed out to me that I hyper-focused with anxiety to get anything done and then had to clean up messes that occurred when I focused on only one thing for a long period of time. I continually get help for that now.

Steps to Build Success
Believe There's More Meant for You

List what you are best at, what you love to do, what you are most willing to learn to do yourself, and where you will need ongoing assistance. Do not pretend you are good at something when it just overwhelms you to no end. None of us can give to our fullest if we are not simultaneously receiving what we need. Do it with love and compassion for Yourself and Others-and Success will find you!

1. Recognize when to ask for help and appreciate the support and direction you receive.
2. Follow through with opportunities and recognize what a gift they are.
3. Get a structured path to get you started if you feel you need structure you can't put it together yourself initially.
4. Keep finding creative ways to help others and use the unique talents you already have.
5. Remember to be laser-focused on what you want in work and life..
6. Love what you do.

First Sign Of Success

My first sign of success was I passed the oral and written test for the first time. I also did well in my internships and was told I have the talent to keep going.

Management told me I listened and followed through. Ron, my second husband, was very supportive when I went to take my L.C.S.W. test. He was very kind and proud of me.

I am here to remind you to focus and celebrate your small wins. If you stay focused only on the end in mind, you may feel overwhelmed

Dedication

This book is dedicated to Ronnie, my husband, who has been with me through thick and thin. I truly am thankful for his support and patience throughout the process of this book. Also, to my darling daughter, Brittany, who has sung and danced and cheered me on.

My mother deserves recognition for teaching me the great value of "being who you came here to be" and "letting no one keep you from your dreams."

This book is also dedicated to anyone who sincerely desires to experience more happiness and less stress in his life.

and anxious and may give up. Look for the first signs of success so you can feel excitement and joy.

Ultimate Solution
Path to Success

I found that I could write and express myself well, and I came up with workshops for others that also helped me to structure my life. Mentorship did help me it showed me the importance of learning from others so I could teach and serve better.

The impact I am making in my community consistently involves using my speaking, writing, communicating, listening, and stress management skills. Right now, whether it is with individual clients, groups, workshops, debriefs, or myself I have developed a stress management system to help anyone put a structure on a grid to help them stay as grounded as possible, especially in these times.

The advice I have to women reading this book is to give themselves credit that they

are looking to find mentors. Also, to recognize that whatever comes your way in life is actually "part of your life's curriculum" to deal with- and appreciate what gains you can make in facing them. That can become one of the gifts you are meant to successfully pass on to others.

Ring Shui is my ultimate solution.

Ring Shui is a unique, new, and dynamic way of using old wisdoms to bring a lot of depth, joy and insights into your relationships with yourself and others. It makes the law of attraction more apparent in your life and it helps you learn the laws of flow concerning giving and receiving. What Feng Shui is to the living space, Ring Shui is to the hands.

It's a fun, unique and inspiring way to:

- Gain insights about how you do relationships and how you connect to people and the world around you
- Put your intentions out into the world in such a way that people support you more and you receive more of what you desire
- Bring balance into your life and more satisfaction

You will never look at your hands or the hands of others the same way again!

Having Balance Between Your Personal and Public Life Provides the Best Groundwork for Success

Free Gift

Contact information: I invite calls and texts, and would especially love to do a "Ring Shui" party, event, or consultation for you! - "Move Your Rings- Change Your Life"! For help in Success in your Work and Personal Life- 909-786-7201. barbara@barbaraberg.com ; barbara@ringshui.com; ringshui.com;barbaraberg.com; check out Ring Shui on YouTube and around the net.

https://www.mydigitalpublication.com/publication/?i=265398&p=3&view=issueViewer

Accolades and Achievements

I did a SUE Talk for the Connected Women of Influence on August 26th, 2021, and this was a huge achievement and honor for me.

For my first Ring Shui book, I was awarded the Next Generation INDIE Award 2009.

I was a finalist for the Eric Hopper Award for Excellence in Independent Publishing 2012 for my second Ring Shui book.

I also received the SIMA Global Award Winner 2022 in the United States for the She Inspires Me Award.

I have also done over 300 Ring Shui events and interviews

See What They Are Saying...

"Barb, your delivery is always fluid, dynamic and real. Your humor is awesome, and we learn so much from you. Learn to be the best you, you can be!"
-Joan Wakeland, Menifee California

***

"Excellent information and most enjoyable presentation style, knows her stuff. Thank you so much for sharing the reminder to always be yourself."
-Gillian from Temecula

***

"Barbara Berg writes directly and clearly to her readers, reflecting her conviction that each of us can become our own best helper. She gently guides readers to become calmer, more thoughtful, and more analytical so they can take charge of their problems and their lives."
-Dr. Dojelo Russell Professor Emerita Graduate School Of Social Work, Virginia Commonwealth University

***

Tamara L. Hunter
Branson, Missouri, USA
SpeakerTamaraLHunter@gmail.com

Chapter 24
How Three Words Changed My Life

Tamara L. Hunter is a cancer survivor with a mission to change the world. She is President and Co-founder of a nonprofit cancer support community, CB4L.org; the "First Global Next Impactor"; CEO of Impactor Press; Creator, Producer and Host of two TV Shows; Two-time best-selling author; Coach; Keynote Speaker; Emcee; and Red-Carpet Interviewer.

Mission and Vision

My businesses revolve around three words, "Healing Through Connections." As "The First Global Next Impactor", my belief is that the time for change is now. As a keynote speaker, coach, author, and TV Host, I share we all have a "Service Hero" inside. Together we can change the frequency of the world.

Starting from Scratch
Everything Clicked

"YOU HAVE CANCER." Three words you never want to hear, yet too many have. I have heard them from five people, through four generations of my family. For my hero grandfather and mother, my brother, my nineteen-year-old daughter, and myself. My life changed on the first day of treatment; I nearly died from an extreme allergic reaction. That one experience has inspired every step I have taken since.

From an early age, I knew deep in my core that I was meant to accomplish something that would change the world as we know it. As I lived my life, I kept an eye out, always asking myself, is this it?

In an instant, everything clicked into place. My life's purpose became clear; it was up to me to share and inspire others throughout the world, "There is healing through connections" no matter what disease, trauma, or challenges you have experienced.

Big Why
Time for Change

"**Y**ou're Not Alone!" Three words that drive me each day. On my first day of treatment, I met a "buddy." We traveled our journey back to health together. Our doctor shared how scientists found that if you are alone going through cancer, it can affect not only the quality, but it can also affect the length of your life. Too many are feeling afraid, isolated, and alone. It is time to change how cancer is done.

Aha Moment Epiphany
In My Mother's Honor

"**I** can't help." Three of the toughest words I have experienced. During my own battle with cancer, my mother lived with me and was facing hers. She became affected by "superbugs" in the hospital, and I was in active chemotherapy. The hospital released her; she was still affected. She could not come home. She was afraid, isolated, and alone! I could not help my own mother; therefore, I am committed and determined to help others in her honor.

Secret Formula
INSPIRE * IGNITE * IMPACT

I believe to help heal the world you must find ways for those you are working with to first heal themselves. People I work closely with know that my focus is on them; they are the most important person to me at that moment!

I gained a title, "The Movement Maker." I coach others to grow their business, share their message, and build their movement. Through the nonprofit, I inspire volunteers to join and ignite "healing through connections" thus impacting those facing cancer and other life-changing events. I have TV shows, speak on real and digital stages, have been featured on the news and in magazine articles, have been a guest on radio and podcasts, and have written books. My latest business venture as a publisher has just begun.

Photo Taken by Mikey Adam Cohen

177

Steps to Build Success from Scratch

"**Y**ou are never too old!" I was in my mid-fifties when I received "the vision;" the time is now to change the world. What I found interesting was I would need to use the internet and social media. I had no idea about this technology. I didn't even have an active social media account. When there is a will, there is a way!

My six steps to success:

1. Know your why. You must have a "clear vision."
2. Know your why behind the why. It will become so difficult you will want to give up; your second why will not let you.
3. Find people who are the best at what you need to know or do. Ask for help.
4. Invest in yourself. Find a mentor or coach. Take courses and classes.
5. Create a community of believers. Do not go it alone.
6. Never give up!

First Sign of Success

If it could go wrong, it did. I blew up websites---three of them. I was gone from home for weeks and months at a time, traveling on my own dime, and volunteering somewhere; I was invited to share my nonprofit's vision and message on their stages. It got extremely ugly and painfully lonely!

Then I finally found a coach. That changed everything. She empowered me and helped me to move outside my own box. "365 Days of Awesome, Celebrate Success Through Service" was born. I went "Facebook Live" every day for a year. The "Service Heroes" whose stories I told became those who celebrated my successes and helped me to achieve my global vision.

Ultimate Solution

"**T**he Next Impactor" became my ultimate solution. After the initial success with my first mentor and coach, I knew I needed to find the best of the best coaches in specific areas. The winner of the global "race against time" won five top coaches in those exact areas. I had to win and did.

Free Gift

Do you believe one person can change the world? I do. Is it easy? No. Is it possible? YES! I wrote a twenty-four-page eBook, which shares my ultimate solution entitled, "Changing the World; What It Takes to be a Global Impactor." You can use the QR code here which takes you to my website to get your free copy immediately. You can send me a message once at my website too. I look forward to hearing from you.

www.TamaraLHunter.com – the opt-in area for eBook in on landing page.

Also, receive your free copy of "Celebration Journal".

Scan the QR Code. It will take you to www.CB4L.org. Go to the bottom of the landing page and opt-in.

Accolades and Achievements

When I became "The First Global Impactor" not only did I win the five coaches, but I was also known globally. I share all the awards, recognitions, and honors received with the volunteers throughout our organization from all areas of the world. An example was the "Captain Sir Tom Moore - Memorial Medal for the Covid -19 Hero Award." The international coalition honored top scientists, doctors, government, and business leaders and a handful of others, including me.

See What They Are Saying...

At the last minute, the owner of an exclusive event center contacted me in need of a keynote speaker in four days. I was able to finish out a daylong event with a specially designed ninety-minute speech. The result was the owner was thrilled, and I am still hearing from those in attendance how they loved the closing speaker. She told me I will be the first call made next time.

***

I have been working with someone off and on for years now. In the beginning, she was struggling with focus. Together, she found her "clear vision," became a best-selling author and is now coaching others.

***

A nominated Service Hero came onto my show. She was truly inspiring, yet she knew she was playing small. After an hour with me, she refocused her commitment. She continues to tell me it was that time that made all the difference in where she is now.

***

Books, Social and Business Media

180

Alison Vaughn
Jackets for Jobs & Ms. Goal Digger, LLC
Detroit, Michigan, USA
AlisonVaughnSpeaks@gmail.com

Chapter 25
How To Be A "Goal Digger" And Not A "Gold Digger"

Alison Vaughn is an International Speaker and an award-winning author who focuses on professionalism, leadership, and workforce development. In 2021, she was named Entrepreneur of the Year by the Michigan Association of Female Entrepreneurs. She has graced the cover of several women's magazines and has been featured in FORBES, ENTREPRENEUR & FORTUNE Magazine.

Mission and Vision

Two decades ago, I had the vision to help women that were on welfare to get back on their feet and become self-sufficient. To be a successful businessperson, you have to have a product or service that solves a problem. I started Jackets for Jobs because I saw a need in the community. Our mission is based on the following premise: If a person doesn't have a job, they can't afford career clothing. Yet, without appropriate attire for an interview, they can't get a job. It's a Catch-22. Jackets for Jobs, Inc. opened in March 2000 to solve that problem for low-income individuals.

Starting from Scratch
The Juggling Act

I was on top of the world and traveling around the world, then came "motherhood". Balancing motherhood and business is a juggling act. What I have learned is the all-important word "NO". I realize that NO is a complete sentence; for example, when your friends want to go out after work and it sounds like a great idea and lots of fun, sometimes you have to say NO and go home and be with your kids. Or when your business partner wants to take a trip, you have to say NO because your child has a recital, being a mother is the best thing that has happened for me, it's just learning how to balance work and family. Women seem to be more "people pleasers" than men and we tend to say YES more often than men and we get stressed and burned out, therefore, we get off balanced.

Big Why
Clothe the Poor

Being an entrepreneur can be very challenging yet very rewarding. I feel my "calling" purpose in life is to "clothe the poor". So, in the midst of chaos and challenges, I always remember why I started the company, to help those in need. I truly believe that when you "give" blessings come back to you. The question of why I do what I do is a simple answer. To enrich my life and those around me. I give back in the midst of challenges to connect with my community, people, and ideas that will positively impact others and myself for the rest of my life.

I challenge you to reflect and review; A goal digger always sets aside time to reflect and review their progress in achieving their goals. Do you clearly know what your goal is about? Was everything geared at achieving your goal? The answer to these questions can be had by conducting an honest evaluation of your progress and making the necessary adjustments geared at achieving your goals.

Aha Moment Epiphany
Jackets for Jobs

My "aha moment" to start a business came out of a tragic situation. When my distant half-sister died of cancer, I helped with the funeral arrangements and discovered she was on welfare and didn't have much. At that moment, I knew I had to do something to help other women. So I started Jackets for Jobs to help women get off welfare and to become self-sufficient. I didn't want to see other women struggling. add more engagement and how they should take action now

Secret Formula
Ms. Goal Digger, Success is Sexy!

My secret formula is GOD, and I don't keep it a secret. God opens doors that need to be opened and closes doors that need to be closed. Networking is the best way to attract clients. I believe in networking and being sociable because when you "show up, you go up". In my book, *Ms. Goal Digger, Success is Sexy!* I discuss networking and how to be a stiletto in a room full of flats. I attract customers through social media and my TV Show- "The Alison Vaughn" Show. My show is a 30-minute TV show about spiritual growth and current events. I also tackle issues that busy moms go through such as how to cook a meal in 30 minutes or less and helpful household tips.

Introduction to steps success

Human beings are tuned to the concept of success where everyone strives to achieve respect, wealth, or fame. Do you find yourself caught up in the adrenaline party of finding an interesting concept, writing it down, and then forgetting about it in the next week? Sounds familiar, right? Some of the ways in which we can become successful are by being creative and finding your passion; Finding your passion is everything one needs in becoming successful. Learning and understanding what you are passionate about and what truly makes you happy is an integral part of the realization of your goals. Before setting any goal, it is important to ask yourself, "does this make me happy? In life, you have to do some things simply because they make you happy. This provides a driving force for working towards your goals and achieving them.

Steps to Build Success from Scratch
My steps to Success:
<u>Take care of yourself first</u>

I know that sounds selfish but it's not. If you are not ok, then you can't help others. As a former flight attendant, I was trained to tell others, "Please secure your mask first, before assisting someone else".

<u>Stop trying to be perfect</u>
We all make mistakes. Learn from them and move on.

<u>Have a support system</u>
Find an organization to join that focuses on your interest. If you are not a member of an organization, network as much as possible. We are coming out of the pandemic, so in-person events will be starting back up and it will be very beneficial to go out and meet other people.

<u>Have a sense of humor</u>
Laughter is the best form of medicine. Don't take everything so seriously.

First Sign of Success

My first sign of success was being featured on NBC's Today Show with Al Roker. Being featured nationally validated our mission and displayed to the country the good work we do to help women get off welfare and become self-sufficient. That episode on "The Today" Show opened many doors for Jacket for Jobs and helped us form national partnerships. Other successes included being featured on the Oprah Winfrey Show, ABC's "The View" and ringing the closing bell on NASDAQ twice. I always celebrate my successes with my mother, Betty Henderson who is my mentor.

Everyone has their own definition of success. For some, it may be to lose 10 pounds, for others it may be to add ten thousand in their bank account in a specific time period. For me, my recent success was being crowned, "Miss Fashion Global-Michigan" I define success as the achievement of the desired goal. How would you define success? and how did you celebrate your success?

Ultimate Solution

For more than two decades, I have worked diligently to cultivate the success of others through etiquette and grooming tips, as well as providing professional clothing to job seekers. As a Goldman Sachs Scholar and a Comcast Newsmaker, I have secured millions of dollars for my company and I am committed to sharing first-hand knowledge with other business owners, my techniques—allowing them to maximize profits and partnerships. I have been featured in the world's top business magazines, FORBES, FORTUNE, and ENTREPRENEUR Magazines.

Article- Featured in HOUR Magazine February 2022

My tips are in my book, Ms. Goal Digger, Success Is Sexy!
I share my recipe for success. The recipe is simple: (1) build a library of self-help books, (2) Get a journal. Make it a gratitude journal, and (3) find a mentor/support system.

AS SEEN IN
Forbes, Fortune & Entrepreneur

DETROIT WOMEN IN BUSINESS

Tailored for Success

Alison Vaughn is an international speaker and award-winning author who focuses on professionalism, leadership, and workforce development. She is the founder of Jackets for Jobs, an award-winning nonprofit organization that has been honored as one of the Best and Brightest Companies to Work For in the Nation" by the National Association for Business Resources, for four years in a row.

Jackets for Jobs is celebrating two decades of serving men and women on their path to financial independence. When it comes to job interviews, the old adage about first impressions being the most important rings true. A person might be qualified, but if their clothes fail to impress, they can kiss the job goodbye.

Vaughn thought about this after her half sister passed away. They'd lived disparate lives: Vaughn, a graduate of Michigan State University and the Women's Campaign School

Alison Vaughn empowers women by helping them dress like the successful professionals they want to be.

PHOTO BY ANDRE SMITH

185

My support system is my mother. I do not know what I would do without her. I'm also guided by the LORD. Every decision I make or whatever problem, big or small I talk to GOD.

Free Gift

Why should the readers sign up or get your free offer? What are you giving? I will mail a free copy of my award-winning book-Ms Goal Digger. While the world may define success in dollars and cents, my book teaches women how to work smarter, not harder.

In my book, you will learn:

My mentor, my mother Betty Henderson

- How to network to increase your net worth
- How to develop a millionaire mindset
- How to act, speak and dress like a CEO
- How to set strategic goals and plans of action
- And more!

While many may define sexy as miniskirts, makeup and stilettos, this book teaches that true sexiness starts with a mogul mindset

In the meantime, while you are waiting on my book, I suggest you get a journal. I mentioned journaling earlier in my chapter.

Several studies have shown a strong positive link between gratitude journaling and well-being. Spend a few minutes each evening recording five things that were good about your day. Include big and small accomplishments. Include big things like receiving a promotion or acing a test but remind yourself that the little things are important too.

How To Be A "Goal Digger" And Not A "Gold Digger"

Accolades and Achievements

Ms. Goal Digger, Success is Sexy! copyright 2017-Createspace Publish Company
Book available on Amazon

Facebook & LinkedIn/Alison Vaughn

www.AlisonVaughn.com

Email Address/ website
AlisonVaughnSpeaks@gmail.com   www.AlisonVaughn.com/
www.jacketsforjobs.org

Eline Pedersen
Doctor of Chiropractic
Owner of Health Q. Group of Chiropractic Clinics
Initiator and Honorary President of Birth Forward NGO
Larnaca, Cyprus
eline.pedersen@aberdeenchiropracticclinic.com

Chapter 26
It is a Human Gift and Duty to Contribute to a Better Society

Dr. Eline Pedersen is a Doctor of Chiropractic, a working mom, and a devoted wife. Eline works internationally, aiming for global change, advocating the philosophy that healing is an innate action happening from within the body. She lives in Cyprus, running a wellness family chiropractic clinic with her husband, Costas. Birth Forward – Cyprus Eline Inspires.

Mission and Vision

Birth Forward is an NGO focused on providing information, support, and advocacy for people planning and becoming parents. The NGO works with pregnant women, informing and educating them on their human and birthing rights, and advocates with relevant institutions for keeping the birthing process as close to nature as possible

Starting from Scratch

Creating an NGO or Business from scratch using proven processes and strategies is essential for sustainable change in the community. This does not take away the benefits of collaboration and co-creation with established projects and initiatives. It is a human gift and duty to contribute to a better society and an achievement to create something that you as an individual started from scratch, we need new and innovative ideas, especially of the younger generation.

Birth, Nature, Motherhood

During my education, I faced things I considered faulty in treating patients, which led me to explore how the body heals itself. In my work as a chiropractor, I worked with pregnant women and noted many serious issues humans face, starting from how we give birth. This was also supported by the birth of my second child as I underwent the challenges of natural birth and experienced the challenges and rewards. My work and birthing experience, combined with my previous experience from my university days, led me to the idea to help elevate the birthing culture in Cyprus, a country with a highly concerning rate of C-sections. I was lucky to collaborate with like-minded professionals from various fields, establishing and growing Birth Forward as a veritable entity to help all pregnant and birthing moms in Cyprus.

Big Why
Mother, Baby, C-Section

My **why** for initiating Birth Forward came from working as a pregnancy chiropractor and the ever-growing number of C-section rates in Cyprus. I felt obligated to help somehow as people are often kept in the dark about the

189

importance of respecting the nature of birth, even when intervention at birth is needed. I wanted to help birthing moms experience the beauty of childbirth and have the right to decide how they want to give birth and to feel empowered and respected in the process. I feel a personal win every time I hear a positive birth story because of our work. It helps me on my mission to save one child at a time from unnecessary trauma and interventions with potential lifelong effects physically and mentally.

Aha Moment Epiphany
Serve, Humanity, Motherhood

The very moment I gave birth, I had a vision of all the mothers giving birth at this very same moment all over the world; we were all breathing and pulsating together, one energy birthing the children for the future. I knew I had to do my part to create a culture where other women could tap into this amazing personal but yet so natural experience of un-intervened birth.   Combined with my work experiences, my own birthing experience, and communicating with expecting mothers, I realized I needed to do something to change the birthing culture in Cyprus

Secret Formula
Collaborations, Referrals, Advice

Birth Forward started as an initiative to change the birthing culture in Cyprus; I was lucky to meet and collaborate with like-minded individuals from different fields, and we built an organization that serves to educate, inspire, and support expecting parents. We serve people from Cyprus, supporting the cycle of creating a family. Birth Forward focuses on advocacy, support, and education for families and professionals. We do this with an extensive knowledge base with information, advice, and support for all stages of pregnancy and invaluable advice for all the challenges people face during this time. Birth Forward's Scientific Board has scientists and leaders in different fields to advise and help concerning preconception, pregnancy, birth, and childhood, including health economics, human rights, and ethics.

Steps to Build Success from Scratch
Collaboration, Mentoring, Like-Minded People, Focus, Help

My efforts began as an idea, and I was lucky to meet and closely work with pregnant women and people from the medical field directly involved in childbirth in Cyprus. Things became apparent when I started to think about how to implement my ideas in practice, and here are some of the specific steps I took to make this happen:
1. Thinking of the necessary steps and processes needed to change the established birthing culture in Cyprus
2. Meeting and working closely with professionals from many related fields, creating a multidisciplinary approach to making changes happen

3.   Using all the available means to make things happen; campaigns, pamphlets, social media, public letters, petitions, etc.

First Sign of Success

I initiated Birth Forward, but the result was a joint effort of many individuals; we all worked on changing the already established practices in a culture that is not very open to changes. A vital influence was my mentors, who were always ready to listen and provide advice based on their knowledge and experience. My steadfast support was my husband, Costas, who stood by me through all the hardships as an unmovable pillar I could always lean on. One of the great successes was the public's receiving of our Cesarean Awareness campaign.

Ultimate Solution
Mentoring, Support, Friendship

I've been lucky to know and closely collaborate with many notable people who've made incredible networks for women and made sustainable changes in their communities. From my many mentors throughout my professional career, I can outline Dr. Viola Edward, Dr. Jeanne Ohm, and many more. I believe that everyone can contribute to something and that deep inside we all love to give and contribute to a better society, environment, or world in some way or other. I am here to support and inspire you to bring your passion and vision to life.

Free Gift

I can gift the readers a smile, hug, unwavering mentor support through their efforts, and a free strategy call and free download of my e-book "How to Create a Movement" from my website. Starting something, creating, and growing a business, a movement or an NGO is demanding and challenging, so I advise you to start slowly and build on your efforts. Don't worry if you are going slow, as you can follow proven processes I can share with you, you can follow your progress, make changes, and adapt to the changing trends in your field.
https://www.elineinspires.com/bookacall
https://www.elineinspires.com/freebook

Accolades and Achievements

I've won several accolades for my work, and the ones I'm most proud of are the awards for my inspirational, humanitarian work in Cyprus and internationally. I've received an Honorary Doctorate of Humanity for humanitarian work and Leadership from the Academy of Universal Global Peace 2018. I also received the Inspiration Award for Woman 2017.

It is a Human Gift and Duty to Contribute to a Better Society

See What They Are Saying...

My mentoring style is hands-on, which means I'm getting personally invested in the success of my mentees. Here are three testimonials from people I've mentored while they've started their careers:

Being mentored by Eline has been one of the most beneficial and rewarding experiences. She is an extremely open and caring person with a warm personality that makes anyone in the same room as her feel at ease. She has such a wealth of knowledge in both chiropractic and life and is open to sharing her experiences, as she ultimately wants everyone to succeed and help them get the resources necessary to grow and do well.
– Dr. Sydney Brangenberg
***

Eline was a fantastic support, offering her knowledge, passion, and advice during a challenging time. She is always calm, professional, and open to listening and providing help and guidance. She has been a fantastic mentor!
– Sandra Siljanoska
***

Eline has compelling and dynamic energy; she is focused and passionate about people and their health. When looking for a mentor, I believe it's vital that they have personal hard-earned experience, success in ventures, and the ability to pass these skills on. Eline easily ticks all these boxes and then some.
– Dr. Mike Marinus"

***

Business Links
https://linktr.ee/elinepedersen

H.E. Dr. Sherri Henderson
Founder & President
Global Business Development Firm
Detroit, Michigan USA
DrHenderson@GBDFirm.com

Chapter 27
Launching Women Business Leaders into New Global Markets

I am a global business executive who mentors women to exceed their potential. Appointed by the UN, I curate business relationships with G7 and G20 nation heads of state and the World Bank at an enterprise scale. I collaborate with C-suite business leaders and have executed multimillion-dollar deals on business ventures and opportunities, worldwide.

My collegiate journey began at Michigan State University (BS & MS), then continued at International Chaplaincy Academy, Ashland Theological Seminary and University (Ph.D.), Harvard Business Institute (Business Executive Program), and culminated at Yale University (Business Executive Program), respectively.

My educational profession commenced as an elementary school teacher and Adjunct Professor at Spring Arbor University in Michigan, respectively.

Mission and Vision

Our mission: We are a Landbridge connecting businesses with global opportunities. The GBD Firm leverages our team's expertise through strategic global partnerships and organizations. Our international consultants provide a 360-degree consortium of success.

BUILD SUCCESS!
Ignite your business with Purpose and Passion

Intelligent decision-making defines, then drives success. I chose to take calculated risks to pursue entrepreneurship; failure was never an option. I believed I could make a difference in the lives of women around the world.
There were relatives whom had obtained their college degrees in various subject areas and took risks by forming their own businesses. After teaching as a classroom educator and administrator, I wanted to expand my horizons! The status quo was unacceptable, and I decided I was the only person that had the power to control my destiny.

When you are overwhelmed by your career and day-to-day jobs, women seldom have the luxury of following their dreams. My main hurdle was managing my financial obligations as an entrepreneur. My lifestyle changed from receiving bi-weekly paychecks to being reliant on clients paying for my consulting services. I increased my faith and accepted the challenge to overcome all obstacles.

The Big Why
'Merger She Wrote':

The Big Why for me was having the ability to touch and change lives, personally and professionally. My focus realigned to how my talents and skill sets could help other businesswomen.

While identifying education, business, and ministries, I combined all three occupations which led to the creation of GBD Firm (Global Business Development Firm). That life-defining merger initiated the launch of Global Business Development Firm. Merging my expertise from all three occupations made me efficient and effective.

Aha Moment

On a global business trip to Washington, D.C., I had an aha moment. Attending a high-rise rooftop engagement across from the White House, an epiphany surfaced. I was actively engaged in education, business, and ministry, and decided to marry all three into a cohesive business model. That life-defining moment initiated the merger of my education and mission experiences with my Business Development Firm, conceptualizing the Global Business Development Firm.

We serve clients throughout the USA and around the world, with offices in Nairobi, Kenya with a newly launched office in London.

Secret Formula: Lead by Example
Our 4P Philosophy

Our 4P Philosophy defines our clients' success, specifically People, Purpose, Planet, and Profit.

People
> Our company continues to make a positive impact in the world; we recognize people's respective demographics where they live. We understand and serve our clients' needs in their space, addressing their needs with relevant solutions.

Purpose
> We are purpose-driven in how we serve our clients.

Planet
> We challenge our clients to achieve the United Nations' 2030 17 Sustainable Goals. We define and deploy sustainable solutions on every project and encourage our clients to contribute to those goals as they continue their progress.

Profit,

> Profit is critical to business survival and success and enhances long-term longevity in every business, corporation, and organization. Our 4P Philosophy is a core component with every client we partner with and serve. Government and business leaders worldwide request me to champion our 4P Philosophy, empowering their respective citizenry.

Steps to Building Success

Our commitment: Elevate small and medium-sized businesses by consulting them on strategic planning, organizational development, marketing management, cultural intelligence.

The first task was to make the philosophy our central branding message. The second task was to make sure everyone on our team had a concise understanding of the benefits of the philosophy, internally and externally. The third task was to invite clients to engage, and the fourth task was to assess and evaluate our usage and adoption success rate.

Our success is supported by our network of family members and colleagues. I have relied on my business memberships, professional networks, and organization affiliations. I credit our success to our amazing international teams and strategic partners.

First Signs of Success
Blaze the Trail!

Our first signs of success occurred when our clients implemented new policies, achieved new goals, created annual calendars, launched new products or services, and projected themselves into new markets. One of my first clients was Moneyball Sportswear. I enjoyed working with the company because I was able to see it grow and watch it expand its brand with new sportswear products in new locations. It launched as a basketball sportswear apparel company that expanded into football, soccer, golf, and volleyball. It is a pleasure watching their business and brand grow.

Ultimate Solution

We deliver customized client solutions. When I launched my company, there were no other women-owned, global business development firms in Michigan at that time; I was the first.

It is important to align with other women in business and collaborate with like-minded professionals. Many women have mentored me along the way notably my mother Gail King, Dr. Margret Aguwa, and my current clergy, Bishop Corletta Vaughn.

Free Gift

My gift to all participants is a complimentary, one-year membership to our **GBC** (Global Business Club). The Club offers resources and information on strategic business practices through webinars and success-building tools.

More broadly, we educate our members on how to promote their business in new global markets. Every member has access to exclusive, multi-dimensional checklists, online training, and business networking groups essential to their success.

Join GBC at www.GBDFirm.com.

Appointments, Awards, Affiliations & Education

- ❖ United Nations: Appointed US Ambassador
- ❖ Chair of the Michigan Trade Summit Committee
- ❖ Global Black Women's Chamber of Commerce, Executive Board Member
- ❖ Global Business Professional Award
- ❖ Spirit of Detroit Award
- ❖ Global Business of the Year Award
- ❖ International Real Estate Agent - Sotheby's International
- ❖ Delta Sigma Theta Sorority
- ❖ Michigan State University
- ❖ Ashland Theological Seminary and University
- ❖ ICCC Business and Community Program
- ❖ Harvard Business Institute
- ❖ Yale University / Business Writing Program

See What They Are Saying...

I serve as an international diplomat and was appointed as a United Nations Ambassador at Large. I have received numerous certificates and awards from across the United States for my 25 years in international business. I was awarded the Spirit of Detroit award for hosting Michigan's only two-day global business conference. I received a Community Pillar from the State of Michigan Chamber of commerce and recently received the Global Business Award for assisting women-owned businesses in business development.

***

Launching Women Business Leaders into New Global Markets

My goal will always be to establish, nurture, and exalt women business owners. I began consulting women business owners in 2010. My goal was, and remains present day, to educate and ignite women to pursue and conquer global markets. I offer(ed) information and resources that guide women to new countries as a board member to 4 international organizations. I have mentored women business owners in Canada, Mexico, Dubai, Hong Kong, South Africa, Tanzania, Kenya, Peru, Chile, and Venezuela.

***

A colleague requested a blueprint for students to explore international business markets. I assisted in developing the organization and joined her on one of their first group mission trips to Dubai and Abu Dhabi. We established a weekly virtual course where I taught about the natural resources and tourist attractions located in Lima, Peru.

***

Business Links

www.DrSherri.global

H.E. Dr Desziree Richardson
GLOBAL LEADER, VISIONARY, VIBRATORY VOICE HEALER,
INTERNATIONAL SPEAKER, ENTREPRENEUR,
ADVOCATE, HUMANITARIAN
London, England
desiree.richardson@gmail.com

Chapter 28
Leading With Love

Her Excellency Dr Desziree Richardson, DLA, DLITT is a thought leader, transformation and motivational speaker, International best-selling author, model, humanitarian, and entrepreneur.

Although she is a solid businesswoman, she feels genuine desire and devotion to the well-being and welfare of her fellow human beings. She enjoys being a service to others. Dr Desziree believes her sole purpose in sharing her story and wisdom is to help empower positive changes in the lives of many people around the world.

Mission and Vision

Dr Desziree's mission is to help change lives and positively influence others through her empowering projects. Her wish is for everyone to be happy and to feel inclusive.

To live in a world where peace, love, kindness, and the energy of cosmic love can be radiated and felt through every human existence and experience.

She envisions a world of hope far from the perils of the ego to replace the elements with compassion, kindness, peace, and tolerance.

Face of Woha

Face of Woha, the empowered woman brand, products and speaking extravaganza platform. Our mission is to give a voice to those who have the potential to become leaders and icons. We are providing more significant causes and opportunities for diverse women worldwide to help heal the world through the powerful messages of wisdom and grace. Face of Woha is determined to bring positive changes to the world. Helping women find their voices, celebrating their achievements and spreading awareness around diversity, equity, and inclusion.

Moreover, we are preparing for a future when every little girl will have the chance to chase their dreams and realize them. Voices of women won't be lost in the crowd. Furthermore, their achievements and capabilities will be celebrated. Stories of their journey, struggle, and success will inspire others to do better and achieve whatever they want. Face of Woha aims to become the support system women need for a better and more empowered future. Our platform is passionate about giving back to those in need. Therefore, it is a joy to know that we are making a difference and positively impacting and helping to restore the environment and support the Women of Heart Foundation.

**Starting from Scratch
Finding My Purpose**

I had to start believing in my creativity while practicing self-love. However, all I ever

knew was to share my love with others without taking the time out to connect with my abilities, skills, and talents. Therefore, I had to stand up and look in the mirror and ask myself, who are you, and what is my life purpose?

A few years ago, I had an aha moment. I realized the stories I was told were far from the truth; I was enough and sufficient, and all I can be and more. I was listening to the voices from the wrong crowd, and I was engaged in bad, inappropriate relationships, which taught me the lessons I need to get where I am. Hence, I was grateful for the opportunity to choose and connect with my inner being that brings out the beauty of my hidden capabilities. I found myself because I had to let go of places, people, situations, and things that were not in my alignment.

Taking My Power Back

I took my power when I realized the enemy was trying to change my identity, stealing my sanity, emotions, and energy. I took my control back and realized I had to venture into a world by discovering my true purpose and passion is to serve humanity and empower the next generation; so, it is, so it shall be, and so can you.

**Big Why
Journey, Empowerment, and Impact**

Journey
The journey to date has been punctuated by so many aha moments, despite moments of self- doubts, obstacles, dark clouds, and poor judgment. In today's shaping world, there are still many women and girls worldwide who were born and raised in an environment without sufficient knowledge of empowerment on self-love, self-

201

esteem, self-doubt, self-reliance, and self-confidence. These women and young women never had an opportunity to access this information from an adolescent age because they did not know the data existed, or I couldn't access it because of their humble beginnings. Millions worldwide still cannot access this wisdom to empower themselves because of their circumstances.

Empowerment

With passion and purpose, it is our duty that the messages of hope, love, kindness, healing, and acceptance reach every

Connor in the world to empower those who don't have access to the Internet or any other facilities to watch and listen. I want them

to know that they are special, unique, and worthy of this information, just like everyone else. It does not matter how you were born in the world; you need an opportunity to make a difference.

Impact

Therefore, the only way we can do this is to share opportunities with others and learn the life skills to help us along our journey through life. As a collective, we need to create more opportunities for others to feel a sense of belonging. So that we all feel accepted and have access to the same rights from birth

Secret Formula
Leading With Love & Humility

My secret formula is to lead with love and humility. The results will appear in many different, unique and respectable ways. When you are the master of your emotions, well-being, and

personal development with good intentions, you will foster long-lasting support and connections with a positive outcome in your personal, professional, and business life.

Leading

Having taken counsel with my universal inner voice, the law of attraction drove me to pursue my dreams as God is in control of my destiny. My work is to reach a broader audience to teach and

support women on how to empower themselves from within and find their voice, and become leaders and decision-makers through the stories we share and the work we do, geared towards promoting the values of excellence, generosity, and pride in the actions of women as well as celebrating their achievements.

My mission is to help change lives positively through my empowering projects such as Face of Woha, Women of Heart Awards, Breaking the Ice Talk and Women of Heart

Foundation. All my platforms represent a sense of belonging and a contribution to embracing these factors.

Humility

Humility plays a significant role in creating the platforms to reach a broader audience to impact the lives of every human existence, to make a positive change in the minds of readers, listeners, and viewers, to help change the world through changing lives, and to empower the world to become kinder and to share love towards humanity.

Steps to Build Success from Scratch

Creating, Investing, Building up my Credibility and Visibility, Sourcing Opportunities Giving Rise to Monetary Gains and Implementing Sustainability.

Here are my steps to success.
1. **Idea** - Bring your ideas to start up a brand concept and work on your personal development, business plan, or project.
2. **Investing** - Know your actual value, invest time and money in your passion and purpose, and take action to bring dreams and life aspirations to life. Your time is pure and precious. Monetise and give back.
3. **Credibility** - When you invest in yourself, you are doing the necessary things that show up and to gain access to multi-media platforms. However, this will help you become credible and gain credibility and visibility in your business, brand, and career prospects.
4. **Visibility** - By becoming more credible, you become more visible, creating a path to be observable with your brand, business, and career. You are Long-term with visibility. When visibility takes place, opportunity comes knocking.
5. **Opportunities** - When your brand, business, and career are enlarged and visible, you are open to receiving opportunities. When the opportunity comes, there is room for your finances to increase.
6. **Financial Breakthroughs** - The opportunities you create through your creative ideas, credibility, and visibility will bring you advancement in your financial circumstances.

Sign of Success

My success was realizing my businesses and projects have the potential for long-term sustainability. Even though I had gone through all the bad and ugly alone, my determination resulted in the ultimate legacy of my actions, modesty, compassion, attitude, gratitude, respect, values, and how I treat others. Furthermore, I took care of my emotional intelligence and had good intentions. These are the guiding principles we should endure to become stable successors.

Ultimate Solution
Your Worth Value and Service

My message is to know who you spend time with and what you do daily. How do they or you add value to your time? Also, be mindful of your time spent. Think about the missing gap in the market and how you and your ideas can be of service. With these steps, you will get there in the end.

Offer

Come create a brighter world with us and build a long-lasting legacy with Women of the Era: Leading and Stepping Out Into the World so you can reveal your untold stories and history to empower other women worldwide!
https://womenofera.drbglobal.net/

Accolades & Achievements

I am appointed the UK representative of the emerging African country, Birland State, UK Ambassador to the United States Presidential Services, Diversity, Equity and Inclusion DEI Chairperson for Rotary Club of Global Impact, and International Honorary Distinguished Multicultural Advisor Board Member for FOWCAAS and many other appointments and international recognition and awards, honours, and grants are in honour of my credentials and achievements recorded over the years as a generalist, humanitarian, and experienced broadcaster, writer, and International Speaker.

See What They Are Saying...

Thank you so much, Dr Desziree R, Richardson Princess of this beautiful world. You encouraged me a lot in this journey of Face of Woha; you taught me how to do things in the right way. You listen to me in every difficult time whenever I ask you for the time extension you gave me. Without your encouragement, I really could not make these videos. Maybe I quit in the beginning and realized that if I wanted, I could do anything with your beautiful voice notes every day, and your motivational messages every month inspires me a lot. I did not find a teacher in my school time or during my college times who told me how to do things in the right way with perfectisawt; I saw you, a unique amazing, mind-blowing lady of this beautiful planet. I think I don't have words to say Thanks for whatever you did for me; you are so kind and humble in every situation I found. ce again, Thanks a lot 🏷️🏷️♡
~ Habibah Javed

***

I am honoured to be a part of an incredible fantastic journey!! Thank YOU, Dr Desziree Ri, Richardson, for creating a space for women to embrace their divine feminine leadership qualities that the world needs to incorporate to keep evolving!!
#FaceofWOHA #Gratitude #empowerment #DivineFeminine
~Clarisa Romero
***

Thank you so much for being a constant support to every one of us and for bringing us all together. Hope we make you proud and carry forward WOHA to the whole world! LoveDr
~ Dr Roopa Modha

***

https://blinq.me/GdWPudh7Hwg6

Dr. María Angelica Benavides
Ultimate Legacy Builder, A World-Class Storyteller, Serial
Entrepreneur, and Publisher
Arlington, Tx - U.S.A
dr.angelica@drbglobal.net

Chapter 29
Legacy: The Finish Line

Dr. Angelica Benavides is known as Dr. B and the Ultimate Legacy Builder. She increases visibility, exposure, and influence, helping entrepreneurs be all they can be. Dr. B's, [Angélica Benavides (Underwood) Ed.D.] story is being written and shared worldwide by the Women's World Conference and Awards. She has been featured on NBC, USA Today, and Fox and recognized as an Amazing Woman of Influence. She shared a Global Virtual Stage with Forbes Riley, Bill Walsh, Ragne Sinikas, and Dr. Freddy Behin.

Dr. B. shows women entrepreneurs how to scale their businesses. She teaches them how to become financially literate and how to use financial knowledge to make better decisions from everyday spending to long-term financial planning. Throughout the chapter in bold words, Dr. B. will share her key recipes to help you share your Mission with Millions.

"The only thing worse than being blind is having sight but no vision."   *Helen Keller*

Mission and Vision

Dr. B helps women spread their message through storytelling and delivering the right message to the right audience. She inspires and motivates women entrepreneurs to write books that outlive them and helps them align to their best version of who they are and who they need to become to achieve the bigger version of themselves. Dr. B is supercharging women business owners to take big ideas into reality and help them step into their greatness.

Dr. B. helps women clarify and establish a mission to be delivered to millions of people around the world to raise awareness, empower people into leadership, and elevate them to serving people around the world. A visionary woman leader must take responsibility to create a mission and legacies that will take our future generations to places we never imagined we could reach.

Outliving Life Circumstances is a Success

All women need to inspire other women to do everything in their power to thrive in life and leave a legacy. You see, leaving a legacy is more than giving an inheritance and trust ... a generational legacy is leaving ideas, stories, perspectives, and/or beliefs that are emotionally or culturally passed down from our families to the world. A legacy is an opportunity to change the world. It is an opportunity to live for a purpose bigger than yourself and bless those around you.

Convinced that people have the power to reach their own potential, I know everyone has a story to tell that will transform people's lives around the world who are waiting to hear your story. Today more than ever the world awaits you and is looking for the job, products, or services that you can create. It is time to start your business or reinvent how your business operates. The truth is that your business is not unique; the reality is that **you are unique**. You need to leave a legacy that outlives you by telling your story and sharing your message with the world.

BIG Why
Creating a Mission to Millions

One of my greatest achievements in life is living! I was able to outlive two types of cancer. Before being diagnosed with cancer, I was doing Zumba and six inches of my intestines twisted; I nearly died at that time. During one of my surgeries in dealing with cancer, I ended up with a blood clot that led to a severe infection landing me in intensive care for more than a week. My greatest achievement and honor is being alive. I realized I had a bigger mission to convince, inspire, and motivate women leaders around the world to

live their life's purpose in a bigger way. During my most difficult times of life, I discovered **"Me"**. I realized that to achieve big dreams, you must take big risks. It is scary but Bravery is key. You must simply do it and take action towards your big dreams to achieve any success. Getting a message in front of millions might not be easy, but it is possible.

Create a mission for millions. Make sure to write a book that outlives you. Live and leave your message and story that are your golden nuggets on how you overcame challenges in life. So, our children, and future generations are inspired to keep going no matter how difficult life might seem. We need to encourage and inspire people to find love and joy within. We must celebrate small wins to motivate us and create momentum in our life. Remember to be present in all your life experiences. It is not the destination you seek but the experience of the journey that is brought to your soul. Collaborate and build strong relationships to have a sense of belonging and create supportive communities.

Aha Moment and Epiphany
My Business Born from Times of Uncertainty

My business was born from times of uncertainty. I was living a life that defies the odds. I was the ninth of eleven children born to Mexican immigrants. I struggled in the English (monolingual) classroom and often doubted my ability to succeed. As a native Spanish speaker, I struggled in all classes - especially reading. I was the first in my family to finish high school, but even on my graduation, I wondered. "How did that happen?" After finishing high school, I took menial jobs that did not require

much education. I felt that, despite my diploma, I probably would not amount to much. Fortunately, one of my employers saw what I did not see in myself: potential. Armed with confidence, I enrolled in
Laredo Community College and earned a doctoral degree in Leadership and Specialized in Curriculum. I have proven that success is possible for everyone by creating a plan and sticking to it through thick and thin!

I have gained the unique ability to help people release the mental obstacles that prevent them from achieving their very best at work, in business, and in life. I am committed to empowering others to exchange the chaos of life for the best life possible. Helping people unlock their full potential and believing their time is now. I share my personal story of how I beat cancer and how to heal your body and your life. I share some of my challenges in life and how I overcame the darkest moments of my life, turning them into light, joy, love, and empowerment. I am committed to providing a RoadMap to my online coaching platform. I connect with other passionate women and unique voices who share their challenges and how they overcame life challenges. I empower women in all areas of life, such as health, money, relationships, education, and career, by teaching them universal laws and how to play the game of life. Life is simply a game you must learn how to play to achieve your highest potential and live on purpose to be self-actualized.

Secret formula

I help businesswomen and leaders to master the art of writing their own books within 90 days. Publish your book the right way and make it available to hundreds, thousands of readers. Share your story and message to the world. I offer premium coaching which is one-on-one coaching to help you turn your dream business and book into reality. I take you from blank pages to publishing. I help you identify your writing blockages using Neuro-Linguistic, TimeLine Therapy, and Hypnosis techniques to break through what is holding you back. I not only help you write but heal old wounds. I coach women like you on how to write a book, turn it into an e-course, and show you how to get a speaking gig so you start to share your Mission with Millions.

I am also supporting businesswomen leaders to manage, inspire, and publish collaborative book projects just like this 100 Successful Amazing Women Book. I also have my own book series, "From Zero to Success", where authors from all over the world share their mission to millions on how they started from scratch to where they are now. Experienced in working in a richly diverse school community with bilingual skills, I have successfully led major organizational change and strong community partnership and have demonstrated experience in collaboratively working closely with leaders and supporting initiatives and priorities aligned with implementing a rigorous curriculum in their businesses. I help you design a vision, plan, and clear direction. If you have no vision and plan, you have no clear direction. You will end up going in circles or feel stuck. A Strategic Plan is key, so you have a sense of direction and outline your measurable goals. Strategic planning will help guide your day-to-day decisions. You can evaluate progress to change your approach if it is not working or if your plan works duplicate and use it repeatedly because you have found a Formula that Works!

Steps to Build Success from Scratch

Become the published author you have always wanted to be. The benefits of writing and publishing a book are to leave a legacy, change lives, write to heal old wounds, earn money from profits, speak, and get on other people's platforms, and become an authority in your field. Start with low and no-content books that are not your traditional books. A low and no content book is one that doesn't have a lot of writing or text in it.

- Find a niche and research it to have a better understanding
- Design a sizzling book cover to attract the audience's attention
- Choose a dynamic book title
- Create your low content or no content pages
- Get my mini 5X5 Book Publishing Made Simple System

First Sign of Success

I often say that COVID-19 might have kept us home and stopped the local connections, but it opened an internet portal to connect with the world. During COVID-19 the world shut down and for a minute the world froze; however, immediately we found a solution that changed the way we do things. One of my giant steps during COVID-19 was connecting with women around the world and creating PowerTalk Livestream where I interview women and leaders from all over the world so they can share their messages. Innovation is another recipe for spreading your Mission to Millions. Use the internet, get on podcasts, or create your own; use online TV such as Apple TV or Amazon Fire TV. If it doesn't exist, invent it. You have a greater being within you that has the confidence and power to achieve your big dreams. I believe in you. You should believe in yourself, too! Believing in yourself is a vital key you must use and use again in your Million to Millions journey because if you don't, no one else will.

Ultimate Solution
Dare to do the things you have never done before!

An inclusive and diverse world with a primary focus will be to create transformational learning communities fiercely committed to educational equity and excellence for women worldwide. The need to provide leadership and expertise to

assess, identify, formulate, and implement a mission that will serve millions with goals and objectives to make equity and inclusion a reality. The main key is an Inclusive Culture to spread your message to millions. One way to make inclusion a reality is to collaborate with women around the world and model an open dialogue around race, culture, class, and other issues of differences. We must find what works and doesn't work by finding and researching best practices, innovations, and research across multiple disciplines and subject areas. We must understand historical contexts and the active investment in changing social structures

and practices over time. Create a common vocabulary and protocol for resource allocation and evaluating strategic investments. Just having a seat at the table is not inclusion. It is finding your voice and sharing your message that creates a more Inclusive Culture. I stepped into my greatness when I found my voice, responsibility, and duty to the world that helps you and millions of women to share their Mission to Millions through my coaching programs, publishing books for entrepreneurs, my app, and B-Global masterminds, and business ventures. Visionary Leaders should strive toward optimal inclusion to create a strong community and strong connections, giving people a sense of belonging.

Free Gift

I help entrepreneurs find that story and tell it to the world by writing a book and creating your signature talk to help you overcome the wounds of the past.

Telling your story can be cathartic and makes you grow as a person, gives you satisfaction, and allows you to increase your chances of success. It takes you out of that dark area that perhaps you thought ruined your life forever. It shows you the light. Share your light with others who are waiting for your life-transforming message. You will leave this experience with a feeling of dominance.

You are here to make a big difference in the world. The best way to do this is to use your story, experience, knowledge, and advice to help others be successful. This strategy that I share with you will guide you in a process so that through your story you can package and share advice, systems, tools, and processes, and create a lucrative business that impacts lives. Plus, leave a legacy that outlives you!

Get my free **4-Online Video Series** below called Book Publishing Made Simple System so you can get started with writing your book or start with a low-content book that is a notebook or journal.

Accolades

My certifications are Associate in Arts, Bachelor of Interdisciplinary, Master of Science, and Doctoral Leadership with a Specialization in Curriculum & Instruction. These don't define me but shape who I am now. I have always been curious about Learning Theories, Human Development, and how the brain functions. I am dedicated a decade to researching and discovering how humans learn, develop, and how we can shift our beliefs to shift our decision-making and actions.

I have learned from the giants such as Anthony Robbins, Dean Graziosi, John Maxwell, Grant Cardone, Forbes Riley, Bill Walsh, and Mark Victor Hansen to help me think bigger, make bigger decisions, and take giant action steps toward my mission to millions. I now create even more success for businesswomen owners. I specialize in publishing books, business programs, speaker training programs, certification programs, and global masterminds. I put on the table the best resources that every business needs to learn about to survive and thrive in any economy. My message has been delivered as cutting-edge content.

I am known as Dr. B. I inspire women worldwide to share their Mission with Millions and their stories. I am a Badass Influencer, an Ultimate Legacy Builder, A World-Class Storyteller, Best-Selling Author, Serial Entrepreneur, and Publisher.

I am a Marketing Director, Advisory Board Member, and Publisher for the Face of Women of Heart Awards (WOHA) for 2021. I was recently invited to the International Advisory Board for the 100 Successful Women in Business Network.

See What They Are Saying...

"B-Publisher (Dr. B.) has excellent communication and fully engages the author. Very supportive and helpful from the start to the end of the book project. Starting with the draft format guiding on how to write the chapters."

Nontsikelelo "Ntsiki" Ncoco
The Incredible, Global Epic Leader
***

"Dr. B. passionately speaks about her novel idea to sell hard copy, action-taking journals, and more!"
Maija-Liisa N. Adams, CEO Maija-Liisa Speaks, an Idaho-based global TEDx talk coach
***

I have been a Co-author of more than a dozen books; the experience of having been mentored by Angelica was just magnificent. I am a professional mentor. and I can recognize when I am Mentored by a master mentor, and I bow to the joy and grace to have this chance. I highly recommended Angelica as a mentor for authors looking for a wonderful publisher. If you are thinking of writing, get a meeting with Angelica.
Viola Edward De Glanville, Owner at GRIT Academy
***

Learn More About this Author

Dr Angelica Underwood
WhatsApp contact

Jo Wiehler
La Belle Sabbioneta
Sabbioneta, MN, Italy
jo.wiehlersprklycln@gmail.com

Chapter 30
Life is But a Dream

JO IS A FUN POWERFUL BALL OF ENERGY! Specializing in Sales, Marketing, & Branding. She will inspire you to Dream Bigger & Reach Higher.

Jo Wiehler is a Visionary and Business Owner, with a wonderful combination of Love and Kindness and an Exceptional Eye for Business and a genuine love of people, places & culture. She is the Founder and CEO of La Belle Sabbioneta®, La Belle Sabbioneta & The PowerBall Women®, La Belle Swagger®/ La Belle Brand ®/La Belle Travels®/ La Belle Tours®/ La Belle Sabbioneta Luxury Alcohol Line® /La Belle Whiskey®/The General Scotch®/La Belle Brandy®/Pirates Rum®/La Belle Sabbioneta Wines & Gourmet Olive Oils® La Belle Sabbioneta Sparkles Rosé (Nonalcoholic)®/La Belle Sabbioneta Sparkles Blanco (Nonalcoholic)®/ La Belle Sabbioneta®/ The Duke®/Sabbioneta the Jewel of Italy®/ La Belle Sabbioneta Queen of Beer Golden Lager 100% Pale Ale®/ *La Belle Sabbioneta 100% Italian Luxury Olive Oil®/ La Belle Sabbioneta 100% Italian Luxury Red Wine® /La Belle Sabbioneta H2...Ohhh!!! ® / La Belle Soda Pop Shoppe (Old Fashion Soda 3 Flavors Lemon, Orange, & Cherry)®/ La Belle Sabbioneta Juice Bar (100% Italian Juice/5 flavors: Peach, Pear, Nectarine, Apple, Mixed Berry)® and so many products & services coming soon.

*La Belle Sabbioneta is an Exclusive Licensed Domkapa Furniture Dealer for Sabbioneta, MN, Lombardy Northern Italy Region with Walking Showrooms at our Facility La Belle Sabbioneta. Giving you – your residence, and business, the top-quality furniture and Design for all your decorating needs, giving you the elegance, sustainability, durability, and style of an eco-conscious product.

Mission and Vision

Our Mission at La Belle Sabbioneta is to give a safe place for individuals to come and learn, grow and find themselves- to be connected, and have the peace, love and confidence to heal, overcome, learn, and develop into the person they want to be.

The Vision for our business is that we not only impact you right now but make an impact on your life for good for generations to come, because we know if we impact you, you can impact your family, community, city, state, country- and we want to be that change-that you are empowered to be that change in the world too!

Build a Business From Scratch
Become Highly Positive, Energetic, and Powerful

I had to become Highly Positive, Energetic, Powerful, and was able to be a highly sought Motivational/Keynote Speaker. The key ingredient is to love and laugh. By combining your life experiences with your business knowledge, you will have a unique way of grabbing the audience's attention-while powerfully making your Business Points and delivering a Powerful but loving message. This is how I was able to speak with global companies such as Anon Global Foundation India, RedCorner Show South Africa, BC Cancer Agency, Vancouver Canada, and Intuitive Summit in Australia. On Sales, Marketing, Branding, Positivity, Optimism, Dreams, Goals, Cancer and Various other subjects to name a few. She is an International Bestselling Author & Co-Author in several books, a Writer, Muralist, Freelance Makeup Artist, Designer, Event Planner, Coach & Mentor to Many around the world! I am a big believer in leading with love and kindness.

The Boom Moment

My Life Seemed Perfect...and then Boom! Everything that was secure in my life was taken in an instant- everything but the Dream for a better life! I was 12 years old Watching "Lifestyles of the Rich and Famous" it was Tours Castle, and they were repossessing all of our furniture-we were left with nothing-they did allow me to finish watching the show before they took the tv - and then told me "Kid it will never happen- you are poor- think about it- we're taking the TV" as a little girl that was my reality but in that tragedy... was a burning desire to do more I was fascinated to think there was another way to live, and helped me to navigate the trials in my adult life to be and have more, as well as to help more. Which led me to my lifelong journey to have and own my own business and Brought me to Italy for La Belle Sabbioneta- no matter the circumstances the Dream stayed alive in me.

Big Why
"Why Not Me?"

That was a thought from 12 years old and up that was burned in the back of my mind- "WHY NOT ME?" Why can't I rise up? Why can't I do better? Why can't I be a business owner? Why can't I be more than my circumstances? When it came to taking risks, it became my bulletproof vest... and gave me the courage to rise and not apologize for my success-but at the same time to keep me grounded in humility to always remember where I came from but at the same time keep me focused on where I was going and the Dreams, and Vision for my future.

Jo created the PowerBall Team-a unique coaching team consisting of Global Coaches 46+ and growing rapidly- that teach, and train, on a variety of subjects that is dedicated to helping others to arise and to become their best in all areas of their life.

Jo is dedicated to helping professionals and individuals to level up in life by accessing their inner intelligence, talents, creativity, health, and wellness, - spiritually, physically, mentally, proven, and extremely different—but highly effective marketing techniques Experiences are possible.

Since the origins of La Belle Sabbioneta ® in 2019, Jo has worked extensively connecting with thousands of people in the coaching, wedding/events, and retreat industry-leading to the creation of the PowerBall Team®, which consists of 46+ Amazing International Coaches which will be holding their retreats on a monthly basis, covering a vast learning, and combining with a luxury

tour seeing the most incredible 8 cities that Northern Italy has to offer, while helping those attending the Retreats to dive deeper into themselves and truly find out who they are-giving them the greatest experience & trip that Italy has to offer.

With Love and kindness and excitement for life, love for others and their success, prosperity, and abundance, she is proving that you can actually prosper in business without taking out the love!

Aha Moment Epiphany
Forced to Get Out of Our Comfort Zone

"**W**HY NOT ME?!?" is my Driving force...my A-HA moment happened in the middle of the Coronavirus pandemic- we all were forced to do things differently, to restructure, to evolve... the world forced us to get out of our comfort zone

Secret Formula

What is your secret sauce to success?

Mine is simple-Love is my secret ingredient to success- it's time to pilot the love back into business... and not be afraid to give more, do more, serve more, and do it with a smile, as well as we created a system that is proactive for the coaches and coaching industry and to blend a retreat together with an incredible tour of Italy most beautiful Northern cities

With any business you want to be known, so many people focus on the website, but I believe it's Sales, Marketing, and Branding... they need to know who you are- so for La Belle Sabbioneta- we needed a strong powerful branding, and message—one that stepped out of the normal, and comfort zones... always thinking WHY NOT ME

boosted me so much. I learned to create an unforgettable Brand. La Belle Sabbioneta...and I'm proud to say we have just launched our Italian Luxury Wines, & Gourmet Products

https://1drv.ms/w/s!AkfNQ7w2QroeiAJ18jJ7g5ykLw0e

Steps to Build Success from Scratch

To step outside the box and not be afraid to do things differently.
To keep my sense of humor intact. And sometimes push the envelope... in uncharted waters.
To keep myself laser focused and keep my blinders on and go with what my gut tells me or what feels right - so many people want to step in and give you directions/advice-be strong enough to follow your own vision.

First Sign of Success

Do you want to know how cool success is, and a Yes for yourself? "My very first yes was a coach in Australia- up to then I thought what if no one get my vision? What if it's really not that good? And she enthusiastically said "YES" I cried right there on the spot. And then I got another yes & another yes & now 47+ Global Coaches later and being contacted daily by other coaches to become a part of it. My daughter and 3 close friends and my brothers and sisters were the ones that have stuck by me in the good times and also the very hard ugly times- getting that first yes to me was like landing on the moon it made me believe... if I can get one yes... then I can get so many more (my original goal was 10!)

Ultimate Solution

Have the courage to rise up and Be Your Own Boss!
As a business owner the best thing that we can do is be a solution finder- it makes life more streamlined and stress free if you have already helped to eliminate as many obstacles, objections, and excuses as possible-but sometimes we get stuck- I have had to learn to continue to reach higher to those that have gone before me-we can learn from everyone.

Jo teaches business in a different way to break free from old cycles of limitation, time-and proven results—a loving process for developing "Back-Door" sales in business and in her relationships and approach to life.

This has helped her to quickly rise to the top in Sales in whatever industry she has worked-from selling Industrial Steel Buildings to Industrial lighting, Makeup & Skincare- Long-distance... or whatever is placed before her- she has risen to the top & now teaches others to do the same.

With joy, laughter and her positive power as her weapons of choice, her goal is service to help give you a safe place to help you, your retreats- whether attending one or running one, to flourish your brand to grow and revitalize all aspects of the mind, body, soul, and Creativity and to help you to have the very best Global Retreat/ variety of area's from weekly corporate classes, art, yoga, cooking, writing retreats/events, teaching at conferences, and so much more while combining her love of travel giving her guests the opportunity to combine 8 Incredible Italian Cities and Empowering Retreats.

Jo is a multifaceted visionary and leader not afraid to do things differently to receive different results. Her ability to see things differently and then ask "WHY NOT?" Has helped to navigate sometimes untried waters to success—all the while sharing her genuine love and kindness to all she meets and work tirelessly to help those rise around her in all walks of Life!

Free Gift

Free stuff! Who doesn't want some free stuff?
I'm excited to serve you all with my "BBQ, Burger & Backdoor Sales" Booklet - Free!!! It's Fun Size so it can fit in your bag, pockets, and purse and will really help you with your own sales/branding and marketing as well as give you an additional €400 off your personal coaching with Myself (regular price €997!) @jowiehlerlabelle (Instagram/message) mention code:100SW www.labellesabbioneta.com

Accolades and Achievements

Sometimes our journey takes us on exciting adventures- with this particular Journey I have been privileged to be invited to speak all around the world both publicly & privately, Co-Authored 8 books (including this incredible book; 100 Most Successful Women Volume 2) and have become an International Best-selling Author in two of them, have Received the Hera Award, The Red Blazer Award and Jacket, have been a Co-Star on a TV show, invited as a guest on several podcasts globally, and TV Interviews, newspapers, and now just launched my Gourmet Olive Oil & Luxury Italian Wines - so excited to say we have hotels, resorts, wedding venues globally interested in my products. It's a very exciting time.

@jowiehlerlabelle (Instagram) Jo Wiehler LinkedIn

See What They Are Saying...

People are Talking about Jo Wiehler, And La Belle Sabbioneta:

"Judy S.- Jo has been an immense help in coaching my business from the ground up! With such a gentle heart she has helped to guide me in the right direction.

Tanique E- I Call her Momma-Jo! She has helped me through all parts of my Life & he continued to support and business knowledge & helping me to be bolder and take more Risks in business.

Alex G. -Jo has a brilliant business mind and helps me to truly be different than the competition and stand out in a powerful and effective way, as well as continued business success

Have you ever wondered if there wasn't more to life- than what you have? Coming from humble beginnings do we even have the courage to become more? Or step out of the known to risk the Dream… or ask "Why not me?"

…Well why not you?

Website:
www.LaBelleSabbioneta.com
Facebook: facebook.com/labellesabbioneta/ or
facebook.com/labellepowerballwomen/ Instagram: instagram.com/jowiehlerlabelle (business)
LinkedIn Jo Wiehler
Jo Wiehler®
+393494651968
Owner
La Belle Sabbioneta®
La Belle Sabbioneta®, & the PowerBall Team®
www.LaBelleSabbioneta.com info@labellesabbioneta.com

Nutan Patel
Nutan Patel Insurance
nutan@nutanpatelinsurance.com

Chapter 31
My Mojo is Back

Dream Big, Dream Wide, Dream Long, Dream Deep -
Set Your Goals
And One Day You Will Be Living The Dream

An accomplished entrepreneur with over 30 years of experience across multiple industries starting with family retail businesses, owning, and operating a food franchise, network marketing, and now taking my Medicare business to the next level, my corporate background entails a short span of 10 years as a business analyst in information technology with a major telecommunications company and an independent educational consultant with a global publishing company. In my personal time, I enjoy hiking, scuba diving, traveling, blue beaches, meeting new people, and being a lover of dogs. A couple of my goals are to climb Mt. Kilimanjaro, become a certified pilot, and get an Airstream.

Mission and Vision

My mission is to simplify complex and confusing Medicare Insurance for Seniors approaching 65 and other eligible populations with compassion and sincerity to select the best insurance plan to fit their specific needs.

Starting from Scratch
From A Free Spirit to Darkness and Back

The American Dream: Life was great, everything I had dreamed of—a beautiful family of four, our family dog, a lovely home with a mother-in-law suite, and our two cars living in one of the top suburban communities in the US to live, work, and play in.

I am never gaing to feel this way again!
02-06-2006

Then one day in 2001, IT had a downturn, and I received my pink slip. I was just getting to the peak of my second career. Unable to find a job, as a couple, we decided I should go into Real Estate - that was my second biggest mistake in pursuing my career. The first was giving up my franchise operations to my husband as he was uninterested in pursuing a career in his chosen field.

Be the energy you want to attract

Also, my marriage had been on the rocks for years, and this just added fuel to the fire, leading to clinical depression and eventually
a separation and divorce. The pain, suffering, and guilt of breaking up our home and the impact it had on our children
consumed me for more than 15 years where I could barely manage to hold a job with zero to minimal responsibility.

But I never gave up on my dream of being a successful entrepreneur.

Fast forward 18 years: I found my dream product and clientele with the flexibility to work from anywhere in the world. This goal was set in 2009 when working remotely was never an option. I found Medicare Insurance, serving and advocating for an awesome population where I can actually make a difference, build a successful business, have flexibility, and create time and financial freedom.

Big Why
My son and daughter, to leaving a legacy

I have learned that one should never give up on her dreams even when others say things to you like "you live in lala land". Which I was reminded of all the time.

Yes, I live in lala land and always will because that's the real deal in life. I continue to dream bigger and set bigger and fatter goals every day now and you should too!

I am filled with gratitude each day now for the wonderful people in my life, and the ability to experience some awesome and amazing adventures, checking off items on my bucket list.

I had to break away from the cycle of chronic depression to return to Nutan, who was a free spirit, free thinker, full of life, fun, filled with dreams and hopes, be the best mom, and a great daughter, sister, aunt, and friend that I was. After spending 15 years in the trenches, I discovered a leader, Grant Cardone, whom I started studying religiously every day. It changed my life within two years, and it has been uphill since. Success encompasses all of these things while creating financial freedom.

223

Aha Moment Epiphany
My Mojo is Back

I remember when my mom suddenly fell ill in 2015, I started learning how Medicare insurance works and thought I should pursue a career in Medicare but did not have the confidence to dive into it.

Several years passed, and I had been studying with Grant for two years where I was getting mentally and emotionally stronger and rebuilding my confidence. No one really knew how weak I was or sad I had felt since 2002 because I had learned to smile and laugh. You can do it too!

Right around this time, I had moved to the Washington, DC area and a new friend, David Reagle, who has a successful Insurance Agency said to me "you should do insurance as you would love it and be great at it". I was still not sure. He could see what I couldn't see in me, so unconsciously I borrowed his belief that I could do it. When we got hit with the Covid 19 Pandemic, during the lockdown, I decided it was time to go for it and never look back. That was the most courageous decision I had made in almost 20 years and realized; I got my mojo back! I had that old feeling back, the energy, the stamina, the clarity and the drive I had 20 years prior, and it felt great. I am here to remind you that you can do it, too!

The first two years in the business were tough, to say the least, the hardest I have ever worked in my life. I am not afraid to work hard and long, but this was excruciating due to the pandemic. It was one challenge after another, but I had a dream, mission, and vision for this business. I am starting my third year of business, and it's on solid ground, growing rapidly. I will achieve the level of time and financial freedom I have always dreamed of within the next five years. This will allow me to have a comfortable retirement and leave a legacy for my children.

Again, I am grateful for my mom who has been my strength, my dear friend David, who encouraged me, my mentor Grant Cardone, and my two colleagues Nick and Justin who have been my support and cheerleaders, and my new friend Dr. Angelica Benevedia whom I only met 4 months ago at a 10X event who inspires me and guides me to reach my full potential. And of course, the pandemic that pushed me into taking action.

Secret Formula
Hustle, Hustle, Hustle!

My hustle is the name of my game every day. I have set massive goals and broken them down from yearly, to monthly, to weekly to how many contacts I need to make and how many appointments I need weekly. I write my goals down almost twice every day. I keep my marketing simple and easy with lead generation, networking, and targeting niche markets, conferences, and trade shows. Find your niche!

About 90% of the time, I do in-person home visits with my prospects because it gives us a chance to meet, connect, and build trust. The average drive time for an appointment is 4 hours. This sets me apart because the majority of agents and brokers are not willing to drive an hour. Medicare prospects get hit so hard

with mail, calls, texts, emails, and commercials, that they get even more confused with the complex and confusing product. One of my clients thanked me graciously for a face-to-face meeting and sent me referrals immediately. A referral is the best compliment. Clients call me" my dearest friend, my Medicare angel" and such instead of calling me by my name.

Steps to Build Success from Scratch
Commit! Educate! Massive Goals! Attitude!

Commit
Committing is the hardest part of starting a new venture. It is nerve-wracking, scary, and you're filled with fear of failure. However, once you commit, you have no choice but to follow through. You will encounter many challenges and you will be tempted to bail out, but you simply won't because you have committed. My mentor, Grant Cardone says "Commit First and Figure Out The Rest Later".

Educate-Learn
Again, commit to learning all about your industry, product, competitors, market trends, and marketing, and become visible in your environment and space, attending seminars, training, and events. Additionally, commit to reading at least 25 books a year (that's an average of 20-25 pages per day) and have one takeaway you can implement. I drive a lot in my business, so audiobooks work great, maximizing time. The most successful people read 52 books a year.

Define Your Vision and Goals
Without a vision and a goal, it is just an idea or a hobby. This is where most people fail in their endeavors. They do not realize the amount of effort, perseverance, tenacity, resilience, and mental and emotional strength it takes to launch a business.

Your goals should be very specific and well defined, broken down from a 10-year plan to a 5-year plan, to annual, to monthly, to weekly, to daily.

Niche - Untapped Market
This one piece of my plan has served me very well. It may not be glamorous, fun, or exciting; however, it is doing what others are not willing to do.
> For example:
Driving 9 hours for 1 appointment because others don't want to.
I joined an organization within my community that very few people can penetrate due to language and cultural barriers.

Do whatever it takes and Yes attitude!

There are days when I am too exhausted from working round the clock to hit the road or do mundane administrative work. I say Yes to all opportunities and figure out how to do it and how to find the time to do it later. With clear goals, routine, and discipline you will see incremental growth. It's the rule of doing 1% better each day compounded for one year (365 days) equals 3778% growth.

First Sign of Success

My first sign of success was right at 2 years when I realized I was about to hit the monthly, weekly, and daily goals that I had set out when I started the business.

I had a big grin on my face and took a moment to sit back and absorb the accomplishment. Two of my colleagues and mentors congratulated me. My mom, too, who has been my backbone, is so happy to see where my business is headed. They have been my glue from falling apart.

My clients will say things like: You are my Medicare Angel. I couldn't have done this without your help; you are not only my broker but my friend. This is when you know you are truly helping and bringing value to your clients. It is the best feeling!

Ultimate Solution
Why Medicare Insurance?

I was looking for 3 things in my business:
1. A Great Product and Regulated Industry.
2. A Great Clientele - seniors are some of the sweetest people you can be around.
3. Flexibility - I had the vision in 2008 that when I select a business, I would like the ability to work remotely with time and financial freedom.

I have two mentors for my business who have been my rock in launching my business. We selected each other because we are aligned with the same values, goals, vision, work ethic, and mindset. These five characteristics were non-negotiable because if we differed, we would all lose in the long game.

Free Gift

My gift to you is the free Medicare 101 eBook. If you wish to learn more, you may set up an appointment for a consultation when you opt-in for the book. There is no cost to you or obligation for a conversation.

I begin helping my clients between 9-12 months before their 65th Birthday and other Medicare insurance-eligible individuals when they become qualified to receive benefits.

Ultimate Solution

Just as I am growing my business and creating financial target points to reach before my retirement age, I can guide you to reach your business goals at any stage so you can have peace of mind and financial freedom in your Golden Years.

You may use the QR code below for your free eBook and schedule an appointment if you wish. I would love to speak with you and learn about your dreams, goals, and vision.

Accolades and Achievements

Most recently in my Medicare business, I received the Top Agent Award for 2021. This was a huge deal because it was my first full year in Medicare and a tough Covid 19 Pandemic environment to be working with seniors.

See What They Are Saying...

Nutan is a very energetic, passionate, and very supportive helping people who are seeking to plan their future. I highly recommend her.
–Dr. Angelica Benavides - Mentor

***

Me meeting Nutan at the time of where she was in her life, I learned that Nutan has had experiences and now knows what she wants, makes her own decisions and choices, and knows when to say No. She is willing to try new things being a daredevil, and risk taker, and researches her travel destinations in depth so that when the opportunity arises, she can hit the road.
I recommend this brilliant woman for her love of life, insight, and courageousness.
–Beatrice Stair - Friend

***

My Mojo is Back

Nutan was referred to me for Medicare Insurance. She was thorough and helped me find the best plan for my needs which helped save my vision. My husband did not qualify for Medicare insurance and referred us to a trusted partner in her network who does marketplace health insurance. My husband recently had a heart attack, and his insurance was a lifesaver.We recommend her for Medicare insurance and anything else you may need as she doesn't give up and has a trusted network, she can refer you to get the help you need.
–Nancy Williams and Paul Baker - Client

***

Laylah Rose
VIP Pageantry, VIP Events & VIP Fashion Shows
Sarasota, Florida, USA
laylah@vippageantry.com

Chapter 32
My No Pivot Business

Laylah Loiczly, the founder of Laylah Rose Couture and Co-founder /Creator / Executive Producer of the TV Network, "VIP Pageantry", has been in the pageant industry for over 38 years. She has several degrees in the fashion and broadcasting industries as well as obtaining a Master's Degree as a Holistic Health Practitioner. She has worked for CBS, Sports Media, Film, T.V., and Radio productions. Currently, she is a creative director, writer, and executive producer on her TV network - VIP Pageantry. Laylah Rose debuted her Interview and Red Carpet and Couture fashions at New York Fashion Week in 2019. As she continued to follow her dreams, she was given the honor to be a Red Carpet Host and Interview Host at Miss Universe 2019 and Miss Universe 2020. She was honored to be selected as a judge for Miss Universe Competitions worldwide as well as a panel judge for several USA national competitions. She is a recipient and past title holder of America Achievement 2021 for Ms World Achievement/Dr World Productions, a Visionary Award recipient, and a Board Member of The International Pageant Professionals Organization. Recently, she was interviewed by a writer in Forbes Magazine for all of her achievements to date. Her favorite crown she has earned is being a mom to six amazing children. Laylah hopes to inspire everyone to always create new dreams, have the courage to explore it all, and continue to preserve integrity along the way. "The best is always yet to come!"
Laylah Rose

Mission and Vision
VIP - My Beauty, My Purpose, My Legacy

A new Multimedia, Worldwide TV Network focusing on the BEAUTY, FASHION & PAGEANT Industry. VIP is all about Diversity and Inclusivity. A place to connect while promoting body positivity, confidence, and strength.

Beauty: We all struggle with how we feel about ourselves. If we are too boastful or too confident, too nice, too tall, too short, too big. The list goes on. We find our beauty from within and with growth, with understanding who we are and the life we create. Be more genuine they say, be more confident. The demands are never ending to reach perfection...but beauty is a funny evolutionary word. What it once was and what it once meant doesn't hold true to today. It was suffocated by uncertainty and darkness, by meek expectations and false realities. It was weak and succumbed to ignorance. There is a new era of BEAUTY!
We will always radiate from the inside out. The more beautiful your heart, the more beautiful your presence will be!

Purpose: I have asked myself a million times what my purpose is. I have come to the conclusion that we need others as much as they need us. To love, to grow, to understand, to lift each other up, to nourish others with our gifts. We are all created differently for many reasons. We are here to help those who need what we have to offer the universe to make the world go round. To evolve into better humans.

Legacy: I wanted to leave something more than just a life lived. To be something important, something needed in the world today and tomorrow.

The grace, the education, the commitment to community, and the overall ability to speak to an audience on all platforms and make a difference in the world is what the pageant community is all about.

We are here to empower others and encourage them to lift each other up, reinforce values that set the bar for change, and foster connections to make a REAL difference.

Through these actions, may we all want to create a legacy that will continue even after we have achieved excellence that will impact future generations to come!

Starting from Scratch
No's Pivot My Business

The No's that I have received did a few things for me. They made me pivot and go in a different direction—one that I was reluctant to go in because it was unknown. I

was comfortable where I was. It made me work harder, smarter, and just wholeheartedly. I wanted to create something that made everyone shine from the inside out. I wanted to highlight the amazing leaders with a heart of gold. There were so many people doing amazing things that nobody knew about. They were standing out in their own ways with the biggest hearts I have ever seen, and in that moment for me, we were all the same...leading with our hearts, not taking no for an answer, finding a way, getting it done, and pivoting to the next important thing without missing a beat. All doing their part in helping make this world go around. Don't take no for an answer and keep going. Lead with your heart and people will know you truly are there for them.

Big Why
Breaking Barriers and Walls

I wanted to fulfill love and passion in all aspects of my life. I was determined to break barriers and walls and determined to show others it can be done on your terms, your timing, and however long it may take. Your journey is yours to figure out, to pivot and change, and to continue on the same path. Whatever your hopes and dreams, they are yours! The ones who become so tired, feel like quitting but don't. Your Why is so important. Figure out your BIG Why and go after it by breaking barriers and walls until you achieve your goals.

Aha Moment Epiphany
Whatever it Takes

The world was infiltrated with negativity and sadness. I was surrounded by strength, leaders, and positivity and realized some people were not. I wanted to change the mind of mainstream media to the great things that come from the pageant world. I wanted to fill viewers with happiness and show them true strength & determination from leaders who work so hard for their communities. I created VIP to highlight all POSITIVITY that the pageant world encompasses, together. Starting new, starting again, with wherever you are, with whatever you have! Make sure to surround yourself with great leaders and mentors that will support you when the road gets rough.

Secret Formula
Build the Empire from the Heart

My secret formula is in the TV Network with beauty, pageantry, etc. I highlight that they are working hard in the community As my vision became clear, I was able to share my thoughts and aspirations, with lots of networking, and emails to people from all over the world. I did things complimentary because I know my worth. That may be difficult to understand, but it's just like giving a sample. I knew once people saw  quality, equality, inclusivity, growth, and the ability to have experiences on all levels they would understand why we're here. It created a solid foundation to truly build the empire I have in my heart. You will need to make connections on a daily basis using all sorts of ways such as emails, networking, social media, and events. Remember when you build your empire people will come. You must grow your business even if it is by word of mouth. You need to create a solid foundation and continue to find creative ways to network and reach clients. Also, give your services from your heart.

Steps to Build Success from Scratch
Amplify Your Voice

With that being said, we are here to empower others and encourage them to lift each other up, reinforce values that set the bar for change, and foster connections to make a REAL difference.

Through these actions, may we all want to create a legacy that will continue even after we have achieved excellence that will impact future generations to come! These steps will enable you to become your own TV host!

1. Mood Board and doodling helps a vision become clear.
2. What matters to you? The leaders I know in the pageant world were not treated fairly. I wanted to change that.
3. I wrote down what I wanted to change or improve.
4. I set a time frame that would make sense for launching. It could change if you're not ready.
5. Create your list of contacts, clients, customers, and network lists.
6. WHAT is your launch? Who is it for?
7. Start your passion; announce it to the world.
8. Build the foundation.
9. Give a sample. They will be watching.
10. Constantly troubleshoot, create new, and continue to grow in the forward motion.

Believe in yourself and have the courage to never give up!"

First Sign of Success
It's Just the Beginning...

People believed in us and prospered. People gained experience and knowledge—people who supported us that I didn't even know. People talked about what VIP was currently doing. We received many thanks for our presence that impacted their own stories and why they are doing what they are doing. Success is written in what you have projected onto others, what you are here for, and what you have sought out to accomplish in others along the way. "We rise by lifting others". I see that in full effect every day! Don't give up; it is just the beginning. Celebrate every moment. Find the small wins to celebrate and raise your spirit so you can lift others.

Ultimate Solution
The Start Is What Matters.

Asking for help is the key to navigating your dreams and accomplishing your goals. The best and worst mentors can help fuel your passions and success. What not to do is just as important as what to do. Don't disregard your negative experiences; use them to fuel your next move. This is exactly what I do. It works!

For VIP, Beauty is an evolving word. What it once was and what it once meant doesn't hold true today. It was suffocated by uncertainty and darkness by meek expectations and false realities. It was weak and succumbed to ignorance. There is a new era of BEAUTY. The perception of typical beauty standards are lost but not to be forgotten. We will always radiate from the inside out. The more beautiful your heart, the more beautiful your presence will be!

233

Free Gift

No gift is available at this time. Use my steps above to increase your business success.

Accolades and Achievements

I debuted my Interview, Red Carpet, and Couture fashions at NYFW 2019. It opened up so many doors. I was a Red Carpet Host and Interview Host at Miss Universe 2019 and Miss Universe 2020.   I was a judge for Miss Universe Competitions worldwide & panel judge for several USA national competitions. I am the recipient and past title holder of America Achievement 2021 for Ms. World Achievement, Visionary Award recipient, and Board Member of The International Pageant Professionals Organization.

See What They Are Saying...

It wouldn't have happened without your support. Thank you for everything. You guys are the best people I have ever worked with!"" **~Anjali Phougat**

***

Her words were a defining moment for me. I would have to agree, "that "support "comes from those who lend a hand, a steppingstone, a gesture, a voice of compassion and understanding, support is a way to help others push forward toward their dreams!

***

I am beyond thankful for the VIP family providing a platform to showcase my NYFW debut. The team is amazing and seeks to create community while producing a stellar production. I look forward to returning and having the opportunity to collaborate with the VIP team in the future. **~Sean Bellamy**

***

""Providing a platform"" GOAL as I yelled in my head before the event, and it was accomplished with flying colors!

***

"Thank you, VIP Pageantry, for having me during Season 2 of VIP NYFW. It was an honor to walk in your fashion show and to experience New York Fashion Week. I had an amazing time and would absolutely love to do it again! Lots of love," ~ Miss Universe Iceland 2021 **Elísa Gróa Steinþórsdóttir**

***

Providing opportunities as promised and also for those around the world! Keeping my integrity is something I cannot ever live without. We may run thin, regroup, and ask for help, we may grow tired; take a break and unwind, we may lose hope; refresh, start from the top; but never lose your integrity. Integrity becomes your core strength, value, and your forever legacy."

Media Links
I have never published a book. However, VIP does have a magazine that I have written articles in. Our website, www.vippageantry.com
The VIP Pageantry channel is available on mobile devices worldwide, Roku, Apple TV, and Amazon Fire TV.
VIP is available on all smartphones. You can find it in your Apple Store or Samsung Play Store.
For Roku:
1. Scroll down the Home Menu and tap on "Channels."
2. Tap on "Channel Store." This should launch the official Roku app store, where you can find VIP PAGEANTRY and tools.
3. You may be prompted to sign into your Roku account before the app store opens
4. Tap on "+ Add Channel" to add the channel to your device.
5. Download begins.
Download on Amazon FIRE TV.
1. Use the main menu on your Fire TV to search for apps. You can also use your voice to search for specific apps. Just press the voice button on your Alexa Voice Remote.
2. Select the VIP PAGEANTRY app you want to download.
3. Select Get or the shopping cart icon to start your download.
How to download apps for Apple TV:
1. Open the App Store app.
2. Browse or search for the VIP PAGEANTRY app that you want to download.
3. Select the price or Get button.
4. If you see the Open button instead of a price or the Get button, the app is already downloaded."

https://linktr.ee/VIPPageantry

235

Monica Gomez
Monico Go, LLC
Orlando, Florida, USA
pastormonicaoml@gmail.com

Chapter 33
Nothing is Impossible

Monica was born in New York City. She immigrated to Colombia and lived her adolescent years. She loves sports. One of the highlights was being one of the first women who competed in a twelve hundred Kilometers race for several years. She is an ordained Pastor in the United States and cofounder of La Viva City in Orlando Florida. She has been working for over 20 years in discipleship, restoration, and purpose. She shares this great task with her husband Pastor Osmany Ramos. LOVE4 mission's ministry with the most needed in countries. She holds a leadership diploma from Bel-haven University. In addition, Monica is the Founder and Principal of Orlando Based Media Conglomerate Monica Go. This is also the home of her podcast "Monica Go on Streaming Platforms" Where she focuses on coaching, personal growth, and spiritual leadership for her listeners in more than ninety plus countries who loyally listen weekly. She is focused on women entrepreneurs that are in search of spiritual and emotional restoration preparing them for personal self-development and growth within their businesses. Monica is always ready to GO and as she says, "Let's Give it a GO!"

Mission and Vision

Monica's vision is to work with women leaders, mentoring and empowering them as they develop in their expertise. Currently, in our network, we provide annual events and resources for women to be able to network and participate and develop geared toward helping them balance their life. The **mission** of Monica GO is to bring together a diverse mix of successful women leaders who through their own testimonies are relevant to today's issues, inspire, mentor, and encourage women to reflect on their own goals and their empowerment to be a catapult for their organizations and family.

Introduction

Life is a huge adventure. Things hit you in the gut and try to keep you down. We all

go through hardship and sometimes we can become victims of others. I could tell you that when things come against you since childhood, I know for a fact that there is a fight for your purpose, greatness, and legacy. As a little girl I was sexually molested even though there was love at home in my family it wasn't enough to protect my child-like innocence. That really brought so many deep insecurities that no one can see but they were there. I went through a divorce, and abuse and just became without even noticing it a beggar for love. The rich girl with a begging heart. There was so much to heal and not be aware of it because it's easier to keep on going trying to make the best of all things without searching inside. Behind the happy light of the party girl there was the

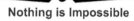

lonely one waiting for that special prince to pick her up and be happily ever after. "I think I got a lot of those chick flick movies inside me"

Sickness came suddenly, so hard to go through. Weeks went by with no recovery in sight. The doctors said I would never be able to bear children. Sickness was inside and out. Only a miracle can save me. I was in a pit with no exit. The happy social and party girl was in SOS mode.

The rescue was out to find me, I didn't look for it or did I call 911 (emergency phone line in the US) the one that had the power to go against all doctor's reports and even the open wounds inside. Life just does not happen; it all has a reason. Greatness in teaching whatever you have gone through or learned is not in vain. Those lessons have a way to bring the true you. Some may call it luck, higher power but I call him God. He found me, he heard, he held me and gave me purpose, tapping in areas I thought nonexistent.

Change is Coming

When things get out of normal, things start happening, it is a sign saying that change is coming, and you are part of it. Who would have thought that in my adolescent years being the daughter of a well-off family I would find myself in the midst of so much crime that hit Colombia and is part of other peoples' restoration. At that time death was the news every day, and panic was reflected on people's faces. (For reasons that I will describe in the near future through a book.) I had access to many that needed to see and really believe in God. I was guided to share the gospel of salvation for those who no one would even think forgiveness could exist for. I started understanding firsthand that love is really what makes the world go around.

How can you see hardship in your life as a turning point to a new path? It is all about the heart, forgiveness is key to being able to enter in the new season of life. Have you heard the saying "someone's trash is another's treasure" Someone who did you wrong, who rejected you is saying and screaming out to you. Let it go! As I had to pivot several times in different areas of my life, I see how it was needed In my love life, in my currier, work, new businesses, putting together teams, mentoring them to achieve the best version of themselves, coaching women and seeing the results tell me one and one again, that we are being trained.

Things may come that are out of our control, but the action and attitude of those moments will cause results and reflect your faith. Circumstances will suddenly come into your life. faith is the ingredient that brings to the picture results you never thought they would ever happen. I can confidently say that: "what looks like is coming against you t is really for you.

Big Why
Pushed by love

Pushed in ways I would never imagine. When I was diagnosed with a sickness and that no babies would ever come to my whom, I kept the faith and believed.

I have three powerhouse miracle sons Simon, Mateo, and Joshua. They mean the world to me and rock my world. Joshua, my youngest, was my restoration baby with a man that had three people for the price of one. He has stood there for me in the bitter-sweet moments. He has loved us in his Cuban, salsa way.

I know that it is being rejected, abandoned, and insecure. That is one of the why's that drives me to help others. My husband is my gift that has helped me change in so many ways, seeing things from another perspective and I have taken him from a full atheist to a pastor with God's glory. I love that man! He is my treasure as I know I am his. Love is restoration and the center of all things

I have worked with broken strong women that need that area in their life restored. I am passionate about seeing them thrive in every area of their lives. Weddings are my thing and many of the ladies that I have mentored we have married.
I am better than Cupid in God's hands. Lol. I am old school in many ways even though my son and my inner core keep me vibrant and relevant. I am living a family life filled with greatness that has never stopped us in the darkest times we have stuck together because we are better together.

I just want to say that the people that surround me are crazy in believing and I love it! We need good crazy people around us all the time. People who believe and stand firm while we work together on the vision that lies ahead are a gift and a miracle in itself.

I **was in a box for years.** You're big, why do you do what you do?
I was in a box for years. Just calling out some of the hardest moments in my life took quite some time to get up. I have the same burden for those women who are strong, and hurt but committed to themselves seeing greatness in their own life. When an opportunity is given, and we need to take it. We expanded in the midst of turmoil. People go through plenty and knowing that I can do something about it, it's

a satisfaction that no money can pay. Why should they find they're big and go? Passion is key to living that life desired. With passion comes hope, and hope will not be embarrassed.

That skill, talent that you have, that you don't need to get paid to do it, you just are driven, that is part of that calling my friend. Tapping into your true self is the best thing that can happen to a person. So, if you see yourself in the next three years, loved and surrounded by the right people, my friend, is a true Go to a life filled with value and success. Little beginnings lead up to big results.

Aha Moment Epiphany
Tap Into Your Inner GPS

When you have been guided into new territory, even new groups that are the leader in you, some play it off on the safe side and some other leaders are worriers

that are road openers for others to go in easier. I have gone through a lot in my life, and to be sincere I never would have thought to be a pastor or a coach—yes, an actress, it is sexier if you know what I mean. And because of who I am called to be I have been seeing results that have catapulted others close to me. Why not think in a grander mode to give to others in other places, countries, and cities that beauty that is in your heart so many can be nourished guided with their unique GPS so they get ready for the new roads awaiting in this beautiful world.

I think that living in today's digital era it's the best time in human history to be able to make a living through the Internet. The internet has leveled the playing field for every human on earth to make a living from it. It doesn't matter if you are black, white, Hispanic, female or male, from South America, Africa, or Europe. The internet doesn't care who you are or what you look like or what your religion is.

So for women, it's extremely important to build their empires whether it's fashion, creative work, building a sales force, outsourcing jobs, or creating jobs for others or for whatever their passion is. If the internet doesn't care who you are. What is stopping you? It is time to be your own superhero!

Secret Formula
Be Your Own SuperHero

Be True to yourself: I have had my own businesses, an acting career, and because I am a pastor I kind of limited myself and just be complacent. That is not what God called me to do. You are who you are, and until you don't STOP and look yourself in the mirror for your uniqueness you will not understand your calling and see what is in store for you. You could be wealthy but have no passion. It is time to get it and live intentionally. With all due respect to those that passed away as those who I loved that did so as well through the years, it was a bittersweet moment for me to look at myself and say I only have this time in my generation to make a difference so when our world was hit with so much death it was something that did a thorough x-ray check to most of us. I felt the hit, death, desperation, and sadness all over again. I cried yes for the loss of some dear friends and family, but it was time to gear up and go into rescue mode not only for myself but for others. I am truly convinced that if you are serving other people in your business with a true heart you will gain the confidence, respect, and wealth of being your authentic self.

The Monica GO podcast came out in that re-inventing moment to bring out stories to encourage, empower and bring people back to basics. As well, as Monica GO coaching, travel, speaking engagements, and more that my team and I are delighted and honored to serve others.

Steps to Build Success from Scratch

Nothing that you have lived is in vain, it all works on your behalf. I just love a quote that says, "your mouth has the power of life and death". What are you saying? It is more than positive words, it is power and faith in a great combination with results that come in at the right time not before, and never late. So, when you are calling out the truth you come to a place where no one sees you, in that secret place. That place is where you are shaped and sharpened are those that will come out and will be seen by many.

Keys for you my friend so get ready.
- **Have a secret place:** Key—have time to connect with your creator alone.
- **Change your glasses:** Key—look at yourself in the wonderful way you are and call things out in the midst of turmoil.

- **Deception calls to forgive:** Key—take care of your heart and let go of the acts against you; it is liberating.
- **Be Grateful:** Key—you are already abounding in satisfaction First Sign of Success

Ripple effect

Success is wonderful when you know that it has a ripple effect in many that you

are guided to work with. Even though success may mean so many different things to people, it is fine to enjoy their advancements. I have seen firsthand the transformation of people I have mentored; seeing them how they came and how they live now is a gift that has the word success all around it.

My husband and I say "their success is our success "even if they don't say anything or come back and say thank you. We know what we did! Through the hard times which are needed to mold our character and really see who is there for you, I have a few people that for years have surrounded me close to their core they know who they are. I celebrate in a joyful scream and cry just seeing greatness right in front of me.

Ultimate Solution
Lead Powerfully—Get Unstuck

The results and transformations you make. I know well how to kill that thing you have not called out. I help restore leading ladies that are tough cookies, successful in business, and cry alone at night because they are stuck and don't know how to get out. I help them in their relationships and help them love life, so they can live balanced lives and position them to thrive for massive success. My clients come from my podcast, social media, coaching, and speaking engagements.

How to impact people and what changes do you want to make?
We all go through hardships; It has its purpose for learning that brings out character. Trauma is hidden in the hearts and many, and we wing it pretty well. When something comes up, it triggers that unhealed area, we lose power or energy in just thinking; here we go again! Without knowing we become complacent and just adjust to live with the trauma for the rest of our lives. You don't have to live like that! You need to commit to yourself and connect to that person that will be reassuring. If He had not helped you go to your desired level. Yes, I have had a few mentors in my life; my pastors, coaches, and my husband have been influential in my life, but the greatest one of all is the Holy Spirit of God that knows how much is needed in restoration, revelation and done so, I would have never believed. It's your decision GO! There is more than what you ask or imagine waiting for you. Ephesians 3:20

Free Gift or Offer
Commit to Yourself: Give it a GO!

What impact will they achieve? When you work with me and commit to yourself, I will take you to a higher level to be able to view yourself in truth, having been restored, recalibrated, and revived so you can live with passion and joy. I offer you a 30-minute free strategy session to see that we are a good fit and if so, continue into a 90-day program that will be a life changer.

You can contact me via email or DM to receive the offer. Code: 100SWB

Accolades and Achievements

Some of the extraordinary things I have done in my life are in the masculine territory. Having the courage in boat racing and being the first women's team in this modality we won in our category 2nd place worldwide having hundreds of men compete in this marathon. It was hard but decisive. I was able to see what I was able to do. It started small but we gained the respect of the other competitors. Some of the achievements I am extremely proud of fall within our nonprofit sector. In these endeavors, we have been able to feed more the 200 + Families in Venezuela and Honduras where a lot of these families don't have access to the basic necessities to live a decent life. We also did a campaign for Havana Cuba where we build water wells in areas that have no running water access. These are the things I'm most proud of in my life. Being able to help people in places where they have no help but just a breath of hope.

See What They Are Saying...

Monica found me in an extremely dark place in my life. I was empty inside and in need of love and guidance. My Career was on a great path but my life was in shambles with her help I found balance in my life. I love Monica.
Kennia Barahona
Kenniabarahona@gmail.com

***

Nothing is Impossible

My mentor and my coach had the guidance and support I needed when I lost it all. Let me tell you who I was before I met her. Yaima, is an insecure and angry person who had a lot of inside conflicts with myself and my surroundings. But here she is Pastor Monica coming with her kindness and love and helping me through the beautiful process of transformation from the inside out. She said things straight in my face every time I wanted to procrastinate or give up and this is the thing, I love most about her because she pushed me to be the leader I am today. She believed in me. She kept pushing, and here is Yaima Osorio today. Even though I lost it all. I was able to regain everything back and better. Thank you, Pastora, for coaching me all these years!!!

Yaima Osorio
yaima.osorio@topempowerment.com

Business Contacts
Monica Gomez
Phone (407) 684-4111
soymonicago@gmail.com

Patricia S. Tanner
Multhai International Realty
Sanford, Florida, USA
ptanner@multhai.com

Chapter 34
Real Estate Royalty: Entrepreneur of Innovation

Patricia Tanner was born the second child to the late Mr. James & Mrs. Lamjiak Tanner. She is the founder of Multhai International Realty, Multhai Asset Management Services, and Multhai Investment Group, all located in Sanford, Florida.

She is a graduate of the University of Central Florida, where she received a Bachelor of Science in Business Administration and a minor in Human Resources Management.

Throughout her career in property management, she has a successful track record of increasing company revenues by over $5 million annually.

Mission and Vision

Preparing buyers to become homeowners, while teaching sellers to turn profit into generational wealth. We train investors to become venture capitalists and inspire renters to become first-time homeowners. By doing this, we impact our community by creating value.

Building A Business From Scratch

Building a business from scratch involves mind over matter. To locate your desired success, you must first get your mind together, and be determined that you will accomplish what you set your mind to do. This means women will work smarter and not harder.

Building from scratch means taking the time to write down what your plan for business looks like. Develop your business plan and a clear vision that aligns with your purpose for forming your business. Most women fall short in business because they fail to plan, listen to their intuition, or want to model other people in business. The best advice I can give is to be your authentic self.

You are enough and you have the intelligence to build an empire: just do it!!

Real Estate Royalty: Entrepreneur of Innovation

My Big Why
Determination, Passion, Dedication.

It seems like the biggest hot topic for interviews, and at business, seminars are the 'why' of it all. My big 'why' was because I was overworking for others, and it was simple: I wanted to work for myself. When I went full-time with my real estate company, my father recently passed away. He always wanted me to work a 9 to 5 job and invest my savings into a 401K retirement plan. He believed in playing it safe, and this method would set me up in life. Well, I had some different plans for my life! After his death, in 2016, a newfound passion was birthed within me to experience something I had never experienced before. I took all my education, resources, and knowledge and created a multimillion-dollar real estate business. My drive, passion, dedication, hard work, and determination are all that made Multhai International Realty what it is today.

I challenge you to grab a notebook right now and write down your 'why' for launching your business. Was it for time and financial freedom? Were you trying to make a difference in the world? Did you set out just to help people? Why do you get up daily to do what you do? What's your 'why?' Do me a favor,scan my QR code so you can stop by my site and let me know why you decided to go into business. I'd love to hear from you!!

My Aha Moment
Service, Expertise, Motivation.

I was ready for my real estate career to go to the next level, and I knew my next move: to become a broker. I had taken the test, yet I failed! Imagine that: you're all hyped up for your next level, and you fail when your excitement is at its height.

Failure was in the building, but my motivation was a greater force than my disappointment. I refused to allow that failure to dictate where I was going; I had goals to reach. So, I scheduled to take the test again, and guess what? I passed on the second attempt.

This was my 'aha moment!' I had come to the realization that my career was about to take off, and I was about to gain a better grasp on my future. I was truly in the driver's seat of my financial destiny, with a greater sense of being able to help the people I served.

I have always been the 'expert' at everything I set out to do. If I did not know how to do it, then I took a class, watched a video, or just jumped out and made things happen! I never allowed a lack of education to stop me from doing *anything!*

Secret Formula
The F.A.I.T.H. Adjustment-
Focus | Accountability | Integrity | Trust | Hard Work

Through word of mouth, I am known for my company values, or consistently adjusting our F.A.I.T.H. Most times when we hear about having a 'F.A.I.TH. adjustment, we *immediately* think we have a lack of faith. But this secret formula has everything to do with how we as women business owners should operate our businesses daily. Well, the F.A.I.T.H Adjustment has everything to do with the acronym in F.A.I.T.H.:

- **F** stands for Focus. My number one focus is to help my clients.
- **A** stand for Accountability. I always answer my phone and respond within minutes of a missed call.
- **I** stand for Integrity. I am a woman of integrity and I command integrity from everyone who works on my team.
- **T** stands for Trustworthy. I am very trustworthy. I show up on time and do what I am supposed to do. My goal is to help you establish and identify your needs, plan a way to meet them, take steps to accomplish them, and execute.
- **H** stands for Hard work. I work hard, and I am open-minded, which allows me to navigate through challenges. I maintain balance and get the transaction to the closing table. I am here to support my clients and my team in every aspect of the goal: secure the home!

I developed this secret formula (oops, the secret is out) to make sure that every experience that my clients have with me is seamless and successful. I am sure what most business owners miss are the simple steps of following patterns and systems. These are the 'secrets' that have made fortune 500 companies gain their notoriety: a proven system.

Steps To Build Success From Scratch
My BestAgent-The Success Of Others

I build success because I am a B.O.S.S.: Believing Others Should Succeed. With that motto, I live by my word. I always put others before myself and create successful paths for my clients. I turn pessimistic clients into optimistic clients.

Here are 5 steps to building success from scratch:

1. **Gain Knowledge**. Education being at the foundation and core of my success, helped me to take my real estate career to the next level. There is NO business you can operate successfully without obtaining some sort of knowledge. I started exploring other branches in real estate such as land

248

acquisition, real estate development, new construction homes, real estate investments, renovations, remodeling, and commercial leasing.

2. **Set Yourself Apart from Your Competition.** What sets me apart from my competition is my years of knowledge that helps buyers and sellers be prepared to make the right decision to buy or sell their homes.

3. **Be Customer Driven.** There is no business without customers. I have yet to see a business that survived without customers. Whether those customers walk in off the streets, or they are business owners, you must have customers to fuel the economy of your business. Be mindful to ensure each customer has an experience that keeps them coming back and referring others to have the same experience.

4. **Locate Your Business Mentor.** The beauty of having a mentor is you can learn and glean from them from a distance or up close. Your start-up budget may not include thousands of dollars to invest in a coach or consultant. Most women in business throw in the towel when they cannot afford such types of services. But gaining knowledge (#1 on this list) can come in all forms. You can find your mentor and buy their books, watch their videos, and put yourself in their company: all for FREE! Find someone whose success you can emulate and make your own.

5. **Gain employment with perseverance.** This one requires no cost and no down payment! You must have thick skin if you are going to survive out in these business streets. This journey is not for the faint at heart. Perseverance is what you learn when you encounter failure after failure. This is a
job you can sign up for and no one has to officially hire or fire you if you do not get it right. PERSEVERANCE: You just got your welcome letter to your new full-time job!

My First Sign of Success

My first sign of success was the growth of my community. Notice I did not say when a certain amount hit my bank account, but when my community started growing!

When my community was growing, I knew my success was in view. One of the first lessons of Business 101 is providing goodwill in your community. When you provide goodwill, you show the people you serve that you are not *just* there to make money, but you honestly care about people's wellbeing.

Growing my community became my number one priority when I learned the impact I was making.

Real Estate Royalty: Entrepreneur of Innovation

My fiancé, Terrell Hunt, and I built the first custom home in Sanford, Florida; this had never been done in the history of my city, so we became instant history makers! Not only had we built the first custom home, but it sold at the highest price point in Sanford, which opened doors for our real estate market. Real estate investors, developers, and I started building single-family homes for a diversified class of individuals. Sanford became the New Lake Mary based on real estate value.

My fiancé Terrell and my best friend Cassandra Barnes are my biggest fans. My first client always thought they were my only client based on my passion for real estate and my excellent customer service. I'll never forget how ecstatic they were to be working with me, and I wanted to give them all that I had to assure their happiness.

My Business Mentor/Coach

Taking My Own Advice
Realizing that I do not know everything, I hired my business coach and mentor: Mel Bowers. I am always open to learning, and I remain teachable. This is the main reason I have a mentor. I had to be open to constructive criticism to grow to the next level.

Free offer or Guarantee

My track record speaks for itself. If I list it, I sell it; if I assist it, I accomplish it. I don't make excuses. I make it happen because I am a workaholic and a career-oriented individual. Winning is my concoction, and 'no' is not an option.

After having many conversations with small business owners, I learned that many had been in business for many years but lacked the structure to elevate themselves financially. This prompted me to develop a formula that I call the Triple 7 formula ™. The Triple 7 Formula helps business owners gain the structure they need to earn a seven-figure income in seven months.

I offer a free download teaching business owner how to block their 7-hour days for effectiveness. This blueprint helps business owners to increase and jump-start their business revenue.

You can obtain this download here: https://bit.ly/triple7timeblocking

Real Estate Royalty: Entrepreneur of Innovation

Accolades and Achievements

I have earned a Bachelor of Science in Business Management from UCF with a specialization in HR; a Master of Arts in Human Resources-Webster University and a Master's in Public Administration from Troy University.

I am licensed in real estate brokering, land acquisitions, and real estate development. In addition, I build new construction homes and perform real estate investing, renovations, remodeling, and commercial leasing. I am the owner of a property management company, and a Florida certified notary.

I added author to my achievements in 2022, creating a path for mentoring and coaching. I received all these accolades based on hard work, remaining career driven, and goal-oriented.

I received the Black Women Handling Business Award and was a participant in the Ms./Mrs. Corporate America Pageant represented as Ms. Sanford, Florida. During the pageant, I was awarded the 'People's Choice Award.'

Books, Articles, Media Links
Books:
- 30 Days of Grieving: Given By The Inspiration of God
- The 30 Days Challenge: I tested Positive for COVID-19
- It Was the God In Me
- The Triple 7 Formula

*Publisher: IBG Publications, Inc. (Jacksonville, FL)

News/Periodical Features:
- Sanford Herald Newspaper, March 20-22 Article Sanford Native to Compete in Ms Corporate America Pageant.
- IBG Mag (September 2022 Edition)

See What They Are Saying...

I needed some assistance on a deal and Multhai International Realty (the broker) is a, 'Say it/ do it' type of company. I have yet to see the type of service I received from this team on the real estate circuit. From relocation knowledge to business professionals and just a family feel. Whether you are selling or buying, they're the answer.

~Mel Bowers

Real Estate Royalty: Entrepreneur of Innovation

Patricia is a wonderful realtor to work with. She is very professional and knowledgeable about the entire home buying process and knows a lot about the property management side of the business. She really cares and wants to make sure you get the best deal possible. I highly recommend her for any real estate needs including buying/selling or managing rental properties.
~Jessica D

Patricia is a true professional. In my experience, while working with her, she returned my calls, texts, and emails rapidly. My requests for documents were also turned around quickly. She is thoughtful, courteous, caring and an excellent communicator. During our transaction, Patricia represented the seller, and me as the buyer. I found her to be trustworthy and a really terrific realtor!
~Dan Corbin

Learn more at
linktr.ee/ptanner

Be sure to collect your FREE giveaway!

Dr. Joy T. Vaughan
Baroness Productions, Inc.
Fort Lauderdale, Florida, USA
Baronessproductionsinc@gmail.com

Chapter 35
Rise of the Phoenix: My Story of Resilience

Dr. Vaughan is a passionate brain and behavior specialist who specializes in shifting mindsets one neuron at a time. A native of Barbados and graduate of Columbia and Nova Universities, she specializes in personal development, and cognitive, and emotional intelligence training. Dr. Joy has helped many individuals and companies to increase their employees' performance and bottom line. She is the author of Powerful People: Powerful Lives, the 7-Step Empowerment Series for the Secular and Christian Souls, as well as her online Seminar Empowerment Series, and The Art of Resiliency Phoenixes Rising.
Rising.

Mission and Vision

My mission is to help female Executives, Entrepreneurs, and Veterans BREAK FREE OF FEAR, PROCRASTINATION, and SELF-SABOTAGE MINDSETS to fulfill their desired goals. I shift mindsets one neuron at a time. My vision is to build a global business where everyone I have the privilege to work with masters the art of reinvention and resilience so that they can achieve the freedom that they deserve.

Forced to Face the Grim of Reality

Have you ever been devastated, frightened, and felt helpless? This was exactly how I felt after a not-so-simple trip to the dentist resulted in a rapid onset of Rheumatoid Arthritis and Fibromyalgia. Physically and emotionally paralyzed and fighting for my life, I was forced to face the grim reality that my lucrative six-figure career as an occupational therapist and entrepreneur had come to a screeching halt. In my drive to be successful, the one person that I neglected over the years was me. I had become emotionally, physically, and yes spiritually bankrupt, running on empty but pretending that I was ok.

Can you relate to my story so far? Should I live or die? That was the question that haunted me as I struggled to do even the simplest things. The combination of prayer, acupuncture, and a mindset shift helped to pull me out of my mental and physical abyss. Ever so slowly, I allowed my mind, body, and soul to absorb the miraculous and long overdue healing that they deserved. In addition, one look at my child had me fight to live as I realized that to leave him now would be incredibly selfish. I had to finish raising him. It was also clear that God was not finished with me yet. By the way, He is also not finished with you. Rather, like a phoenix, I was given a second chance to rise up and fulfill His purpose which is to positively impact the lives of others on a far bigger scale than I could ever imagine.

Big Why
Live Your Legacy Now!

Without question, the experience of losing my health and income forced me to re-evaluate my life. Was chasing the big bucks while neglecting my child and myself worth it? If so, how could I achieve the same goals differently? Furthermore, what did I really want? What do you really want? If I could achieve freedom in all areas of my life, peace of mind, and leave a legacy for my two granddaughters, family, and future generations, then life would be worth living. Those three goals propelled me to fight the agonizing, physical pain and depression caused by the double whammy of Rheumatoid Arthritis and Fibromyalgia.

As I continued to pray and focus on my healing, my prayers were miraculously answered. I began to walk and function again in spite of my gnarled hands and feet. I had to live my legacy NOW! What is your legacy, and do you want to live it NOW?

Aha Moment Epiphany

As I reflect on my life to date, there have been so many opportunities where I

could have given up. These include losing my mom at an early age, coming to America, facing racism, harsh winters, and working diligently to achieve success only to lose everything because of a dental procedure, Paralysis didn't stop me because while I lay helpless, my son walked into my room just as I reached for the bottle of pills. Had he not been present, I would not be writing my story today. It was at that moment of seeing him that I had the epiphany that I must get up. I must fight. I took stock of what I had left – my faith, mind, hands that now work, and a story to tell.

Reinvent, find my purpose, and make an impact were the thoughts that ran rampant through my mind. However, who should I reinvent myself as? As if God heard my thoughts, the answer was as clear as a cloudless sky on a sunny day. Putting pen to paper, I wrote my first children's book "Three Mean Alligators" to address bullying among children. Then came "Powerful People Powerful Lives." Those two successful works impacted the lives of many children in the school systems in Indiana and Florida. They were also the foundation of my third book The Art of Resilience: Phoenixes Rising and my brain and behavior transformational coaching business.

Secret Formula
One Neuron at a Time

As a brain and behavior specialist, my secret formula is to be able to have people quickly shift their mindset one neuron at a time. I teach female Executives, Entrepreneurs, and Veterans how to consistently manage their thoughts, words, emotions, and actions by rewiring old neuronal patterns that have kept them stuck. My clients struggle with fear, imposter syndrome, procrastination, loss on any level, and self-sabotaging behaviors. Many of them are in career transition because of corporate "downsizing," ageism, or they are just stuck in life.

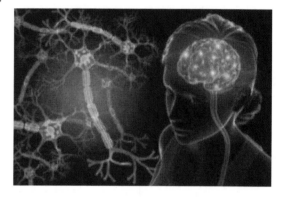

My brain-based personalized one-on-one, 30, 60- or 90-day group coaching programs help them to break free and create a life that they can love. If they are willing to do the work, my clients gain freedom from negative thinking and exponentially increase their performance in areas of life that they choose. Within the first session, clients are moved to tears as they discover the secret to dismantling disempowering thought patterns.

Building Success from Scratch
One Step at a Time

It started with my research and work in transformation and neuropsychology followed by my book Powerful People: Powerful Lives. This work chronicled the transformational journey of seven troubled youth who transformed to become productive citizens in society. From there, I looked for opportunities to tell my story. I also began to coach others to write their books and free themselves from their life's shackles because writing is cathartic.

I developed successful 30, 60- and 90-day online group coaching programs for the faith-based and secular communities who were struggling with their fears and faith.

That expanded into individual coaching for my private clients who wanted to do the deep brain and behavior work to re-invent themselves and learn how to be resilient. Achieving the results, you want is amazing. However, sustaining them over time is challenging because you must pivot quickly. This venture of reinvention, resilience, and sustainability became the fuel for my latest book "The Art of Resilience: Phoenixes Rising" which to date has won national and international awards. Twenty-three women from around the world shared their secrets of resilience. If you are willing, anything is possible. So, how willing are you to start the next journey of your life?

If you are ready and willing to create the next chapter of your life. Here are the seven keys to successful entrepreneurship, financial success, and peace of mind
1. Discover and know your worth and gifts.
2. Develop a solid marketing plan that includes multiple   passive streams of income
3. Write a book and develop related coaching programs, paid speaking engagements, and multiple product spinoffs.
4. Hire a coach, social media expert, and marketing team to market you and your products/offerings on multiple social media platforms.
5. Partner with organizations and others to collaborate and get referrals
6. Nurture referrals, build your funnel, and keep delivering quality programs
7. Pamper yourself in the process and keep fulfilling your purpose.

First Sign of Success

My first sign of success was when I sold my first high ticket item and the look on my client's faces when they achieved their first breakthrough. I was moved beyond tears when my clients shared what a difference my coaching made in their lives long after our agreement ended. I thank God that the fruits of our labor were not in vain. I celebrated my success with my family and close friends. My main source of support is my business team, faith, family, friends, and funds. The ultimate solution to my success is to create and live a life that those I coach, and I can love. What difference would it make if you could wake up to a stress-free and abundant lifestyle?

Ultimate Solution
Create the Life You Love | The World Is Yours to Conquer

The ultimate solution to my success is love. It came from my faith, son, family, mentors at Landmark Education where they deliver seminars in transformation, Kingdom Builders Academy, and my mastermind that holds me accountable for being successful particularly when I don't feel like it. My ultimate solution is to do what you love and love what you do.

Free Gift

My free Gift is "How to Be Fearless: 3 Powerful Steps to Move Past What Holds You Back." The Ultimate Solution that will transform your business is your willingness to quickly shift your mindset and be coachable. Take action **NOW** so that you won't be left behind.
https://www.drjoycoaching.com/free-gift

Accolades and Achievements

Although I have won many scholarships for my studies in Occupational Therapy and Neuropsychology at Columbia University, my most recent accomplishment was receiving my Doctorate in Education and Brain-based Behavior later in life. Since writing "The Art of Resilience: Phoenixes Rising", I have received the Haitian Nurses Network Award, the SIMA Award, LOANI's Beautiful Survivors Award, and now The 100 Most Successful Female Entrepreneurs Award. This and more are also available for you. Just download my free gift and let's chat:
https://www.drjoycoaching.com/free-gift

See What They Are Saying...

Dr. Joy's Boot Camps solve the problem of complacency, self-deception, failure to plan, and loss of purpose. She empowers the individual to identify and solve their own problems through introspection and self-analysis to arrive at the best possible solution for that individual at the time.

Kierra D. Educator
***

Dr. Joy's coaching challenges those who work with her to quickly address the issues that people know they should address, but simply don't have "time for". However, it's interesting because when will anyone have time for anything? When it's too late? When everything you're dealing with shows up in your attitude, your health, your lack of effort, or God forbid when you pass away? We tend to make time for everything else but ourselves.

Claudia M., HR Manager
***

People teach about "how to do" whereas your program is unique because it teaches "how to be in order to do." There is a great difference - they go hand in hand in order to be successful. Thank you for transforming ourselves and our organization.

Dr. J. Weschler
***

Books, Social and Business Media
"The Art of Resilience: Phoenixes Rising" by Dr. Joy T. Vaughan
https://www.amazon.com/dp/1889306045/ref=cm_sw_em_r_mt_dp_FJ498P4VNP9 P6690RCS9

https://bling.me/c84qvFyG7PKL

Dr. Real N. Kunene - MBA, BA, CTC
Rise to Greater Heights Network
Calgary, Alberta, Canada
www.risetogreaterheights.com

Chapter 36
Rise to Greater Heights

Dr. Nompumelelo Real Kunene is a highly sought after energetic certified Les Brown International speaker. Real is also a PhD graduate - Leadership and Business, International Human Rights Analyst, Award Winning Author, Life and Business Coach, Corporate Travel Consultant, Publisher, and an eMCee, well known for encouraging many to rise from mediocrity into greatness.

"The sky is no longer the limit, but our point of view...SO, let's all RISE TO GREATER HEIGHTS." ~ *Dr. Real N. Kunene*

Rise to Greater Heights

There are many reasons why people don't reach their dreams, and it is important for you to get to know the things that hold you back from achieving success. As a CERTIFIED TRAVEL COUNSELLOR (CTC) and a member in good standing in the Association of Canadian Travel Agencies (ACTA), I subscribe to its Code of Ethics which requires that a member's relationship with the public and the travel industry be of a high standard. I've realized that in the past, I did not commit to my dreams and postponed the fulfillment of my ideas, which could possibly be something that was holding me back from achieving my dreams. My goal is to make incremental adjustments to my everyday life, so I uncovered varied opportunities to see what sticks and what doesn't.

The good thing is that you can overcome them if you acknowledge them, so keep reading to discover the top things that may be holding you back, instead of denying the truth.

Mission and Vision

My presentations not only motivate but empower audiences with a fresh perspective and inspiration they require to pursue success and drive sustainable outcomes in a seriously funny way. My mission is to meet the needs and transform the lives of my clients and my audience. My #1 bestselling book "Rise to Greater Heights" has inspired and empowered many to pursue their personal and professional passion to become go-getters. My goal is to study your current situation, identify limiting beliefs, and then design a plan of inspired action to empower you to achieve specific outcomes in your life.

RESILIENCE TO GREATNESS

Following my dreams gave me the purpose to see my goals through and understand that I do have everything I need to reach my full potential. There is another layer to the fear of success; many of us have been conditioned to believe that the road to success involves risks, and I have no doubts you have made attempts at pursuing your goals. Setting and achieving big goals can be difficult.

Big Why

There are many ways in which we need to persuade governments to adopt human rights-related legislation. Some of these include organizing protests and demonstrations, providing information for the general public through exhibits, side events, and formal speeches, or lobbying officials during meetings and negotiations.

Aha Moment
Let Your Voice Be Heard

We all have a voice, but not everyone knows how to use it. As an advocate for human rights, I encourage change makers and educate them on the issues at hand so that their voices can be heard too. I work with the individuals in charge, listening closely before calling out issues that need change. I serve not just as a vocal protester, but I go one step further by encouraging these changes, through education instead of merely telling government leaders, why something needs fixing (which happens quite frequently). So, our organization fills a critical role in society, by providing valuable services that governments may not always be able to deliver. From poverty relief to human rights advocacy, we are vital for supporting the most vulnerable members of our communities. We are an integral part of society, and We are involved globally in human rights, climate change, and humanitarian aid.

Mediocrity into Greatness

Letting go of undesirable opinions allowed me to turn out to be the best version of myself. Apart from being the CEO and Founder of Swati Canadian International Corp, I also run a charity called Swazi Canadian International Foundation, which is worldwide humanitarian relief and development organization dedicated to supporting the less privileged with basic needs through communities, churches, and schools in order to create a more just and balanced world by bringing hope and tangible help. Building solid, consistent habits withstood me through lackluster eras to shake things up in my life. As I was going through life and working towards my dreams, I made sure to position myself on a track to becoming who I really wanted to be.

Secret Formula
Full Control of Our Choices

I believe that we are in full control of our choices. My book "RISE TO GREATER HEIGHTS" has inspired and empowered many to rise from mediocrity into greatness. "Rise to Greater Heights Book" is a comprehensive guide to turning your fears into greater success while seizing new opportunities. Setting your mindset for success is significant; thus, this book has the potential to completely revolutionize every aspect of your life and career. Being a HUMAN RIGHTS ANALYST, I had the opportunity to attract clients from all walks of life. I believe that you really don't have to be politically involved to learn about your human rights. All human beings are entitled to them, and you can never ever be prohibited from your own HUMAN RIGHTS. These are God-given fundamental rights and freedoms! Human rights are not just about the law; thus, human rights are non-discriminatory... meaning that all human beings are entitled to them! I believe that we need to challenge ourselves to turn our resilience into our platform to be true advocates for all human rights. It

doesn't matter where we are born or what kind of family we are born into, we all have the internal recognition of the moral quality of one's motives and actions. Be inspired by my weekly podcast at RISE TO GREATER HEIGHTS NETWORK www.risetogreaterheights.com

The 4-Steps to Goal Success

I've established a strong foundation as a Certified Mentor and Coach by learning industry best practices, helping my clients live passionate and meaningful lives and discover their greater life purpose, old programming empowering them to unleash their happiness from within, and instilling the 4-Steps to Goal Success in their lives because I believe that all success depends on achieving meaningful goals by having a solid short- and long-term plan. Anyone who is successful in consistently achieving their goals are also consistently reviewing their goals, but if you spend too much time daydreaming, your brain sees the big endgame without noticing the problems. When you can reflect on what is going wrong, you can try again and find the solution to the problem instead of repeating the same mistakes and not achieving your dreams. I've mastered training in life purpose, business professional, millennial Mentorship, happiness, goal attainment, market goal, and purpose coaching with Sales Presentation Blueprint and coaching methodologies. I want to encourage you to stop allowing your progress to hold you back; after all, it's easier to reach your destination if you have a road map to assess your mistakes. It's important to have goals and to make adjustments early so you stay on course. Overall, yes, reviewing your goals regularly allows knowing the direction that you want to head in.

First Sign of Success

I am overwhelmed in all humbleness and gratefulness to acknowledge my depth to all leaders who had faith in me and allowed me to empower their team with a fresh perspective and inspiration they require to pursue success. To all the individuals I have had the opportunity to lead, be led by, or watch their leadership from afar, I want to say thank you for being the inspiration and foundation for my life. I am grateful to all of those with whom I have had the pleasure to share my life. They kept me going on, and the success of my business would not have been possible without their input in my life. I would like to express my deep and sincere gratitude to my pastors and church family (both in Canada and Eswatini) for their love, prayers, sacrifices, and continuing support. Nobody has been more important to me in the pursuit of my businesses than the members of my family who provide unending inspiration. Any attempt at any level can't be satisfactorily completed without the support and guidance of you my family. Engage the reader's example to celebrate small milestones gained.

Mentorship the Ultimate Solution

My advice for those interested in mentorship or coaching is that being mentored is one of the most valuable and effective development opportunities you can get. I have been mentored and coached by Les Brown with his high-impact, customized message, and a standing ovation. You need to be clear about your career goals to gain guidance on professional development. As a coach or mentor, my goal is to study your current situation, identify limiting beliefs and other potential obstacles you face, and design a plan of inspired action to empower you, to achieve specific outcomes in your life. Tell the reader the results they will achieve by connecting with you.

As a human rights analyst, my purpose is to teach everyone about human rights and help organizations understand and promote human rights. I also make a difference by bringing solutions and educating others. I am a true advocate for creating new policies that uphold human rights and prevent human rights violations from even happening in the first place. I *Consult* on policies and procedures related to human rights compliance. I *Advise* on best practices for implementing human rights programs. I can assist with audits of operations against international standards. I *Help* develop training programs for employees. I *Research* and help draft human rights-related policies on discrimination at work; harassment at work; diversity and inclusion; patient rights, and others. I *Advocate* on behalf of the company. I have the duty of raising awareness of people's rights and providing solutions. I believe that an essential thing in human rights is based on the principle of respect for the individual. I work towards raising awareness and providing solutions, believing that the most critical thing in our species' rights is based on moral grounds: each individual deserves respect no matter what they do or who they are.

Free Gift

I have a free TRANSFORMATION Guide and free 30 minutes consultation for you on my website at www.risetogreaterheights.com which will turn your fears into greater success while seizing new opportunities. I provide clarity, and I will teach you everything you need to know to succeed! I will teach you the best modern coaching methods in the specially designed stages. I will hold your hand, support you throughout, and hold you accountable for the work you need to complete. You will explore Leadership-Empowerment-Purpose Driven-Mentorship-Coaching-Mental Health-Positive Mindset-Resilience to Greatness-Spiritual Growth-Emotional Intelligence-Successful Parenting and many more topics.

Accolades and Achievements

I have received the following award: Canada Trailblazer Award 2021 - Promoted relief and development by making a difference to the vulnerable; North American Media Award 2020 - Hosting a Podcast that has the potential to completely revolutionize audience life and career; Alberta Strategy Award 2019 -   Successful Business Owner; Top 10 Upcoming Entrepreneur Award 2018 - One year in Business; and Women in the Travel Industry Award 2017 - Going Full time in Business

See What They Are Saying...

Dr. Real Kunene is a stand-out.
I first selected Real in 2019 as an afternoon speaker for an international trade association's annual meeting. Our meeting theme that year was "connect," and our celebratory speaker had done little to help with that message. Real took the stage and dazzled us all for half an hour. She has the ability to read her audience and deliver the energy and messages they need.
Christina Hopewell, Vancouver CANADA

***

Dr. Real Kunene is part strategist, part thought provoker and part cheerleader.
Real Kunene has been invaluable in my search to find the right landing spot as I pivot careers. She is a strategist, thought provoker, and cheerleader. And she has a masterful knack for knowing when to invoke these various skills to bring out a clarity of purpose and desire that is often hard to pinpoint on your own. She has a way of repackaging your own, sometimes confusing, thoughts in a way that adds meaningful direction.

Mariah Cox, Toronto CANADA

***

Rise to Greater Heights

Dr. Real Kunene will hone your craft and turn you from a hobbyist into an authority.

I wish I could have read this book years ago. It would have saved me months of false starts. RISE TO GREATER HEIGHTS Book is a collection of lessons that will hone your craft and turn you from a hobbyist into an authority. It's a definitive and deceptively simple book that has boiled out all of the irrelevant minutia and pretense and bites deep into the bone of what makes you chase after success.

Sisana Mavuka, Edmonton CANADA

***

Books and Business Links

Dr. Nompumelelo Real Kunene, May 3, 2020, RISE TO GREATER HEIGHTS, Swati Canadian International Corp, https://risetogreaterheights.com/book-community-magazine/

BOOK Dr. Real N. Kunene FOR YOUR NEXT EVENT Tel: +1(780) 803-5891 admin@risetogreaterheights.com www.risetogreaterheights.com Connect with Dr. Real N. KUNENE daily: Website: www.risetogreaterheights.com E-mail: admin@risetogreaterheights.com

Dr. Tia R. Tatem
Tatem's Financial Services
Avon Park, Florida, USA
tiatatem@gmail.co

Chapter 37
Rising Above All Odds

Dr. Tia R. Tatem is the CEO of Tatems Tax & Financial Services. Senior Tax Preparer, Financial Advisor, Entrepreneur Coach, Author, Philanthropist, and Treasury of a non-profit organization. She serves countless clients through her passion to educate individuals and business owners to manage their finances. She helps children and families and is a wife and a mother who has dedicated her life to God and Humanity.

Mission and Vision

My mission and vision for my business is to provide accurate and knowledgeable services to my clients in tax preparation, financial consulting, bookkeeping, and business coaching. My top goal is to help educate my clients to make the best financial decisions and experience prosperity in their personal and business Life.

Starting from Scratch
I face many challenges; however, through it all I have always kept the phrase Winners never quit.

Winners never quit! I was working a 9-5 job. I had to relocate. I moved 3 hours away. I wanted a change for me and my family. With no work, I commuted from Miami, FL to Avon Park, FL. I spent weekdays away and weekends at home. I knew this could not continue. Being experienced in my career, I had the ability to start my own business. However, I lacked confidence, and I was afraid of failure. I prayed and decided to get an office space, but it failed. I never started the business. I lost money, and I was in the same position as when I started but with less money. I then began to believe in myself and be true to the reason I wanted to start a business and discover how many people I could help while creating a comfortable life for me and my family. Then I decided to take the necessary steps and launched my business. I worked on my confidence; I received coaching and help, and since then I have helped hundreds of people, and I continue to expand every year.

Big Why
Keep on Pushing!

I kept moving forward in my life despite my challenges because of the love I have for what I do. I have a purpose to help others. I always remember who I was created to be. I affirm myself daily and keep a mindset to strive. I built my business to serve and to offer integrity, trust, professionalism, and knowledge to everyone. Whenever things get rough, I always remember my purpose. I understand the importance of helping others in areas I once struggled in. It brings me so much joy to see others excel in their careers. Also, I'm really big on building a legacy. I want to open doors for the generations after me and to let everyone who is attached to me that we all can reach our purpose in life. For this reason, I keep pushing!

Aha Moment Epiphany
Finding Courage!

The most amazing feeling is when you are doing what you love. I realized I was seasoned in my career. Then I did the math and calculated that I could make my year's salary in a month. Then a light bulb came on. It caused me to get the courage and step out. Because not only am I doing what I love now, I'm doing it and getting benefits, too. A mindset shift changed everything. Being that I'm a mother, I was able to create a life that gave me financial freedom and time freedom. It has allowed me to be more present in my children's life. I have also gained more freedom to travel locally and internationally and network, while also making a difference in other peoples' lives, careers, and finances.

Secret Formula
Trust the process!

Accountability is a secret formula. It's important because it helps develop the mindset and provides a sense of worthiness. I serve individuals and businesses with tax preparation and bookkeeping. As a coach, I serve entrepreneurs, business owners, mompreneurs, and freelancers. As a philanthropist, I serve children and families. I find that most of my tax, bookkeeping, and coaching clients are through word of mouth and social media. I promote using my book and being featured on podcasts, as well as coaching. I educate my clients. As a result, my clients reduce their tax liability and submit accurate reporting to the IRS. My Coaching Clients thrive and flourish in their businesses. My family non-profit has been able to reduce hunger and uplift the community with giving.

Steps to Build Success from Scratch
Mapping Out My Success

One great tip to being successful is to stick to what you truly love and desire to do; it's very important to map it out. Make it plain and visible and put it on paper. The first thing I did was to pray and create a daily routine that kept me focused and motivated daily. Secondly, I began to research others in the same industry to see what their pros and cons were. I wanted to avoid and decrease my mistakes while learning more in my industry. Third, I created a business plan. This helped me to lay out what I wanted, who I wanted to serve, and what I was looking for financially within my company. Fourth, I began to build and work on it. I marketed. I made myself do things like speaking and promoting. These are things I had never done; they were unfamiliar, but they were necessary.

First Sign of Success

My first sign of success was when I met a group of friends who thought about starting a business. With no business experience, they were imagining they could own a business but because of the lack of knowing and being Afraid of everything that could go wrong. I was able to coach them to start a partnership, guide them to start, run, and manage their finances, and I saw the way their business took off; it inspired my spirit that I had the ability to help water someone else's dream. My husband and parents have been my biggest supporters. They see the sleepless nights and stressful days, but it's all worth it when I get the feedback that I was able to make a difference in someone else's life.

Ultimate Solution
Water the Vision:

In order for me to get to the ultimate vision, I knew I couldn't get there alone. I needed mentorship. This provides accountability,

and it helps me in areas I was weak. I wanted to be of most value to my clients, so I knew it was important to get coached. This gave me a great sense of structure. One thing I love to tell people: a teacher has a teacher; everyone has learned something from someone. Even if it's not directly, they have read about it, heard about it, or seen it. Feed your vision and learn about it because the more you know the better you are at helping others become better than them.

Free Gift

My free offer will be a digital expense tracker which is a tool that an individual or business owner can use. This will allow you to manage your finances for a twelve-month span. It's already pre-calculated; all you have to do is add your income and then add your expenses. This allows you to keep track of your cash flow and keep you up to date with your finances which will show you the areas in your finances that need improvement or if you are producing more income.

Accolades and Achievements

I have received my Honorary Doctorates Degree in Humanitarianism. I was awarded this for my continued efforts to contribute to making a difference in the community. In the non-profit organization, we prioritize, changing the community one day at a time by bringing nourishment and love into it. We have served thousands of children and families year by year. I have also been featured in the "100 Successful Women in Business" magazine, which highlighted the impact that I have made on the lives of the people I served.

See What They Are Saying...

A woman, who owned a restaurant and made income but was uneducated with her finances couldn't get funded. I helped her manage her finances and book; she was able to get funded and pay the entire restaurant off debt-free.

***

My second client was a mother, who was opening a new restaurant. She was working with vendors, trying to keep deadlines, and trying to maintain everything.

She hired me and I consulted with her, signed her on, and coached her. She is currently scheduling her grand opening.
***

The third client is also a mother, and she had a talent for party decor she passionately loved. The people loved her. She collected tons of money but had no business structure, I was able to help her create her business structure as well as manage her finances; now she is able to hire her daughter and still have a salary for herself.
***

https://www.tiatatem.com/ Free Offer

Media/Business Links

Facebook: tatemstaxservices
Instagram: tiatatem
www.tatemtaxservices.com Website

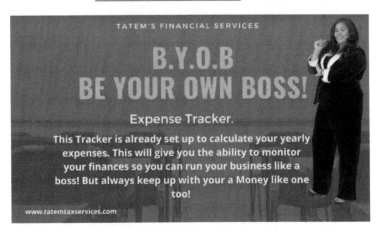

Yaima Osorio
Top Empowerment Inc.
Groveland, Florida, United States
yaima.osorio@topempowerment.com

Chapter 38
The Mustard Seed

Yaima is the Founder of Global Business Group Companies and Co-Creator of the business leadership network Level Up. She is a Latina entrepreneur and business owner who has developed in recent years as a personal brand coach and content creation specialist with more than 100 success stories in helping entrepreneurs build their confidence when exposing themselves on social networks and becoming memorable brands.

Mission and Vision

I firmly believe that our strengths, gifts, and abilities should be shared with others who will learn and grow from them. My main mission is to help the Latino community of entrepreneurs to scale their businesses by creating a positive influence with their personal brands. I want us to plant a seed that will impact generations to come because we all have a very important story to share.

Starting from Scratch
The Mustard Seed
Despairing, challenging, but at the same time rewarding.

When I thought I had my life totally planned and that I had become what I had dreamed of since I was a child, in the blink of an eye everything was taken from me. I had been married for 10 years between ups and downs I could say like any other marriage, and I considered myself a happy and satisfied woman— a Business owner, leading corporate teams, with a healthy social life, and with my greatest gifts my son Christopher, and at that time I also recently given birth to my baby girl, Genesis. My husband at that time, the Co-founder of the company we built together, decided to disruptively break up with our family, and because of his infidelity, my great castle collapsed in front of my eyes. Infidelity left me without a company, without the house where my children grew up, without money, with a broken heart, and with dreams totally destroyed. But the one thing that was never taken away from me was my faith. So, I had to start from scratch.

My faith, the size of a mustard seed at that time was enough to move my inner strength and everything started falling into place.

I firmly believe that everything happens for a reason. And this was not the exception.

In less than a year I met the one who currently makes me fall in love every morning for the great human being he is, my husband. He is the one who held my hand one day and told me, come on, you can do it and he became my biggest fan—the one who gave me the idea to find the great company that we have today together. He is my manager, my photographer, my public relations agent, and my life partner.

That's why I say everything happens for a reason. I lost everything, yes. But I got it back and better. That hard process that I went through with my children made me a braver, more determined, firmer woman, and, above all, I learned to see the bright side of every circumstance. Every process has its learning curve because the best lessons are drawn from the worst failures.

My family is restored…

I owe it to myself!
My testimony, my family, and myself.

My biggest "Why" is proving to myself that I can do it no matter what. I am my biggest competitor, and I am very determined to show up as the best version of myself. I want my testimony to change lives. My family, of course, my children, and my community give me the encouragement to keep going. No matter the obstacles or the stones on the way, there is always a reason to fight, get up and move on. As I always say about cowards, nothing has ever been written…

I always push towards the goal, always forward no matter the circumstances that surround me, and never backward. My "Why" has become a competitive race where I want to take that first place. For me, the most important thing in achieving my goals is to feel proud of never having given up.

When everything falls into place

All I can say is that God was already calling me to my life purpose.

In just a few months I changed my vision of the future. It was the beginning of the year 2020, a year that would go down in history and where many books would be written when my husband and I decided to get fully into personal development, and we began to attend many events, workshops, masterminds, and face-to-face courses. We looked like sponges; we wanted to grow and fill ourselves with knowledge. All this as a new year's resolution, the year 2020 before everything turned into complete chaos.

At the beginning of March at T Harv Ecker's mastermind "Secrets of the millionaire mind" in Orlando Florida, at lunch break, we sat down to dream of the future and analyze what we wanted for our lives. My husband Jean, my soul friend Sara and myself. It was there when dreaming awake I saw myself on a stage empowering and educating thousands of people through my knowledge.

At that moment everything was revealed. God put in my heart my purpose in life to help raise leaders and educate them and that's where we decided to open Top Empowerment within our corporation.

Founders of Top Empowerment Yaima y Jean

Every Obstacle Promises

"**E**very Obstacle Promises" is my great motto and the slogan of

my personal brand. This is where the TOP acronym of the company name was derived.

I do not believe that there is a secret formula for success or for the growth of your business; everything is due to your determination.

During the company's growth process, I realized the need to create strong leaders who impact large communities and who are the true influencers of the future. That is why I took on the task of specializing within the company as a personal brand coach to guide and educate more people to create a high-impact personal brand through social networks.

Technology has advanced much before we could predict it and many of us had to start in diapers. I develop intensive courses and personalized mentoring to guide entrepreneurs to create and develop their personal brands on social media, turning them into excellent content creators so that they leave a memorable stamp
as they grow a large community of fans of their products and services.

I developed myself as a speaker to educate about the digital world and how we can be one step ahead that allows us substantial growth in our businesses.

We all know the power of social networks and how we can reach not hundreds but thousands and millions through a camera. Today more than ever, more leaders are needed to empower, change lives, and impact future generations and what better way to use technology and the world of social media in our favor.

Steps to Build Success from Scratch

It all starts with determination, focus, character, and knowledge, and most of it comes from having the right guidance.

I think knowledge is everything. Knowledge gives you the power and it's the one thing they can't take away from you. So, if you had to start from scratch it would not be a problem if you have the knowledge. You could fall a thousand times and a thousand times you can get up.

That was the first step on the road to becoming the woman I am today. When I lost everything, and I had to evolve and start over I felt very lost.

I didn't know of anything other than what I had been doing in the past 10 years of my life as a Business Manager and corporate sales trainer. I was so hurt by the breakup that I didn't want to continue working on the same thing. I wanted to write a new book in my life and that is why since then I decided that I needed to know more, learn more, and fill myself with knowledge.

But knowledge without actionable steps becomes useless, which is why my next step was to get out of my comfort zone and act on what I had learned. It requires creating consistency, good habits of a true leader, forging character, and being filled with determination so that the motivation that allows you to continue fighting for those dreams does not die.

I once heard Bill Walsh, America's small business expert, say if your dreams don't scare you, it's because they're not big enough.

First Sign of Success

In December 2021, my husband and I participated as attendees at the Social Media fest. It occurred at Florida Global University in Miami, Florida. We were invited by a great mentor, friend Yazz Contla.

We had been in business for 2 years, and despite having started in the midst of a pandemic, we were still stable and growing little by little, but we had not experienced the next-level growth as I was expecting. And in this event, everything was about to change.

We met several international expert speakers in various areas and industries, including Daniel Iriarte, better known as the sales shark, and there were so many

278

alliances that were achieved from that great event that in January 2022 we founded a new company together with new international partners (Daniel Iriarte and his wife Stephanie) BSC Global an academy to train leaders in sales and leadership worldwide and endorsed and certified by Florida Global University which currently holds more than 150 students of different corporations.

I strongly believe in the power of networking. It was there when I discovered that we were on the right path and that now we would experience greater growth on the way to success.
I have the privilege of being surrounded by people who love my growth and push me to get ahead in life. Not only my family but my friends. I am very selective, and I believe a lot in the power of
association. You are the reflection of the 5 people around you so choose wisely.

Step out of your comfort zone
It all starts when you decide to tell your story.

That's what creating a memorable personal brand is all about. Jeff Bezos, founder of Amazon says, "Your brand is what people talk about you when you're not around."

I believe that there are many people with great talents and abilities who have not dared to put them at the service of others. I was one of them—an introverted girl who preferred to stay behind the scenes. After my purpose was revealed to me, I couldn't stay down anymore. That is my mission today—to raise the voices of thousands of leaders who can bring greater growth to others with their own stories.

Create a memorable personal brand that provides greater growth to your business.

Many do not believe in social networks, but that is the future where technology moves today and the best communication channels. Today having a guide to grow your personal brand in a favorable way is imperative.

There is no business growth without a good brand strategy.

My mission in building memorable brands is that you can tell your story and give your gifts and talents in service to your growing community.

For that you need a personal brand of impact on social media that sets you apart from the rest. A unique brand that stands out from your competitors, and therefore you need to become an excellent content creator.

Free Gift

Today my gift to you is my E-book: Storytelling which sells - skills for your social media content. Get it for free with the guide on how you can become an excellent content creator with the QR Code link. Do you want to work closely with me? Book a call now for a free consultation.

At this time and date, there's only one thing to keep in mind and that is; "if you are not online, you do not exist."

Accolades and Achievements

I have worked since 2009 for large marketing and sales companies in the State of Florida; helping them to globally expand their marketing and sales system.

In 2016, I won the Business Mentor of the Year award. For having carried out more than 100 successful training in the corporate tourism chain. In 2020 I achieved advanced certification as a digital consultant certified by FGU to work with firms, trademarks, and companies as a digital agency.

I have founded several successful educational companies for businesses and entrepreneurs.

I have created more than 20 training and courses with more than 100 success stories in helping entrepreneurs build their confidence when exposing themselves on social networks, becoming memorable brands.

I am now a VIP mentor to a global community of over 10,000 active small business entrepreneurs in over 50 countries designed to provide education, training, and mentoring operations through the latest online marketing strategies.

Follow me and learn more about me at IG- *@yaimatop*

See What They Are Saying...

See an Increase in Your Instagram Following

Thanks to Yaima Osorio and TOP EMPOWERMENT. His work team and his availability make us feel accompanied and safe in the process of growth in social networks. We have managed to see an increase in my Instagram followers due to their guidance and training, so if you have plans or projects and want to see results... you must first move yourself to make the decision to learn alongside those who have come far.

Malyory Rangel from Florida
***

Manage Your Private Schedule to Be More Productive in Your Business

I started following Yaima when I wasn't a business owner and all the info I learnt with her gave me the courage to start my own business! I absolutely recommend Top Empowerment, it will help you to manage your private schedule to be more productive in your business, also how to run a successful business, and how to use social media to improve your sales and have a great team!

Emi Mejias from Illinois
***

Take Your Business to Another Level

Thanks to this wonderful team at Top Empowerment, I have been able to take my business to another level, Yaima and her entire team are excellent human beings, and I managed to leave my fears behind and do things that I did not dare to do before, my business has grown by using their excellent techniques.

Netty Casa from Virginia
***

Learn more at
https://linktr.ee/topempowerment
Be sure to collect your FREE giveaway!

(DocV)

Dr. Virginia LeBlanc
Defining Paths
Crystal City, Virginia, USA
connect@definingpaths.info

Chapter 39
THE Pivot Maestro

Dr. Virginia LeBlanc (DocV) is a highly sought award-winning international bestselling author, <u>Podcast</u>/<u>TV show</u> host, multi-disciplinary expert, scholar, and global thought leader, delivering value worldwide across industries in holistic wellness, development, and online business transformation, mastering the art of the pivot through career-life transitions and earning the nickname "THE Pivot Maestro."

DocV is putting you back in business through her heart-centered company, movement, and network—Defining Paths—where the mission is her personal story: "Transformation through Transition." She specializes in helping women leaders, retiring military, and veterans heal, rebuild, and stand up as purposed entrepreneurs to be your own boss in mind-body-soul and business.

THINK WITHOUT A BOX
Building Success From Scratch

Building success from scratch is more than a process. It starts with psycho-emotional stability, strength, and fortitude. Tend to your wellness in mind-body-soul. Cement that foundation first; then you can build sustainable success by thinking without a box.

Redemption

There was a point in my life when I momentarily lost my identity and forgot my worth because of boxed-in thinking and pursuits. The pace, rigors of life, and conditioned expectations had me in a cycle of insanity, playing the game of life on someone else's board. Not until life happened in the workplace for the last time, did I realize life was leading me and not the other way around. I was pursuing the "American Dream" following the rules and normed formula, believing a career ladder (meant for one person at a time) would get me to that dream. I was gainfully employed; punching a clock; obeying orders (to ethical dilemmas); biting my tongue; and accepting a lesser role, even possessing unrivaled knowledge and ability because of hierarchical constructs.

When the game began to affect my well-being and snuff out my soul, my intuition became conscious; I woke from my haze. Before removing myself from employment, I withstood unparalleled challenges and treatment, including attempts at constructive discharge that caused me to question my judgment, expertise, and decision-making like never before. I did not consciously realize that when playing the game according to someone else's rules, no matter the facts, being right is irrelevant and out of one's control. I was left asking myself two questions: who was I, and more importantly, who did I want to be? My perspective shifted, and I realized that I was serving an incongruent, unagreeable mission. My soul began to speak loudly with clarity, igniting a decisive choice to stand my ground, speak truth to power, honor my oath of office, and speak up for myself and others facing injustices in the workplace. The path I believed would deliver me to that American Dream and applaud my courage for pursuing it did not. I was at a crossroads with only one choice—to love the skin that I was in.

Big "Why"

My pain turned to passion and became my client mission: "Transformation through transition." I could have given up, but instead, I found my willpower and strength by leaning into faith, hope, and self-love.

As a Black woman in America, I have always been counted out or positioned in last place on the gameboard of life. But quitting life is not an option, nor accepting fate controlled by someone else. I chose to be the Captain of my fate and the Master of my soul by embracing fear, and it became my ally on my journey to "soul" purpose (the reason we exist).

One would think leading major transition initiatives, climbing the ladder, and excelling in everything I touched in assignments with Joint Forces commands and the Department of the Navy at the Pentagon, Booz Allen Hamilton, Indiana University, and the National Pan-Hellenic Council that I was operating in my soul purpose. I was not. I was performing "on" purpose, managing reality, and simply surviving. I was outside the box but still endeared to and blocked by it, suppressing my calling. That revelation allowed me to change the game and pivot into purposed entrepreneurship.

It was "conscious intuition" that finally brought me into unconditioned reality, reminding me of my worth and that free will WAS in my control; the deafening noise of comfort and false security kept me complacent. I was at a crossroads with diverging paths needing to pivot. I leaned into my source (God) and embraced the fear of being light amid the darkness. THAT made all the difference in rediscovering my individuality and being my own boss in mind-body-soul and business.

Aha Moment

Societies were founded on the entrepreneurial path, which is one that allows us to exercise choice to capacity and see using true vision to ignite joy and prosperity in our life. We are more powerful than we realize, and our greatest gift is CHOICE. The ironies? Our neglect of that birthright and the complexities that unfold with it. Society's box is meant to keep you in, out, or hovering about it. So, abandon the box!

Have you thought about being your own boss? Don't know where to start? Great news! You've started by reading my chapter. Want to know your next steps? Consider this my invitation to visit our virtual home at DefiningPaths.online. Our passion is helping you define your path and stand up in your soul purpose. At Defining Paths, we are a heart-centered, socially conscious global movement and network of thought leaders, change agents, legacy builders, and purposed entrepreneurs seeking to heal, rebuild, and transform not only their lives and online businesses from the inside out but that of others for sustainable wins in holistic wealth and profitability, i.e., inspired living. We endeavor to be the brightest light amid life's darkness.

Secret Formula

Our secret sauce to defining your path is in our Journey Stages—Revelation, Reconciliation, and Renaissance (3R)—and Activation Pillars: 1) Going against the Grain - Reclaiming Individuality; 2) Be Anything but Normal - Reprogramming Mindset; 3) Tune into YOUR Channel - Activating Conscious Intuition; 4) Think Without A Box - Abandoning the Box; 5) Connecting the Dots - Following Your Flow, and 6) Finding Purpose - Attracting positively. Some of our foundational messaging? Perspective is everything! Find your willpower; find your strength. Think without a box. Embrace fear, and it will become your ally.

DEFINING PATHS

When I got tired of being sick and tired, my perspective on life and living shifted, activating positive attractions and flow in my health, wealth, and personal relationships. In other words, I chose Abundance, and it chose me. Abundance IS a choice, and stress IS a free and costly disease. I finally broke free of a collective mentality to reclaim my individuality with the unconditional love and support of those closest to me, including philosophies planted in me by my life-giving coaches: Gerry Robert (Book Publishing Coach), Lisa Nichols (Speaking & Transformational Coach), Susie Carder (Business & Profit Coach), and Mike Saunders (Authority Positioning Coach). Moving through reconciliation, I realized it was all about moving from a fear-based lack mentality into joyful, abundant vibrations to live 'in spirit' and co-create with the divine through my soul for a renaissance that has manifested prosperity and wonder every day.

Next Steps for Success

The path I have walked has empowered me to build myself from scratch and be the strong, diverse, focused, loving, caring, and accomplished woman I am today. Embracing the revelation that I am perfect in my imperfections, as well as reconciling my past, owning my truth, and realizing that I had been in my "soul purpose" Beta all my life gave me the voice and strength to take the journey to become fearless. It became clear that the days of traditional thinking—that a lifelong career in one industry is a sign of success—were gone. An unfortunate number of people ignore the fact that reality can change at any time. Change is life's assurance. What to do? Be prepared. Take action. As one diversifies a financial portfolio for a greater chance of sheltering from risk, adverse loss, or total ruin, how much more should we apply the principle to diversifying our lives? Think about it. Does it not make sense that diversifying your skills, experiences, and streams of income might prove the same protections?

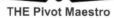
Ultimate Solution

Choose YOU and be your own boss in mind-body-soul and business. If you're frustrated, out of sorts, restless, or conflicted, these are signs (synchronicities) trying to guide you to where you were meant to be. Walking away from accolades, ladder climbing, resume building, and a need for validation revealed the truth that all is hollow and fleeting. I have discovered operating in soul purpose is its own reward and elevation that fills the holes left by validation. If you are a woman and you know that you are called to lead and you're sitting in the background accepting a "less than" role, it's time to be "more than." If you are a retiring military or a veteran, and are ready to define your own path, it is time to lead from the front. If you're already down the entrepreneurial path about to give up, DON'T. We are here to help heal, rebuild, and transform your circumstance from the inside out and put YOU back in business.

When I finally answered the purposed entrepreneur call, my heart began to see with true vision. Yours can too. Let us help you reconcile your past to rebuild your present, so that you may step into your future of infinite possibilities. The choice is NOT a luxury; it IS your birthright. Go where there is no path and leave a trail, and that WILL make ALL the difference. Are you ready to think without the box, connect the dots, and define your path? Let's connect through our Candid Conversations TV show, Define Your Path podcast, masterclasses, Boss Nation Rallies, retreats, social media, and evergreen courses and communities.

Bottom line: It all begins and ends with you. It really is YOUR choice. You have the power to fuel or smother your soul. Perspective is everything. Change yours, change you. Your pains were meant to ignite the passion inside and be the pressure revealing the diamond you are. Your fiery trials were meant to set you up to emerge from the flames and ashes like the phoenix you are, shining bright unapologetically with sustainable success.

Free Offer

Do you have a great idea or passion and wish you had the perfect online business built for long-term success? Then our turnkey solution–True Vision–is your path! Click on the banner below or go to https://definingpaths.online/true-vision and schedule your FREE consultation and 1:1 training.

WAIT, that's not all! Pull out your phone and scan the QR code to download DocV's entire eBook collection for FREE, meant to help you pivot, course correct, and think without a box!

See What They Are Saying...

"DocV Is One of The Best!"

DocV is a 5-Star speaker and a highly-qualified expert! She dazzles her audiences with her knowledge and powerful presentations. I recommend DocV with two enthusiastic thumbs up!!

Dr. Paula Fellingham
Global Mentor and Founder of www.WINWINWOMEN.com

***

"DocV Was Born To Be A Lighthouse!"

She's 100% the type of Speaker & Coach who was born to be a Lighthouse for others. She expertly touches in with her audience's fears & pains and helps them change their thoughts and then brings them UP into a new light – that of a Transformed Mind. When you change your mind, you change your life! She gets it & I highly recommend her to people & companies seeking a well-spoken, relatable and fun speaker who stands for heart-based service to her communities. You can thank me later!

Kevin Lee
International Best Selling Author, Transformational Speaker & Purpose Coach
www.iamKevinLee.com

***

"DocV Is Best In What She Does!"

I attended DocV's International Women's Summit 2021, and it was so full of value. I think she is really called for this mission because she knows how to inspire and guide other people who need guidance, and she is best in what she does!

Charms Trinidad
Meta-Certified Community Manager

Learn more at
linktr.ee/definingpaths

Be sure to collect your FREE giveaways!

Maria Alejandra Castaño
VP People Culture & Services
SierraCol Energy
Bogota, Colombia
alejandracastano73@gmail.com | alejandra_castano@sierracol.com

Chapter 40
The Power of Being Me

Maria Alejandra Castaño is the VP of People, Culture & Services for SierraCol Energy, a full-cycle oil & gas exploration and production company with headquarters in Bogota, Colombia. Alejandra has more than 20 years of experience leading various Talent Management areas and working in multicultural environments in America, Africa, and the Middle East and within the Oil & Gas, High-Tech, and Consumer Goods Sectors. Alejandra Castaño holds a bachelor's degree in Psychology from Universidad De Los Andes in Colombia and a Master's Degree in International Management from Oxford Brookes University in the U.K. Her purpose in life is Serving People.

Building A Successful Career
Mission and Vision

From the very early stages of my life, I knew that my mission in life was **"Serving People"** and that has driven many of my decisions in life.

Reflecting upon what your mission in life is, what your strengths are, and what you enjoy doing the most sets the foundations for a Successful Career.

Starting from Scratch
My father was killed when I was 20 years old as a result of a violent situation in Colombia. My mother, my sister, and I had to figure out how to support each other and continue with our lives despite the profound pain we were in. This was a very difficult experience but gave me the strength and the courage to face any other challenge in life.

I learned the value of a support system and the importance of taking your life into your hands and making the most of it. My father could not do it anymore, and somehow, I understood he could continue existing through me. This very difficult experience helped me affirm my purpose in life: *"Serving My Family and Others Around Me".*

Big Why
The next step is to visualize what success looks like for you; in other words, how you would live your Mission.

For me, success is being able to leave a legacy and a blueprint by doing what makes me happy, which is working with and for people.

I think I made the right call when pursuing my studies in Psychology. That equipped me with tools and elements to better understand and help those around me.

Aha Moment Epiphany
Opportunities and Options

Later, I had the opportunity to travel to the UK and complete a master's degree in International Management. Being exposed to people from different parts of the world with different backgrounds and perspectives about life and education encouraged me to be open-minded and become better at problem-solving by considering an abundance of options to explore. I then visualized my professional career working, learning, and influencing people with a borderless mindset. That visualization became a reality when I came back to Colombia, after completing my studies in the UK, and started working for Sun Microsystems, Unisys de Colombia. I then joined Occidental Petroleum where I had the opportunity to work in Colombia, the United States, Libya, United Arab Emirates, Bahrain, and Oman.

Secret Formula
Build Trustworthy Relationships and do it genuinely!

My secret formula to succeed in business is to build trustworthy relationships with my stakeholders. To accomplish that, the following is paramount:
1. understand the context you are operating in;
2. understand the interests, motives, and characteristics of your stakeholders and that is done through active listening. For instance, if being empathic is one of your talents, as it is mine, use it to connect with others;
3. be open to exploring different perspectives and try new ways to do things;
4. propose a solution that attends to your interests and your stakeholders as well. It is paramount to agree on a win-win solution; and
5. deliver on your agreement in a quality and respectful manner.

291

In conclusion, and as per my experience, when I have managed to build trustworthy relationships with others at home, at work, and with the communities around me, I have always obtained the respect, support, and commitment of others as I strive for success.

Steps to Build Success
Growing in the Corporate World

Alejandra working with her colleagues at SierraCol Energy, 2022

You might not want a business but want to pursue your career at a corporation and that is an option, too. From my experience, there are some tips that could help you grow and advance in the corporate world:

1. Align and harmonize your goals with your corporations.
2. Be confident that you can achieve what you want. Own your future and build your own career within the organization. Seek opportunities to grow.
2. Be persistent and passionate about your goals. Put your entire soul into action.
3. Be authentic in all you do. Understand your talents and strengths and put them into play to achieve your and your organizational goals.
4. Pursue win-win solutions and always promote a collaborative work environment.
5. Be compassionate and empathic. Be aware that you have others besides yourself and that what you do can affect others.
6. Do the right thing. Act with integrity.
7. Be humble. Keep yourself down to earth and have a sense of reality.

8. Be politically savvy. Each corporation has its rules and culture codes. Understand those so you can operate effectively in that environment.
9. Foster creativity and innovation through a continuous improvement mindset. There is always a better way to do things.
10. Keep training and improving your technical and interpersonal skills. That will enable you to be part of healthy competition for merit within your corporation.

First Sign of Success
You Can Do It. We all have difficult times during our life and career journeys. However, the key is to have confidence and believe in your capabilities to turn any difficulty into an opportunity.

When my father left this life, we felt lost and unprotected. Life turned dark and difficult for me and my family. Despite the adversity, we had to be strong and be there for each other. My faith in a better future for my family and me kept me strong and decisive to succeed personally and professionally.

Ultimate Solution
The pandemic crisis put humanity against the wall on many fronts. Many lost their jobs; others had to work endless hours helping the communities to handle the crisis, many others went through COVID-19, some survived, and others did not, leaving their families in pain. Despite the difficult times and the uncertainty, we are emerging as stronger individuals, stronger families, and stronger companies and nations. The pandemic helped us reconsider our relationship with ourselves, our loved ones, our communities, and the planet. It also helped us learn how to be resilient, be more creative and resourceful, and transform challenges into opportunities by supporting each other.

The pandemic brought me back home. I realized that I needed to come back home, be with family, and join SierraCol Energy as a VP of People, Culture & Services with the firm purpose of giving back to my country what I have learned through my career and contributing to the growth of Colombia and its people.

Free Offer

My additional advice to you is to be disciplined and persistent and you will achieve what you have in mind.
Remember that Life is to be lived. There is no time to procrastinate. Work hard every day and you will soon be ready to harvest your golden seeds.

Accolades
In 2008. I received a recognition award for developing a program called the leadership journey for first-line supervisors.

In 2011, I participated in a Joint Venture and a start-up of a company, and in 2020, I participated in the integration of two companies as a result of an acquisition. I received recognition awards for my contribution to the success of those projects.

See What They Are Saying...

Alejandra is a bright and genuine human being; her way is direct with a high sense of humanity. Those characteristics made her the right fit for our organization; she inspires and drives the culture change we are looking for. Alejandra brings the knowledge and international experience to project the organization as a great and diverse place to work.

She is a reference for all women for how determination and commitment lead to success in the corporate world.

Bernardo Ortiz
President & CEO
SierraCol Energy

***

Wickedly smart, driven, and with a huge heart, Alejandra has boldly looked for challenging opportunities throughout her career. Her worldview has been shaped by years of living and working around the globe, giving her a broad and deep perspective on business, diversity, and leadership. Working with her is a joy and challenges you to be a better person and leader.

Patrick R. Powaser, PhD
President & Executive Coach
Ho'ohana Coaching & Consulting

***

Being part of Alejandra's team has been a challenging and joyful experience. She leads by example and balances in a very effective manner results and people orientation. Her leadership style based on trust empowers and fosters creativity and risk-taking. In short, she has been to me an inspiring leader worth following.

Jason Satova
People & Culture Manager
SierraCol Energy

The Power of Being Me

Follow me on Linkedin
https://www.linkedin.com/in/alejandra-casta%C3%B1o-4864938

https://blinq.me/x73bQsMwaliGKju2lD1L

Beatrice Omowumi Yesufu
Bettyjoy Food, Ltd; Major Property; Invotech Educational Services;
and NGO Christian Widows Empowered Initiative Nigeria
Lagos State, Nigeria
yesufubeatrice@gmail.com

Chapter 41
Tragedy to Triumph

Beatrice Yesufu is the founder and executive director of the highly esteemed Christian Widows Widowers Empowered Initiative. A non-profit organization operating in Nigeria that has brought healing and empowerment to no less than 100,000 widows and widowers with their children in Africa in the last five years. She is a co-author of the book a widow's Resilience. Beatrice is certified in Leadership capacity from shattering the limits master class U.S.A. She is a Pastor of an RCCG parish in Nigeria. She has a BSc Ed in Mathematics from Lagos state University Ojo Lagos Nigeria. CWWE as Non-profit organization has the main goal to empower, educate, and equip Widows and Widowers with their children to have quality mental health, an abundant and happy lifestyle, doing this through a monthly program of workshops, conferences and empowerment activities during the last 5 years. Beatrice Yesufu has developed a curriculum for widows and widowers that focuses on the five principles of total human well-being. The scheme has been recognized by international organizations and is being implemented by other widow's organizations inside and outside Nigeria.

Mission and Vision

My mission is to empower widows and widowers with their children to become self-sufficient and sound-minded individuals.

Starting from Scratch
The Story Behind the Success

"I come from Oro Ago in Ifelodun Local Government Area of Kwara State. I was happily married to Late Moses Akahome Yesufu. Tragedy struck in the form of devastating Illness, which led to his premature death twelve years ago, leaving me with three amazing children. Throughout the tumultuous journey of my widowhood, God has shown his faithfulness, being so gracious to my children and me in the last twelve years. Despite this, as the years went by, I found myself a victim of loneliness and depression. This prompted me to search for a way to seek companionship in other women who are suffering from this situation. With this in mind, I searched for an organization that addressed my situation, but unfortunately, there are no widow organizations in Nigeria online then.

With the help of the Holy Spirit, my spiritual understanding was open, and I saw the need to reach out to other young widows in Nigeria who found themselves in my previous dilemma. This inspiration birthed the idea of The Christian Widows Widower Empowered support group Nigeria. A group of young widows and widowers finding strength in God to overcome the trials and tribulations as they go through their journey. An online support group reaching out to over 10,000 widows monthly through differs training programs virtually and physically." It's okay to want to be healed, but healing is a gradual process on this journey. In my case, I'm order to be healed and encourage others to heal, I must ensure I prioritize the methods to

achieve the aim of total well-being for every widow, widower and their children which revolves around the total human well-being, these are:
Spiritually well-being, Social well-being, Economic well-being, mental well-being, Behavioral well-being, and Emotional wellbeing. Our prime objective at CWWE is to empower widows and widowers to sound mind in all ramifications. This we do with our periodic monthly events, conferences, webinar, seminar and workshops. I have also ventured into many other businesses after the death of my beloved husband, Moses, I started a food business where I supply foods to banks. It was such a great deal. I am blessed with dedicated staff, and this makes the work stress-free for me. This outfit of my business helps my family to work in fulfilling one of my late husband's wishes, please let the children eat balanced food. My business is doing well. I am glad and grateful for my many blessings.

It has been an amazing 12 years on my widowhood journey and 5 wonderful years of empowering widows and widowers to become sound minded individuals

Big Why
Widow Syndrome

My big Why has become a passion to empower widows and widowers with their children. I want to change the narrative of "I am a Widow Syndrome" in Africa to "I am an Empowered Woman" that is capable of making difference and changing the world into a better place. To describe this challenge, it was traumatic during the early years of my widowhood. Then it became an eye-opener to birth a vision, and now the vision is so bright, wide and clear. And it's being interpreted, it's changing the narratives of the widowhood community globally.

I am glad I yielded and am passionate about it. I am now flying with my vision. It's been so wonderful transforming lives from tragedy to triumph. I hope you are getting yourself fixed in the journey of life. We must create a voice, and we must turn our pain to gain. The world is waiting for the manifestation of God's grace in our lives. Let's awake from slumber. The time to act is now.

Aha Moment Epiphany

Oh my God, the moment I was able to complete the apartment my late husband left behind. We were building a house, a twin
building that was half finished when my husband passed away. I made up my mind to complete it before his third-year anniversary. On the second anniversary, I was able to complete all the flats and rent it out to tenants. This is generating so much income for my children's school fees. Many widows have to sell their property. I am making money from mine. It was my first aha moment. I realized I could do many things if I put my mind to it and always trust in God. The investment is helping me grow and live my life well.

Aha Moment Epiphany
Widows Are Becoming Big Business Owners

My passion for widows is creating so much positivity and empowerment for the widowed community in Africa. So much beautiful feedback. Widows are becoming big business owners. Lives are being transformed and we are building great capacity to empower more. So many testimonies of total restoration and transformation in the lives of my widow community. I have become a sought-after Inspirational global speaker. We also signed up for an Academy this year to help widows and widowers to learn new skills. We got a more collaborative organization to help us achieve our objectives. I was honored to collaborate with an organization in the USA that sponsored the first part of the project. We believe in God for more collaborations with more organizations as we empower the widowed in Africa.

Tragedy to Triumph
Secret Formula

My soul shall make her boast: My secret formula is to give praises to God every time, pray, and believe in the unfailing promises of God. I love Psalms, 34 verses 2-4. It says "My soul shall make her boast in the Lord: the humble shall hear thereof and be glad. Come magnify the Lord with me, come let us exalt his name together, I sought the Lord, and he heard me and delivered me from all my fears."
I serve a living God—the creator of heaven and earth. I am passionate about the empowerment of widows and widowers in Africa

My business is doing well, clients are all over the world.
The program and my events to empower the widows' community keep on attracting more collaborations with organizations and individuals to join me to do more which makes me glad.

Steps to Build Success from Scratch
My Widowhood Journey

I became successful in the work I do with the widow community based on these 6 steps. Be resilient; Be determined to become successful; Dream and bring your dream to manifestation; Work hard and diligently pursuing your passion with all positivity; See opportunity in every challenge and don't let go without turning it for good and be tenacious and international in your pursuit. The results of my past event are for me to be a leader to grow higher. I started my work with the widows' community with just my phone. I encourage widows and widowers, but today it has birthed so many arms of organizations that make my widowhood journey to become smoother for my community. Determination, Persistence, Perseverance, and Passion have been essential in this journey. I am making so much difference in the widowhood community in Africa.

First Sign of Success Phenomenal Support:

My first sign of success was the May 2019 conference. We received so much help. I began to see clearly that there was so much to do. The people and the community I serve are phenomenal. My children are always in my support, especially my younger son, Victor Akahome Yesufu. Victor is always around, being the younger child of my three children. He is the first person I discussed things with. He is indeed a gift of God to humanity. At times I wonder why I bother him so much; It is probably because he always has a word to cheer me up. He is an encourager and a fun person to be with. He is knowledgeable. He reminds me often to include widows' children in my program every month. He is a gift. My other two children are not always around with me, but they love what I do with CWWE Nigeria. I have their backing as well. Actually, I just started doing what I was inspired to do with the widow community. Year after year we were able to build a strong structure that has come to stay today.

I really want to say a big thank you to Pastor Ajibola Opeoluwa-Calebs who saw greatness in my little beginning in 2018. He called me to tell me I should register the name as an organization which I did, and that was the beginning of a new success. That was exactly what happened to me, I asked for help, and he became my mentor; he really tried his best. It's those that believe in your passion and are aligned with you that will help you actualize your objectives. Our hands are open for collaborations from different organizations from around the world.

Ultimate Solution
Never say Never

Love is key in Mentorship. Be encouraged today that you are capable of bringing to existence whatsoever you dream. Imagination propels you to achieve your goals. Never sleep in your dreams. Work it out by yourselves first and then call others to help you take it to the top; networking with right-minded people is key in building capacity. Never say never as you never can tell who that person is that has the right tools to get you to your next stage of accomplishments. Be intentional and stay positive. You are a masterpiece, working it out. You carry such a gift. Keep birthing it. Position yourself on how you will support and transform the world.

Accolades and Achievements

CWWE Nigeria Facebook Public page @ https://www.facebook.com/CWWEIN/
I am grateful to God for all the accolades I have received in the past years. I am honored to be a proud recipient of 100 successful Women in Business 2021 for my amazing work with widows and widowers in Africa. I have received the Hall of Fame Award 2021 for Empowering Widows; Peace Ambassador Yenwa Indian 2021 for Advocacy for Peace within Family and Widowed Community in Nigeria; Global Peace Award UNESCO 2021; Humanitarian; Award Medal by Nelson Mandela 2021; and Mentor Award Canada for Women Empowerment.

CWWE Nigeria has empowered over 100,000 women around the world through her monthly seminar and has helped them in the past 5 years to improve their economic well-being, emotional well-being, spiritual well-being, and social well-being. My Academy called CWWE Academy has trained over 200 women in skilled acquisition programmes in the last 2 years.

We hosted one of our Global Speakers on Conscious Parenting in Nigeria last month—Val Alino in 3 conferences in the month of June. The experience brought a total mind shift to every participant about being intentional and conscious in relationship with children to bring learning to sustainability development in Africa.

Be sure to collect your FREE giveaway!

Susie E. Mierzwik
Lifewave: Non-Drug Stem Cell Regeneration/Pain Relief
Yucaipa, California, USA
kinderkat9@gmail.com

Chapter 42
Transforming from Pain into Passion

Susie Mierzwik is a retired teacher who received the Teacher of the Year Award and volunteers with Samaritan's Purse charitable foundation. She devotes herself to a unique wellness business that promotes nondrug phototherapy and stem cell regeneration technology which enables the body to heal itself with light. Her memoir is coming out this September. Susie and her husband Steve live in California and share six children and five grandchildren. They stay active by biking, hiking, square dancing, and traveling.

Mission and Vision

My mission is to empower women over 40 to build a business they can weave into their current lifestyle. This business offers great health and the energy they need to be successful. For as little as $100, a budding entrepreneur can begin to achieve great health and a part-time business that can grow into a full-time income.

I feel there is a lesson in life we can learn from every trial we go through. I used my journey from pain to wellness as an opportunity to launch my Lifewave business. Trials, unrest, difficulty, and pain is often what can catapult us into a new adventure in life. Use the uncertainty in your own life to assess what opportunities are presented to you to move forward. Freedom and opportunity open new doors to us when we have the courage to say yes and go for it. Having the determination to start your own business will empower you, especially if you have a solid product and supportive people to show you the ropes. People around the world are searching for relief from pain that prevents them from fulfilling their goals. Lifewave is the business that can help busy mothers and others get the income they need to provide for their children and live the active lifestyle they deserve.

At age 39, I was plagued with chronic back pain, aching joints, stiffness, and chronic allergy symptoms like headaches, head and chest congestion, coughing, and frequent bouts of illness. The various prescriptions I took daily for years did nothing to eliminate my suffering. Then in 2009, a breakthrough came when the mom of a former student entered my classroom. When she saw my painful hands, she suggested an anti-aging solution that had helped her. It was a little phototherapy patch that removed inflammation and pain. Although I was skeptical at first, by the end of my first month of use, I was pain-free for the first time in twenty years.

Big Why
Determination...Motherhood...Courage

During all the years, I suffered from chronic back and joint pain, I carried on because I had two daughters to raise. My husband was a pilot who was often gone flying airplanes. We had no family at all to help. My daughter remembers worrying about me while she was growing up since I suffered so much. I prayed that God would help me, and he did. But I soldiered on alone without any support except my psychologist who listened to my tear-filled laments. I never stopped in my determination to create a better life for myself and my daughters. If you have a passion to do something new, try it. Find a mentor to support your big dream. Take a step every day towards your goal. Never stop. You have to walk through the trials to reach your triumph.

Aha Moment Epiphany
Joy ...Thankfulness...Inspiration

The "Aha" moment occurred to me after my divorce when I realized that the Lord had a different plan for me. About six months after my divorce something clicked in my heart. Just as it says in Jeremiah 29:11, "I know the plans I have for you...plans to prosper you and not to harm you...plans to give you hope and a future."

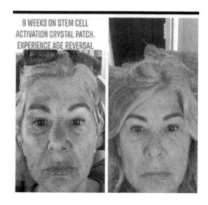

After the pain from many ailments finally ceased by using Lifewave phototherapy, I was filled with joy. My depression had ended because I was now divorced from my emotionally distant, unfaithful husband. Now I was healthy and happily married to a

supportive husband who helped me create a new life. While still teaching, we built our Lifewave business by sharing this NON-DRUG, pain relief technology that helped others live pain-free lives.

Secret Formula
Stop... Look...Listen

Wherever I go I show women how they can live pain free joyful lives; for example, Sarah suffered from a serious anemia problem that left her with fatigue, insomnia, and brain fog. She used the stem cell regeneration patches, and within months, recovered her good health without using any drugs. In my yoga class, I saw a woman in severe distress. I asked what was happening, and she said she was having trouble breathing. I quickly put the Lifewave patches on her chest, over her shirt. Within minutes, her breathing became normal, and she was so grateful. Another time, I had a business appointment at Starbucks. I noticed the woman I was meeting had a very swollen, red face and her lips were distended. I asked her what had happened to her. She said she had just had a dental appointment and the doctor gave her some medicine, which was causing an allergic reaction. She said she would go to the Emergency Room after our meeting. I gave her a single Lifewave patch and a bottle of water. Fifteen minutes later while we were talking, her symptoms disappeared. She said she didn't need to go to the ER now, and since then she has incorporated the Lifewave patches into her massage business.

Another example, Gloria was living in Assisted Living because of a severe medical situation that left her on oxygen and unable to care for herself. Her adult son contacted me to ask if there was any help, I could offer his mom. Within several weeks of using the Lifewave stem cell regeneration patches, she was discharged from assisted living and returned to her own home. The first thing she wanted to do was to get her hair and her nails done! All these stories of success start in pain and end in joy. *I am not a medical doctor and Lifewave technology does not treat, diagnose or cure any condition.* But these anecdotal testimonies are what I saw and experienced with myself and others. The stories speak for themselves.

Steps to Build Success from Scratch
My Method for Building business:

- Wherever I am I stop and notice there are people around me who may need my business. I talk to everyone in a sincere way. I make connections with people everywhere. I observe how they feel.
- **Look**: Observe if someone is walking in pain, wincing, or out of breath. Approach them and ask if they need help. This is easy to do if you are a friendly, outgoing person. There is usually someone around who may need assistance and my solution. While this may seem intimidating, your desire to be of service will guide you.
- **Listen**: Listen to what the person is saying. Ask questions to determine if there is a way I can be of service. Listen more; speak less. See if I can help. Are they listening to what you are saying, and do they want to solve their problem.? Not everyone is ready or willing to look for a solution to their health challenges.
- **Connect**: Depending upon the situation, find a common ground with the persons/ their experiences/ the places they are in at present/ people you have in common. They will listen to me, once I have established rapport.
- **Persist**: Remember, everyone does not want to be helped. I have no control over this response. Follow up with everyone. Situations may change, the person you are talking to may not see the need now, but our health changes and the person will probably know someone else who wants to be pain-free.
- **Continue**: looking for opportunities everywhere daily. Always look to provide service every way you can. Even a kind smile and holding open a door creates goodwill.

First Sign of Success.

First, my husband and I won a cruise to the Bahamas with the company and Suzanne Somers who was the Lifewave ambassador. She is a well-known health advocate and author who has written many books about treatments that build up the body instead of tearing it down. Next, a client with a salon spa held weekly meetings with me at her shop with prospects. When I saw the wide range of people who were helped by the Lifewave products, my spirits soared. My current husband is an enthusiastic partner, and we often showcase our products at various events. Our Lifewave income made it possible to start our rental property business. From one rental property, we have grown to ten.

During Covid, I used Zoom to open up my market to clients across the globe. Even on Safari in Tanzania, I gained clients. THE LIFEWAVE BUSINESS OPPORTUNITY enabled me to start a business that is now in 100 countries First, by changing my own health, I was able to impact the health of people everywhere. This would not have been possible if I had not taken the first step and tried a new solution to my chronic health issues.

Ultimate Solution
Home-Based Solution

My solution to the woman looking to start her own business is to join me in the Lifewave opportunity. This is a true home-based business, which you can run from home with a $100 starter purchase of the patches. The product is proven, and the stem cell regeneration technology has a twenty-year patent. The cost is low, and it is possible to build a substantial income while being your own boss. The company and your direct team provide all the training, infrastructure, and support that is needed for a new person to start their business.

1. Be CURIOUS. Ask questions or lose opportunities.
2. Be COURAGEOUS. Persist; healing doesn't happen overnight.
3. Be CONFIDENT. If prospects reject my solution, don't get discouraged. Success requires effort.
4. Be COMMITTED. Be determined to help those willing to take responsibility for their health
5. Be CONNECTIBLE. Find ways to connect. Preconceived notions eliminate many opportunities.

Free Gift

My Free offer is a $50 retail value of Lifewave patches to experience the product after signing up as a distributor under me. I will provide two consulting calls. They will get weekly coaching calls from me as part of my team. Contact me at kinderkat9@gmail.com

Accolades and Achievements

In 2000, I was awarded TEACHER OF THE YEAR from my California School District. In 2014 I was awarded Woman of Distinction by Senator Mike Morrell. I was also awarded the Crusader award from my Company upline. In 2019 I received the Lady in Blue Appreciation Award from GSFE. In 2021 I received the World Kindness Day Award from GSFE and the Director's Award. In 2022. I received the Sima Award(She Inspires ME) from GSFE. I was also nominated for an Honorary Doctorate by Dr. Robbie Motter, the CEO of GSFE

See What They Are Saying...

Jill was a busy teacher who was diagnosed with a serious disease. After completing her chemotherapy, she was exhausted but she had to resume teaching 30 elementary kids. She used the Lifewave patches to restore her energy and her immunity so she could resume her demanding schedule. The following year she gave birth to a beautiful baby and is now even busier and healthier as a teacher, wife, and mother.

***

Mindy suffered from a debilitating condition that gave her chronic headaches as well as body aches everywhere. She utilized the non-drug phototherapy technology and, in a few weeks, her pain was gone and her energy returned. She now works full-time as well as being a busy mom and grandma.

***

Monica is a self-employed woman who heard me talking about the power of stem cell regeneration technology and purchased it to use for her husband who had a lot of pain following an accident. He recovered and she decided to try it for herself as well. After only a few days, she called to report that for the first time in twenty years her severe monthly pain was gone.

***

Books and Media Links

My Memoir "Sow in Tears, Reap in Joy" will be published this September 2022

Collaboration Chapter in " 2020 A Year of Faith" "My Faith Journey" with the Information Diva

copyright 2021

Collaboration Chapter in "Love your Haters" "A Shocking Homecoming" with Angela Covany June 2022

Collaboration Chapter in "The Impact of One Voice" "A Child Without a Voice" with Arvee Robinson July 2022

https://linktr.ee/susiemierzwik

Nareshini Ranganthan
Environment Language and Education Trust (ELET)
Durban, KwaZulu Natal, South Africa
nareshini@elet.org.za

Chapter 43
Transforming Lives

Nareshini Ranganthan is the Director of the Environment Language and Education Trust (ELET). She began her career as a Primary School teacher following which she spent a few years in Corporate Educational Publishing. Her academic and diverse professional experience spans 30 years in the Education, Corporate, and NGO sectors. As a results-driven leader, she is exceptionally passionate about serving marginalized communities, creating opportunities for access to Education and Social Upliftment, and helping people to reach their full potential. She accomplishes all this whilst living her own motto: *"We make a living by what we get, but we make a life by what we give"*. Her success in life can be attributed to her wonderful and supportive family who subscribe to the philosophy that places compassion and empathy first in purpose-driven lives. This underpins every sphere of her personal and work life

Mission and Vision

Vision: Empowerment of women and youth through education.

Mission: The organization I lead, the Environment and Language Education Trust, intentionally contributes to the development and transformation of a democratic South Africa through accredited skills training programs and community-based developmental programs with a focus on rural women and youth.

Human Potential Wasted

"The future belongs to those who believe in the beauty of their dreams." Elanor Roosevelt.

I believe that the biggest source of motivation is our thoughts, so we must think big and motivate ourselves to succeed. Do not wait for the right time; start where you stand with whatever tools you have at your command. The right tools will be found as you go along. Success is achieved one step at a time.

My career began as a Primary School Educator, and this period proved formative in developing and evolving my consciousness, especially to find ways of providing change and hope for those forced to live on the margins of society. During an engagement with learners, parents and visits with other members of the community, the brutal existential reality of the kids in my care was starkly brought home to me. As debilitating as this can prove to be, as an optimist and someone who firmly believes that every tiny step in the right direction moves all of us forward, I lived in hope that the platforms do exist to implement small but positive changes to make a difference. Gazing across a cramped classroom of children, the realization that all these children were just surviving in a world that had made them shelve their dreams away was an epiphany that catalyzes most of the work I subsequently engage in. Daily life for these children was characterized by crime, poverty, inadequate nutrition and healthcare, and gross neglect. In this situation, I found ways to make even a tiny difference to as many of these kids as possible, but my thoughts often lingered on how it would be possible to find tangible and long-lasting solutions to improve not just their lives but to improve the communities of which they came. To me, one of the greatest tragedies in life is when human potential is destroyed or allowed to just waste away. I gazed at my young learners and found myself wondering if maybe there was a Maya Angelou, Rosa Parks, or Nelson Mandela sitting there, whose challenge at that moment was just to find a meal. I asked myself if there were platforms out there that could be used to effect positive change more broadly and effectively, one small step at a time. A further question I posed t0 myself was – 'How can I help more people to escape the hopelessness of mere survival to allow them to blossom, reach their full potential, and make positive contributions to their communities and society?'. Hard work, perseverance, learning, studying, sacrifice, and the determination to bring about positive change are the reasons for my success. Positive change does not happen overnight. Never change your goals, be open to new ideas, and adapt the plans you implement.

Improving reading & literacy

Big Why
Education is Transformative

Every individual has the ability to make a difference in this world. One of Madiba's most famous quotes is *"Education is the most powerful weapon you can use to change the world".* Education is the first building block of knowledge creation, and its value truly lies in effecting positive change in the world. As an educator spending many years serving children from extremely poor communities, the power of educational opportunities and its ability to change the fortunes of those that live in poverty is the motivation that drives me to continue transforming lives.

311

I remain grateful for the opportunity to lead an NGO driven by a singular vision to provide opportunities for the most vulnerable in our country. In my most reflective moments, I think about all the experiences that guided me and increased my yearning for this precise platform which now allows me to contribute to effecting change on a much broader scale. I am proud to say that the organization I lead gives wonderful expression to the quote of Madiba in all that we have achieved and will continue to do so. I believe that if we put our heart, mind, intellect, and soul into even our smallest act, we will succeed in achieving our end goals. We need to grow confidently in the direction of our dreams to realize our set goals.

"I AM BECAUSE WE ARE" Nelson Mandela

In South Africa, our abiding philosophy is called Ubuntu, which is all about the interconnectedness and interdependence of humanity. As director of an NGO that was on the brink of collapse at the time of me taking the helm, the importance of pooling together all available opportunities and resources and building strong partnerships to revitalize the organization was extremely instructive to me.

The importance of leveraging support and formulating partnerships and synergies to achieve your goal is a lesson that will remain with me forever as our organization grows from strength to strength.

I believe that a difficult time can be more readily endured if we retain the conviction that our existence holds a purpose, a cause to pursue, and a goal to achieve. Work until you no longer have to introduce yourself.

Secret Formula
PASSION, PARTNERSHIPS, PURPOSE

In South Africa, our abiding philosophy is called Ubuntu, which is all about the interconnectedness and interdependence of humanity. As director of an NGO that was on the brink of collapse at the time of me taking the helm, the importance of pooling together all available opportunities and resources and building strong partnerships to revitalize the organization was extremely instructive to me. The importance of leveraging support and formulating partnerships and synergies to achieve your goal is a lesson that will remain with me forever as our organization grows from strength to strength.

A difficult time or challenging situation can be more readily endured if we retain the conviction that our existence holds a purpose, a cause to pursue, and a goal to achieve. Work until you no longer have to introduce yourself.

Steps to Build Success from Scratch
BUILD STRONG ROOTS TO FLOURISH

I believe the strongest roots in an organization are its people. My master's research on a 'value–centered approach' to managing your business is fundamental to my success. I inculcate the foundational pillars of honesty, integrity, mutual respect, and stewardship into my daily business practices. They constitute the starting point and crucial building blocks, determining the fundamental ethos and direction of what I want to achieve both personally and within the organization.

1. Engage with a diverse cross-section of people and identify partners, associates, and fellow staff that are intrinsically motivated and have the same passion as yourself to pursue similar goals.
2. Provide effective stewardship and mentorship to ensure the team embraces and understands the core values and aspirations of the organization.
3. Set firm and achievable goals and ensure that the organization's objectives are aligned with its core mission.
4. Put in place protocols to uphold and constantly strengthen accountability, transparency, high levels of ethics, and good corporate governance for the organization.
5. Treat every individual irrespective of rank or position with respect and dignity.

First Sign of Success

'It always seems impossible until it is done'. Nelson Mandela

Success is a journey that is almost totally dependent on drive and persistence. Consistent hard work, always making the extra effort, and the willingness to try another approach is critical. If you want to be successful, you have to follow your passion and not your paycheck.

Currently, I lead ELET, an NGO with a significant record of transforming lives. ELET was severely financially constrained when I joined. My first objective was to source funding to ensure both financial stability and growth within a three-month turnaround time. Successfully steadying the ship and setting it on a rising trajectory are achievements I take great pride in, and we now continue to grow whilst positively impacting thousands of lives. The successful implementation of our Early Childhood Development Learnerships, together with local tertiary institutions which began in 2015, is our most significant achievement and it speaks directly to my vision of empowerment through education. The program focuses on rural women with more than 750 graduates 6 years later being able to contribute to a foundational education, forge successful careers, and impact their communities. This alone inspires us, providing momentum to forge ahead. I draw inspiration from being part of a process to transform the life of a rural woman largely marginalized by the system. Our partners have been strong pillars in the midst of some of the greatest challenges the world has seen and together we are able to forge ahead and make a difference in the lives and livelihoods of marginalized women.

313

Ultimate Solution

"...continuity of strategic direction and continuous improvement in how you do things are absolutely consistent with each other. In fact, they're mutually reinforcing."
– Michael Porter

The work done by ELET is self-motivating because of our project locations. Our firm operational protocols, together with a committed team of facilitators, associates, and staff synergize to reach successful completion. I deem it important to constantly draw advice and inspiration from a range of sources, globally and locally. I believe that people with a shared vision and determination can achieve everything that they set out to do. Every individual can work, but together as a team we can soar to greater heights and accomplish our set goals.

Free gift (Advice)

Stay positive, work hard and make it happen. You are the master of your own destiny.

Finding your intrinsic motivation, believing deeply in the work that you do, and always giving off your best are vitally important. I have created my own motto: "We make a living by what we get, but we make a life by what we give". The dignity of every person comes before all else, and we must help people to realize their full value and potential, live dignified lives, and escape cycles of poverty.

Accolades and Achievements

Master's degree in business administration (MBA).
Dissertation - Human Values and Business Management. A value-centered approach to the way Business should be managed.

City Stars Award (2008)
In contribution to the eThekwini Municipality Community Outreach category for Math, Science and Technology, and Early Childhood Development

Nominated for the Businesswomen of the Year Award in the category of Social Entrepreneur in 2011
Nominated by Engen for outstanding contribution to CSI initiatives in KZN

Paul Harris Fellowship Award
Received the Paul Harris Fellowship Award in 2016, recognizing her outstanding contribution to community development, humanitarian and education programmes,

Mangosuthu University of Technology
In MUT's 2018 Woman and Philanthropy category for outstanding contribution to educational programmes.

Global Partnership: African Institute for Health Leadership
As Director of ELET, instrumental in formalizing this partnership. The CEO is Professor Rubin Pillay, medical futurist, and Professor of Healthcare Innovation and Entrepreneurship, and Assistant Dean for Global Health Innovation in the School of Medicine, University of Birmingham, Alabama.

See What They Are Saying...

"The ELET Learner Support Program helps learners from rural areas to obtain better marks in Mathematics and Physical Science. Since being in the program, my marks in both subjects increased steadily and I have so much more confidence. This program has enabled me to improve my marks tremendously and I have secured a place at the University of Johannesburg to study in the Health Sciences. Thank you, ELET! ~ **Lwazi Ngcobo (Ohlange Secondary School)**

***

"I come from eMagabheni, KZN. Growing up, I had to drop out of High School to take care of my siblings. I managed to complete Matric whilst working and was given a chance by ELET to enter the Early Childhood Development (ECD) learnership program over 2 years to study towards becoming a practitioner. I have since graduated with a Diploma in ECD and am now employed by ELET as an ECD Facilitator Assistant. I remain grateful for this life-changing opportunity offered to me."
Zanele Magubane

Transforming Lives—Our proud ECD Graduates with Zanele Magubane in the centre

"A partnership between the Durban University of Technology (DUT) and ELET was inevitable because ELET has been a trailblazer in Language, Education and Early Childhood Development. ELET's involvement in this sector has been necessary and insightful, whilst being headed by a visionary, scrupulous and action-oriented leader. Their method of delivering ECD learnerships is innovative and goal-oriented, maximizing their role in society. We look forward to growing in strength together."

Professor Surendra Thakur
Director: The Short Course Unit (DUT)
InSETA Research Chair in Digitisation

Business Links

Learn more at
https://za.linkedin.com/in/nareshini-ranganthan-312186148

Be sure to collect your FREE giveaway!

Amelia Fjellvard
The Queen of Joy
Larvik, Norway
post@ameliafjellvard.com

Chapter 44
Unleash the Power of YOUR Inner Flame

Amelia empowers women from all walks of life to regain their inner peace, flow, and joy in the NOW. She has compassion for those hurting and has significantly transformed those she serves. Amelia is an expert and scholar who has researched and trained on a holistic view of health and wellness for more than 30 years. She's also an international transformational speaker and author who hosts worldwide retreats to awaken women's inner flame that lights all areas of their lives. Amelia uses a wide range of body-mind techniques, dance, and body movements and connects bodily states with emotional and cognitive elements through dance and body movement activations, forest baths, meditations, breath- and energy work. Amelia is all about discovering your personal power to create an extraordinary life you love.

Mission and Vision

Her ongoing mission is to bring holistic health and wellness to women worldwide and to give them a more positive outlook on life - even in the face of hardship. She aims for you to stand firm and be connected with your higher self through self-care and self-love so you can thrive in life and business.

Her vision is to empower women to put holistic health and wellness on their agenda worldwide for a more peaceful, loving, and joyful life—a life filled with meaning, purpose, and a feeling of excitement and readiness to pay it forward.

Power to Express - Amelia Fjellvard
Starting a Business From Scratch

Every person has a diamond that needs to be polished that you can turn into a business. Chaotic moments polished me, and my business began.

Have you had any chaos or considerable challenges in your life?
If yes, I am here to tell you to take that challenge, turn it into an idea, and build a business around it from scratch.

Tell other people about how you overcome your challenges.
Use your story to change and impact the world. Play bigger, be bolder and live authentically.

Dirty Secrets Transformed Me

In 2004, I lived my dream life. But one day, it all changed! I lost every asset I had built for my children and myself, along with my physical and mental health.
I collapsed on the floor.

I had used my entire life being a people pleaser with no self-worth and a perfectionist with few or no boundaries. You see, I had a dirty secret! I was a survivor of 15 years of sexual abuse and everything that comes with it. I was broken. I had never faced my demons!

Today I believe that my collapse that day was a blessing because it led me to where I am today, filled with deep inner peace, flow, and joy in my life. I feel free and fulfilled.

Once I began to talk about the dirty secret that kept me in the dark, my world transformed. Today I'm working with women worldwide to help them unleash the power within, no matter their
circumstances. For a deeper dive into my dirty secrets, read my book *'The Dirty Secret: Polished My World.'*

Hey, it doesn't matter how many times you fall; what matters is that you keep getting up and keep going forward. Understand your value and worth, align with your purpose, and share your unique brilliance with the world. Stand tall and never give up!

My Big Why
Breaking Out from the Chains

I felt imprisoned and locked in by my dirty secrets, but the moment I decided to reveal them, my healing process started; I found my authentic self. My big WHY is *daring to be me* just the way I am. I'm focused on filling my cup first and loving myself unconditionally and unapologetically. I stepped into my power, found my courage, became responsible, learned to let go, and trusted the process. I eliminated deep-rooted negative emotions and now live a life of freedom and fulfillment.

I naturally sought the healing energy nature could provide;
It grounded me. I found peace using my senses, observing, and being in the present moment. Dance and general fitness allowed me to experience flow, and joy became my roadmap as an action taker who wanted real change.

What is your biggest Why? GO FOR IT!
Your biggest why will turn into a passion, which will drive you to keep going. Commit to finding happiness within and living a life with meaning, purpose, and the feeling of excitement.

Aha Moments
Trust Your Inner Voice

My most significant **aha moment** was when I zoomed out and saw my past, present, and future appearing in front of my eyes during a soul purpose session. Suddenly it became as clear as day; my purpose was to use my life experience with different stressors to help others heal and transform by finding inner peace, flow,

319

and joy in the now.

At that moment, everything turned around for me. I went inwards instead of listening to all the chaos that surrounded me. *"Inside every human being, there are treasures to unlock."* -Mike Huckabe

Letting go of the past is not easy but necessary, and yes, you will find yourself in the NOW.

Everything will become clear if you trust your inner voice.

Everyone has had an epiphany, and I'm sure you had one too. What was your aha moment to continue, move on, and build your business?

The moment I started to pay attention to my inner wisdom it offered me guidance. With all the outside noise and stimuli confusing you, you must not lose touch with your ability to connect inward. Trust that you have this inner guidance waiting patiently for you to notice it and to guide you through the tempestuous waters of life.

Secret Formula
Find Your Inner Flame That Lights All Areas of Your Life

My golden secrets to transforming women's lives and business are through healing with nature, dance and body movements, meditations, breathing exercises, and energy work—
a mix that created wonders for me and later my clients.

My life experience of being traumatized and lost has taken me to work with women experiencing different stressors in their lives.
My secret formula helps you boost self-confidence, practice self-love and self-care, find your voice, and use it authentically.
With me, you will re-connect, realign, re-energize, heal, and transform.

I attract my clients by writing, speaking, creating programs, and hosting retreats, workshops, seminars, and webinars. I'm available on social media platforms where I share and serve weekly.
I invite you to come to one of my retreats or join my program to find YOUR inner flame.

Remember to realign, and re-energize your mind, heart, body, and soul. Go out in nature, go dancing, and have fun. Joy is inside you, so don't look for it in someone or something else. It will not make you happy. Find your personal power, the inspiration, and the clarity, to just "do it." With peace, flow, and joy in your life, it will feel easy.

Unleash the Power of YOUR Inner Flame

Steps to Success
Tap Into Your Divine Energy

My greatest passion is to help women to realign and re-energize to find deep inner peace, flow, and joy in the now, even amid the chaos, through the healing power of nature, dance- and body movement activations, meditations, deep breathing techniques, and energy work. My desire is for them to heal and transform FOR GOOD. I would love to connect with you to help you realign with your higher self and re-energize your whole system. Below are some steps that you can follow to tap into your personal power.

1) Heal with nature

While in nature, slow down, walk barefoot, relax, breathe, tune into your senses, observe, stay in the present moment, enjoy the stillness, meditate, and connect with mother earth and yourself. Tap into gratitude and just BE.

2) The power of dance

Dance to express yourself, to heal. Dance for fun or dance your stress away. Dance or move to promote emotional, social, cognitive, and physical integration. Process, observe, assess, and intervene in your overall health through dance and body movement.

3) The timeless benefits of meditation

Refocus your attention on something calming like meditation. When we meditate, we calm our mind so the soul can speak. Become aware of your infinite potential, strength, love, and power.

4) Tap into the incredible power of breath

Become aware of your breathing. Breathe consciously and systematically, disconnect yourself from the mind and connect with your body and heart. Return to wholeness and make yourself more equipped to handle stressors.

5) Manage your energy

Understand how energy works and get your vitality back when you are drained, your health back when you are ill, and joy when you are down. Outsmart stress and surrender to happiness. Instill strength, resilience, health, and vitality into your body.

Unleash the Power of YOUR Inner Flame

Do you make sure to practice any of the above so you can see the world from a new perspective, enjoy life, and have fun?

First Signs of Success
One day I sat down and reflected on why I felt more aligned lately. I felt a sense of awakening, making me feel like a complete human.

You must be consciously aware of the first signs of success.
I felt so open and heart-centered. That's when I stopped to celebrate my milestone of success.

I became aware and laser-focused on having peace, inner flow, and joy with me in everything I did or created.
Many forget to stop and smell the roses. Learn how to STOP and pause. Don't wait to be on the top of the mountain; enjoy it and celebrate every little milestone. Celebrate YOU! There is success at every level. Find the people that will support you, surround yourself with like-minded people who love you for who you are, value you, and lift you up to whatever next level you want to reach.

The Ultimate Solution
Change Your Life Today.

My path led me to guide my clients into inner peace, flow, and joy in the now.
They learn to express themselves through activities like dancing, forest bathing, energy work, meditations, and breathwork.

How would it feel to burst with self-confidence and energy, lungs filled with the maximum capacity with fresh air, ready to vocalize your intentions, feelings, and rights?

How would it feel knowing that no one and nothing could stop you?

To have mentors has been life-changing for me. My mentors raised my confidence and problem-solving abilities. No matter your level, a mentor helps you get to the next level much quicker.

Do you have anyone helping you on the path of self-discovery and growth?

Inner Flow of Joy
My gift to you is to give you access to my free *"Inner flow of Joy"* 3-Online Video Series, an ultimate solution that will transform your life and your business.

Here are just a few things you will discover in this free 3-Online Video Series:

- ***Peace is a quality of your divine nature***
  Deep inner peace gives you an overall sense of serenity.

Unleash the Power of YOUR Inner Flame

You will be more connected to your higher power, have more harmony, meaning, and purpose in life.

- ***Flow gets you where you want to be***
Through dance and body movement you will bring forth the inner flame that will light all areas of your life. You will feel free and energized - ready to take on the world.

- ***On the other side of despair, there's joy***
Prioritizing and intentionally seeking more joy could be the magic ingredients for your success. Find your mojo, open up to pleasure, and feel those sweet moments in your life.

Are you ready to choose **you**?

Join my free gift now, and let's unite to lighten our mind, heart, body, and soul and brighten the world.

Here is my business card: -------------->

Come join my Facebook group community where you can connect, participate, and grow with like-minded people.

Accolades and Achievements

Amelia is a trained teacher, a certified belief clearing practitioner, a mindset practitioner, a dance-and-body movement therapist, and a 'heal with nature' guide. She is the CEO and founder of her company, Power to Express - Amelia Fjellvard. She is also a co-writer in the *"Find YourSELF Handbook,"* and the *"100 Most Successful Women Around The World. "* Amelia writes for magazines like "B-Global Magazine". Her book *"Dirty Secret: Polished My World"* is in print. She is honored in Paris as a Global speaker and a Norwegian Country Chair - Oneness and Wisdom. NLP and Hypnotherapy Certified Practitioner

See What They Are Saying...

Elisabeth Bergsholm Hansen
Amelia is a beautiful soul who meets you heart to heart.
I am so grateful for her work; the dance classes are super fun.
She provides a space where I feel incredibly safe, allowing me to go deep both
mentally, emotionally, and physically.
She has become a good-hearted light sister.
Therapist

Helene Berven Johansen
Forest bathing and dancing intuitively at Amelia's workshops have taught me
numerous things. She has many beautiful tools
for opening up creativity, staying conscious in the present moment, silencing
thoughts, and getting deeper into a
meditative trance state.
Artist

Hilde Ring Sørensen
Amelia is very knowledgeable and wise; her calm and comfortable way feels good
for a tired body. It shows that she has the experience. Her work is perfect for my
mind, body, and soul. Thank you so much for giving me great experiences and for
helping me transform my life.
Business owner

***

*Remember, your health is your wealth. Give yourself a break, and celebrate
who you are, your uniqueness, and your amazingness.*

Dr. Ella Ford Mthethwa (hc)
Ellagence Wellness Boutique & Ellagence Foundation
Pretoria, Gauteng, South Africa
emthethwa@gmail.com

Chapter 45
Wellness & Beauty Meet Confidence

The Inspiration: A God-Fearing Praying Mom

Dr. Ella at age 26 (left) in the military and age 50 (right) at an Ellagence Bootcamp in Ellagence gear.

Dr Ella Ford Mthethwa (hc) is the founder of Ellagence Wellness Boutique & Foundation, a Health Professional, entrepreneur, Healthy Lifestyle Coach, Marketing Strategist for Africa, USA and Middle East, Motivational Speaker, Multimedia Contributor, a National Director for the International Youth Society SA and Chairperson Ladies of All Nations International SA.

Mission and Vision

Dr. Ella's mission is to build healthy communities across South Africa and beyond through holistic health and wellness initiatives - empowering women and youth to live healthy, to be confident, and for families to work together to prevent lifestyle diseases in order to raise children who are healthy, well balanced so that they can reach their full potential.

Starting from Scratch
From Barefoot to Stilettos!

Whilst Ellagence has stood the test of time and overcome disaster, the question often raised is: "How did it all begin?"

From humble beginnings running barefoot on the streets of a township called Machibisa in KZN South Africa to jet setting across the globe with corporate responsibilities in Africa, the USA, and the Middle East - this has been my journey. We had a serene childhood until my dad passed away at an early age which meant that my widowed mom and all of us struggled financially. The drive and entrepreneurial spark were ignited by her and the number of women who surrounded me in the township, some widowed, some heading single-parent households who built their own small businesses, religiously working under strenuous conditions in the "apartheid" era, to ensure a better future for their children - a good foundation for understanding the value of good work ethic. Ellagence Wellness Boutique was founded and grounded on these values and has been successful in fostering change in families towards living a healthy lifestyle globally. It is upon this grounding that Ellagence has been resuscitated and rebuilt from the depths of ruin.

The journey of Ellagence is a testimony of how important it is to respect the learnings from one's humble beginnings and to use these as your guiding principles that keep one grounded as the brand grows. These key learnings and principles have certainly helped in building the Ellagence brand and they can do the same for you too!

Big Why
Bouncing Back

I keep bouncing back as a brand and in corporate from the toughest of circumstances through **Resilience, Grounding**, and **Faith in God** inculcated by my parents from an early age. Losing my furniture and merchandise to various factors including burning down to the ground during the SA riots in 2021 as well as theft was an obstacle I overcame through the principles and values of my parents and faith in God. They always encouraged us to embark on ventures

that we were passionate about where we fulfill our purpose and are able to flourish whilst serving. They also taught us to pray and encouraged us to always be grounded in the word of God.

For me, the misfortunes have served as an opportunity to start afresh, to go bigger and be bolder, this in pursuit of my bigger "why". I would encourage anyone going through the same to go the extra mile, to trust God, and take the "ruins" in their lives, clear them and start rebuilding at a much higher level. Go for your Bigger Why!

Aha Moment Epiphany
The Light Bulb Moment

There are times in life when you're in the depths of disaster, on the brink of depression, you've lost it all and you feel like a failure and then you see the light. For me, it came through divine intervention after a period of prayer, fasting, and serving God. I had to forgive myself for some of the choices that I had made and made an extra effort in self-care so that I could help others who were in the same situation as myself through living healthy. Because other women could relate, they triggered another major revelation and idea to launch a range of well-fitting, comfortable activewear for women of all shapes and sizes. This is an idea that came during a series of women empowerment workshops where women voiced their concerns around the negative impact of not having the right gym attire on their health journey. After the launch, the Ellagence range grew into a lucrative brand serving customers across South Africa and is set to expand across the globe.

This really illustrates that your aha moment can lead to your breakthrough so go ahead and act on your aha moment to unlock your potential.

Secret Formula
Finding Beauty Inside and Out

Self-love grounded by God is the secret formula that has enabled me to serve and share a love for people. The genuine passion to empower women to find their true beauty (inside and out) for the benefit of themselves and their families has also impacted communities and has also propelled Ellagence as a brand with purpose. My faith and grounding in God enabled me to take a "leap of faith" to focus solely on the business during Covid 19 which resulted in a successful brand that was able to sustain me financially during the difficult times. Prior to the hard lockdown, Ellagence Wellness Boutique conducted

workshops for women and youth as well as healthy lifestyle family boot camps and also participated in various health and wellness initiatives, including expos. The target audience was engaged directly in these activations across South Africa and in various virtual communities across social media and radio. Clients have developed a close affiliation to the brand which has stood the test of time given the ability to transform the lives of so many that have been attracted to the solution-based approach of engagement and marketing.

My advice to potential entrepreneurs is to build an emotional connection with their customers by providing value-added solution-based services which will sustain their brands.

Steps to Success To Build from Scratch
Rebuilding Ruins

The most important steps to rebuilding from scratch have been through Self Care and through a Consumer-Centric approach to rebuilding the brand.

THE JOURNEY CONTINUES:

🏠 ELLAGENCE Enterprises (Pty) Ltd
1466 Breyer Avenue, Waverley 0186

📱 +27 (0) 76 312 6073

✉️ ellagence@ellagence.info

A healthy lifestyle: The key to Longevity of Health and sustaining Ellagence

Self-care means looking after oneself through living a Healthy Lifestyle so that there is a rebirth and revival, a transformation that enables one to find their inner beauty that shines on the outside, building the confidence to pursue the dream of a global brand.

From a brand perspective, consumer centricity has been key.
Understanding and fulfilling client needs remain the key to success.

1. Invest in understanding the latest client needs to drive your comeback strategy
2. Understand the value chain of the product/service otherwise, the business loses money
3. Invest in a robust customer recruitment strategy from the onset incorporating the brand positioning, product, price, promotions, and place.
4. Influencers have become key in recruitment - rope in nano and micro-Influencers to help with awareness of the product whilst building credibility
5. Reward loyal clients who voluntarily become your brand ambassadors
6. Be a business with purpose by giving back to build a strong emotional bond that keeps clients coming back

First Sign of Success
Brand Loyalty

The face of success has been evident in the increased brand awareness of Ellagence, the sales as well as loyalty through repeat purchases of clients with some requesting a brand extension to a male range and various other products. Brand awareness increased across South Africa and beyond as clients shared their appreciation of the brand through Word Of Mouth and on social media. The best was when women began sharing personal stories about how the brand transformed their lives and made them feel confident and helped to accelerate their journey to healthy living.

Ultimate Solution
Transformation - Results - Consistency

The testimonials from women and families whose lives have been transformed have been vital. Consumer centricity through investigation, investment, and consistent quality continue to be key in finding the holistic solution for my clients. This comes with being thorough in understanding the need and then sourcing the best products and services with a unique proposition.

Free Offer

Take the leap to your transformation and connect with us on Facebook through the founder Ella Ford Mthethwa and on Instagram at ellagence_wellness_boutique for your healthy lifestyle and activewear solution. Ellagence is also a hub for information to empower families to live healthy so connect with Ellagence on these platforms for the latest Offer!

Accolades and Achievements

Accolades include awards from the South African Military Service and several corporate awards from multinationals including Nestlé, Mondelez, Marico, and others.
In 2020 I was also celebrated with the Nelson Mandela Foundation Award during women's month.

Additional awards include Mrs. Uniworld South Africa 2019 2nd Princess; Mrs. Intellect; Mrs. Fitness and Business Woman of the Year; Influential Women of the Year 2018 and 2020/2021; World Class Top 20 Female Leaders 2022 and others.

I was awarded the Doctorate in Humanitarianism from the GIA University based in Georgia, USA. Additional global awards include the Woman of Wonder Award, Red Blazer Award, and the Olympus International Women's Day Award 2022.

See What They Are Saying...

"Thank you, my sister, for changing my life with all your support. You have transformed my life by exposing me to the world. I am not only looking after myself on my journey of self-care, but now I have a global network that will help me with my business and my financial stability! "
- *Londiwe Mchunu,* SA activist with disabilities and Vermiculture Farmer

" When I walk in the gym wearing my Ellagence gear I feel so confident. I can see people watching me and thinking that perhaps I'm a new trainer! This boosts my efforts in pursuit of being healthy! "
- *Sebe* (30 Something, Female)

" Working with Ellagence is an absolute pleasure. Not only do I value the fact that this business supports local small entities in the township, she has also helped me tremendously as a mentor in defining my strategies and adding value to our customers."
- *Qondile Concepts* - youth-owned, township-based black business.

As a successful businessperson, many challenging times often require one to dig deep and rebuild and restore what is lost. This is what happened to me at the height of Covid 19 and when the mall containing Ellagence material was burnt to the ground during the riots in South Africa. What is evident from my story and many who had the very same experience is that resilience pays off. Whilst the pandemic was an unwelcome tragedy, it also presented numerous opportunities in the health and wellness space, which I leveraged, and which helped me to be financially afloat. This is a sure sign of the importance of building brands with strong equity and never giving up.

Wellness & Beauty Meets Confidence

Connect with me:
Contact Ellagence to start your journey.

Blinq Link :
https://blinq.me/8ZPkRFB4PWXTywxsixpZ

Eva Maria Dias
Phoenix Human Capital Solutions
Miami Beach, Florida, USA
evadias@phoenixhcsolutions.com

Chapter 46
Winning With and Through Others

Eva Dias is a Senior Business Executive, who has developed her career in Human Resources within 4 of the biggest Corporations in the world, all leaders in their industry – Philip Morris, L'Oréal, Novartis and IFF – International Flavours & Fragrances. She has worked in different industries and countries around the globe, such as Brazil, Portugal, Switzerland, France, and since 2003 in the US. She is currently the CEO & Founder of Phoenix Human Capital Solutions, a Human Resources practice with the mission of helping people and organizations to unveil and unleash the best version of themselves. She is a certified Coach on Core Energy Leadership, Public Speaker, Co-Chaired the Diversity, Equity & Inclusion Council at Miami Beach and one of the Board of Governors of the Chamber of Commerce, Co-Founder of the Life Science Women Network, and a member of the Global Trade Chamber from which she has been granted the Global Award "100 Successful Women in Business". She speaks English, Portuguese, Spanish, and French fluently. A Brazilian American, she holds a B.S. in Business Administration, is married to Augusto, and has a little dog called Bela. Her mantra is: "Always shoot for the moon; if you miss it, you may still land amongst stars"

Mission and Vision

"Helping people and organizations to unveil and unleash the best version of themselves."

"Life is a journey, enjoy the ride" - I love this quote and would only add that we are a choice in our lives. It is really up to us to choose the lives we want to live. Whether you are a woman or belong to any other "minority group" do not hide behind any stereotype to justify why things do not happen to you! Women are about 50% of the population of the planet! - This is not by definition a "minority". Look at the mirror every day and tell yourself: I want, I can, and I get it!

Starting from Scratch
Biggest Opportunity-Interrupted!

It was the year 2015. I was living the best phase of my career as a Human Resources professional with my 3rd company, one of the top 3 pharmaceuticals in the world. I've worked there for about 10 years. I was responsible for one of the 5 regions of my division, supporting the President and all employees, having the opportunity to implement high-impact projects throughout the region, receiving all the recognition I've always desired, regionally and globally, and having the opportunity to work and influence important changes in the talent management spectrum until that day that a headhunter from New York knocked on my door. That has changed my life forever. I've decided to accept the GREATEST position of my career with my last employer, a company that produces fragrances and flavors for its clients, headquartered in New York City. Many reasons drove my decision: returning to live and work in the Big Apple for the 3rd time - you know ... if you make it there, you can make it anywhere. Taking global responsibility for the Fragrance

Division, a great promotion from my prior role, working in a business that was close to a "fairy tale" - yes, somehow, being part of the artistic and exclusive environment that permeates the creation of a fragrance can be beyond inspiring and attractive (at least in my frivolous imagination). Do you know that there are more Astronauts than perfumers in the world?? And the compensation was a "Yes" deal! I've just informed my poor husband that we were moving to NYC which he's agreed on with some reservations. We packed up everything, rented our beautiful apartment in Miami Beach, took our 2 dogs, and there we went…

Unfortunately, I have to admit that the signs of a very bad decision started to shed very early in that experience. Nothing was the way I was expecting: New York has become one of the worst places to live - noisy, dirty, polluted, and outrageously expensive - remember my "Yes" deal compensation? I could barely pay my bills and have some money to spend for the rest of the month. My apartment was the size of one of my Miami Beach apt. bedrooms, and I still remember going to bed at night and thinking of how low that ceiling was that I was so afraid of getting crushed during my sleep. Then there was my "glamorous job", which in consideration to the people who hired me with all the best intentions, I will not talk about it, only I'd say my expectations were way above what I found, adding up to the ocean of frustration that raged my life. But....despite all the great disappointment and regrets I've kept going for about 18 months - as always, fighting to succeed!

BIG Why
Why on earth am I here in this world?

Failure is not an option! I have been a very determined person since I was born, I believe. I think my big "WHY" has been my life purpose: Work with people and living an International life. That's been my fuel to have accomplished everything I did. Coming from a very tiny city from the west of Brazil, being raised in Sao Paulo and for 24 years now being outside my country, and living my foreigner life, have been a real blessing! 5 of these 24 years were spent in Europe, in Portugal, Switzerland, and France and I have been in the US for 19 years now. And every time, I've faced a big challenge in the course of my journey, I would go back to my purpose to remind myself why I was doing things that way. So, my advice? Have a purpose for your life and live by it every moment! You can't go wrong! Believe in yourself and your power to accomplish things. You will have all your dreams come true. Your motivation to accomplish what you want will be way more powerful if what you want is aligned to your life purpose.

Aha Moment Epiphany
Making lemons into a lemon pie!

He started to visit all the vision specialists in New York and nobody could diagnose his disease. Meantime, I had to make a decision whether I should continue in NYC or do something else. In the absence of an answer and with all the backlashes of my decision, I have decided to quit my job and get back to Miami. In the beginning, it was one of the most difficult and challenging times of my life. I had spent practically my whole life working for Corporations and counting on the "security" they offer without having to be concerned about anything except "being successful" doing what I was doing there. And of course, my success was dictated by their standards, not mine. I was really afraid and felt my floor disappear, and my little confidence faded away to almost "zero".

For quite some time I could not sleep well and still remember waking up with my body shaking and thinking that perhaps that decision could be even worse than moving to NYC to my new job and what on earth I could do to fix that. Augusto's loss of vision took about 3 months to be diagnosed. We found out through a doctor from NY that he has a congenital very rare disease known as Leber or LHON - Leber Hereditary Optic Neuropathy transmitted by the mother, normally developed in the male children, and yes, since then we had to leave with it as yet there has been no cure for this disease.

This was the driver for me to "reinvent" myself. I've decided to put together my own Human Resources practice to have the flexibility to take care of my husband. In July 2017, Phoenix Human Capital Solutions was born! I've taken a coaching certification with iPEC, one of the most credible Coaching institutes in the world. By learning and applying their Core Leadership Energy methodology, I have changed my life. I have to say that looking back, gratitude is the biggest thing that comes to mind. I am so grateful for what happened to me because that made me a much better person. I've had the opportunity to reconnect with myself and start loving myself unconditionally. Today I am even more caring of others but what they think of me does not define me anymore as it used to be in the past. My level of stress went down significantly as I've learned how to block it, and I am a much happier person, despite the challenges that come my way. All I can say is that I am very proud of what I became over the past 6 years, and I do celebrate it every day!

Secret Formula
Detachment, self-acceptance, and much more....

Focus on others' success! That's my secret formula for my own success. I dedicate 100% to my clients, one client at a time. I really care about spending time understanding what it is that they want to ensure I would design and deliver the best solutions to help them be very successful individually when coaching them. Or, managing the most important asset of their business - Their People! I prospect clients through network groups - Chambers, BNI(biggest network in the world), Social Media - LinkedIn, Facebook, Instagram, etc. However, what I found to be the most effective way to get new clients are referrals - being referred by someone who has used our services means you are being powerfully endorsed to success. Human Resources is a function that can be delivered to any type of business - small, medium, big. It is what I deliver those changes according to the size of the business, industry, and my client's wishes. For small businesses I deliver full HR support, medium and big business can benefit from different offers I have, such as Team alignment or Powerful performing Teams, Coaching, Leadership Training,

Diversity & Inclusion Training, etc. I also work for individuals on Coaching, Outplacement. I just want to go back to my secret formula: when you love and accept yourself unconditionally, your self-confidence, awareness, consciousness will go up without limits, as I consider this to be a non-stop job. As a consequence, you start to lower your judgment and your energy goes very high! That's the

pathway to make those surrounding you your focus, not the other way around. Looking back into my career in Corporations, I do remember doing everything most of the time for my own good. This is a big burden that I and all colleagues I see around in the same situation have to carry on, to be "successful". I can share with you that it feels good to get rid of this burden and focus on other's success, just because you know you are already taken care of.

Steps to Build Success from Scratch
"A dream without a plan is just a wish" Antoine de Saint-Exupéry
I believe in the meaning of this quote. Here are the steps I took:
1. Put together a business plan - I've used the Canvas Model as it is quite comprehensive to help identify everything, we need to be successful: From Key Partners to Income Streams,
2. I've started to execute my business plan: Identify Key partners, Key activities, Business Value Proposition, Develop Client relationships, Define Customer segments, Identify suppliers, Cost structure, Key resources, and revenue streams.
3. Focus on the Prospection of clients based on the Business Plan.
4. Take a very positive, resilient attitude. Becoming a "Solopreneur " coming from my background is NOT an easy thing to do, but I've never doubted it was the right thing to do for me.

First Sign of Success
My first win

The first sign of success came with my first client! This was critical for me to believe I could continue my journey as a "Solopreneur". My biggest support came from my lovely husband. It feels really good that he "has my back" and he is here for me, incentivizing me, believing in my potential, and many times contributing with great ideas! Celebration of successes is also very powerful in helping you to stay the course and not look back on your decisions. When you celebrate you put an important milestone on what you accomplish. Another important building block is to surround yourself with positive, energetic people who believe on you and will be there to help with the walks of your journey!

Ultimate Solution
The power of the 7 energies!!!! Core Energy Leadership Model

I think my coaching certification was instrumental to consolidate what and how I wanted to work with my clients. Through my learnings I went through a big transition and shifted paradigms as a consequence. I've found that I was very successful in my life and career - no doubt with the corporations I've worked for, but somehow the focus of my success was "my own self". In this new life, I am fully concentrating on others' success. That means I am helping my clients to get rid of the ghost of stress that chases them 24/7, unveil and unleash their potential to achieve whatever they want, increase self-awareness and consciousness, lower judgment, and live a much more accomplished life. For women particularly, I help them to connect with themselves, increase their self-confidence, and just take on their place because a woman's place is where she wants to be! I go around and meet with women from around the globe. For some reason, there is still this stigma that we do not have yet our space fully established. My advice: Get rid of this limiting belief! The space and the place are yours! Go get it!!!!

Free Gift

We have been gone through very important changes in the world over the past 2-3 years, driving the VUCA effect - Volatility, Uncertainty, Complexity, and Ambiguity in all dimensions of our lives and of course tremendously affecting the workplace. Besides the list of offers I have - you can access it in my website: www.phoenishcsolutions.com, I can be the person who will help you, Leaders, to deal with this so turbulent moment in your companies! How? give one example: HELPING YOU ALIGNING AND ENGAGE YOUR HYBRID TEAMS (IN AND HOME OFFICE WORKERS) AROUND THE SAME OBJECTIVE AND BEING VERY EFFECTIVE DELIVERING UPON EXPECTATIONS OF YOUR BUSINESS, DESPITE THE DISTANCE BETWEEN THEM AND FLOW OF COMMUNICATION - I.E. VIRTUAL VS. IN PERSON.

Accolades and Achievements

I am one of the co-chairs of the first Diversity & Inclusion Council and Board of Governors at the Miami Beach Chamber, Awarded the 100 Most Successful Women Award in 2020, Co-author of the book "Empowered Women" Cover of Global Trade Chamber and Most Successful Women in Business magazines, and public speaker in several Human Resources related conferences

See What They Are Saying...

I coached a client to cope with a life-threatening disease of her husband and helped her get the strength and resilience she needed to deal with such a challenging moment of her life,

I helped one of my women clients to unblock serious "limiting beliefs" to become fully accomplished in her life, professionally and personally

I helped a woman to unveil her life purpose and live by it in everything she does. She's found much more pleasure and feel way more accomplished in her life now.

***

Books and Business Links
Book "Empowered Women" - launched in 2022, Several articles in LinkedIn and other social media: IG, FB, Tweeter. Cover of Global Trade Chamber and Successful Women in Business Magazines

www.linkedin.com/in/eva-dias-1a80388

Gail P. Birks (Williams)
CMA Enterprise Incorporated
Davie, Florida, USA
Info@cma-ent.com

Chapter 47
You Really Can Have it ALL

Gail Birks is President of CMA Enterprise Incorporated, a full-service consulting and advisory firm since 1990. A seasoned Corporate Director, Ms. Birks attended Tennessee State University (BBA - Economics, and Finance) and Florida International University (Executive MBA (Business/Strategic Management). She completed post-graduate work in HR Administration and Industrial Psychology and is a Lean Six Sigma Master Black Belt Practitioner and Mediator; Ms. Birks is also the Managing Director of The Breakthru Institute, wholly owned by CMA and is a Full-Service Training company.

Mission and Vision

My Mission is to provide innovative Consulting/Advisory and Training Experiences to Individuals and Organizations in Business and Industry globally. The ultimate goal is to guide my clients to own their Sustainable Success Models for long-term market positioning.

Starting from Scratch
My Undiscovered Success

Success for me has come to have quite a few chapters, and while I find my steps ordered, achieving my goals has sometimes proven to be quite an adventure. Most were formed as a result of the universe aligning. This means that when the resources were needed, the levels of confidence and a strong sense of worth were acknowledged. I always ask my clients and colleagues if they have found their roadmap with the ordered steps. As we smile about it, this is truly something that brings about "UNDISCOVERED SUCCESS" along the way.

One **DISCOVERED OPPORTUNITY** was during my cancer battles in 2009 and 2013. Not being able to move much, I was restricted to my computer and found myself creating what is now The Breakthru Institute, my training company. Now, this is where you know that you have a strong village. This discovery was not due to my need to create this company; it was because my husband took my car keys and demanded that I take the time to heal. He walked me into my office, sat me in my chair, and pointed to the computer and credenza with one message..." Figure it out in here (meaning the office)". This was my world for 8 weeks. I did obey.

Probably the only time that I have. So, think about how your discovered opportunity came about and created sustainable success for you.

From these short-term losses, I learned that they were really undiscovered opportunities waiting for me to be acknowledged. My illness, which could have been critical, gave me the blessing that I was seeking but did not know how to access. "BE STILL AND KNOW!!!"

Big Why
Destroying My Business is Not an Option

My Big Why came when I finally decided to end what had been a 9-year nightmare. I was getting a divorce at a time when I really thought I needed that support from my life partner. But that was not in the cards. My estranged husband tried to destroy my business because he thought it would make him feel better about being cast out. I could not understand why there was so much chaos and "hate" in him. But he did not understand that this dream called CMA Enterprise Incorporated was going to be a reality with or without him. I fought too hard to get to this point, and besides, my daughter needed to have a good example of a strong yet caring woman as her example. Without giving too much detail, I can say that I am one of those survivors of Domestic Violence who blazed the trail for women to have better protection when law enforcement is called to a home. My experience brought my village to my aid and watched over me during a wrongful arrest. A judge who had compassion for me knew that I did not belong in this situation. Even my clients said that he probably deserved the beating I gave him when I decided that Destroying my Business was not an Option. I tell this story and have seen over the

years that there are more women who have walked in my shoes than I realized.... Very Successful Women. And this was their incentive to SUCCEED!!!!! This experience prepared me for the fearlessness in business so that I now have business engagements and environments that I was entering even now. I learned to PROTECT my business like a mother hen protects her chicks. The young women who have watched me over the years understand that "FAILURE IS NOT AN OPTION." Neither is allowing others to define your pathway in life or the road to SUCCESS.

Aha Moment
Radical is good...

My Epiphany actually came to me in Corporate America when I looked at my clients and 99% did not look like me but were of other ethnicities, ages, and lifestyles. One year I sent out my personal Christmas Cards because I was being me again. Later that day, a client called me, and she was very upset. Well, I had forgotten about the cards. When I asked her what was wrong, she said nothing and that she was embarrassed. She then shared that she had opened up a Christmas card someone had sent her, and it had Black Angels on it. Well, she said that she did not know any Black people. Then she opened it up and saw my name. She said that she cried because when she thought of me, she did not see color. She said..." You are family to us because you take care of us.". WELL!!!!! My clients are seeking solutions and are not necessarily concerned that I am a woman or African American. Sometimes you have to be a little radical to take people on an Unexpected Journey to a realm of new Discovery.

Life Ingredients for Success

What do you do to transform a life? Impact women to help them tap into greatness? *My secret formula* is just being prepared and having the right attitude to be cast out into the universe. I serve GOD first, my family second, and my wellness third. It then allows me to serve the business, industry, government, and most important the leaders therein. My clients tend to find me because of the results that I achieve with them. But I also make them feel as if they are the only ones that I serve in their times of need. At CMA my teams and I bring NEW PERSPECTIVES FOR SUSTAINABLE SUCCESS that keep a NURTURING TOUCH in the formula. My Father always shared biblical wisdom which included ..." Look to the Hills

from which cometh your help." And I do Constantly.

You Really Can Have it ALL

Being Transparent, Sincere, and Prepared has been key to my Life Ingredients for Success. Your formula is based on those ingredients that best "season" your dish that you want to serve to your universe; take careful steps and insights when crafting them.

Steps to Build Success from Scratch

I attract clients through social media, online open mic, client referrals, and warm introductions. These strategies are important because if you are just starting in business, it immediately gives you the "World as your Oyster." It also gives you the "Big City Image" that is important when courting larger companies.

Some of the other considerations…
1. Investigate the competition because they certainly are checking you out.
2. Determine how to fill the gaps that exist in the service that you are proposing.
3. Create the types of services that clients can benefit from while not over-promising and under-delivering.
4. Bring quality service regardless of the size of the client. This is how you create your choir.
6. Give sustainable results by teaching our clients "how to fish" as opposed to just giving them one.
6. Let your clients know that "you see them", "you hear them", and "you acknowledge and support them" until they are stronger to walk alone. They will tell you that they are "finished for now."

Create your Steps so that you can "move the stones" in the direction that you need them to point.

343

First Sign of Success

The first sign of success was when I signed my first major YES!!!!! It was with Mercedes Benz U.S. International. My spirit said... You are on your way. I celebrated with my inner circle. I have a small circle of people with whom I celebrate the good, bad, and ugly times. I have a large database. The key was that I was not intimidated by the name or the size of the company. I know my focus and OWN IT!!!. I know my VALUE PROPOSITION (what I offer) and I SHARED IT with CONFIDENCE!!!!! Being a Woman in Business is not for the Faint of Heart, and I understand clearly that FAILURE IS NOT AN OPTION IN MY FORMULA FOR SUCCESS. Include in your business plan to take time to do your happy dance on a regular basis... However, you define it.

My Community is My Rock Peer Ultimate Solution

I was mentored by my Father and a few others. My first woman mentor outside of my mom is Beverley Spraggins. She was the first Black Woman Executive I met in my first internship. To this day, I keep in touch with her. The influence that she had on me was not felt until I became an Executive and started reflecting on her positioning, her professionalism, and her kind yet sternness needed to manage her spot in the executive suite.

My Community is meticulously chosen and filtered because it is important to maintain a steady flow of "clean" energy. That means having people who can tell you what you need to know and not necessarily what you want to hear.

Finding the right community for me was peace of mind. Just like for my clients, it is knowing that we switched the right lights on to see the way to Sustainable Success and Transformation. My team and I are practitioners. And they are my business community. Some of them are welcomed into my personal community. And it should be noted that there is a difference. Some things you just don't share with everyone. Your communities also reflect your circle of wealth.

Just keep that in mind. When you need that all-important and necessary support or lift, that is when your communities will step in.

As a businesswoman, I find it important to let my website visitors know who my community is https://www.cma-ent.com/about.

— ●◆ —

You Really Can Have it ALL

Free Gift or Offer

"A short Chat" at my expense. It is my honor to offer five (5) complimentary 30-minute coaching sessions. You never know the difference a short chat can make in your life. In a span of 30-minutes, you can get focused and intentional. Reach out to me at https://cma-ent.com/contact . Put in the subject box "A Short Chat" and your name. I will send you the link to the schedule.

Accolades and Achievements

I have been honored over the years for being a visionary, community, business leader, trailblazer in business, and mentor. Each time it is like the first one offered to celebrate my contributions as a Woman/Woman of Color in Business.

Honors include... Ms. Birks' honors include 100 Successful Women in Business, 2022 - Global Trade Chamber; Luminary MBE Award – U.S. Dept of Commerce/MBDA, 2016; Top 100 Most Influential Black Professionals in South Florida – ICABA -2012; Top 50 Most Powerful Black Professionals in South Florida -2011 Legacy Magazine; Alpha Kappa Alpha Sorority, Inc., Top Hat Award in Business and Entrepreneurship - 2008; Greater Fort Lauderdale Chamber of Commerce Women's Council of Commerce Circle of Excellence Award in Business – 2007; Outstanding Advisory Board Member – 2004-2005; "In The Company of Women", Miami Dade County – 2001; National Association of Business and Professional Women Business Champion – 2001; Florida International University Executive MBA Class of 1999, "Best Presenter"; JM Family Enterprises African American Achiever in Business – 1994.

See What They Are Saying...

Woman Executive who "lost her voice" This client was coached by me for 18 months. We rediscovered her confidence and her "WHY" I am Here and "Where" I am going. When we were done, her confidence was restored, and she was leading for sustainable success.

***

Woman Entrepreneur who was not sure that she could "do" that next step needed to realize success. We brainstormed not only her expectations for herself but those the company had for her. It was like watching a flower blossom as she discovered her gifts and how to manifest them in her chosen market.

***

You Really Can Have it ALL

Young Woman who lost her job and decided that she was not going back to the high anxiety of no stability. I was able to assist her in transitioning into entrepreneurship, and 15 years later, she is still in business and it has allowed motherhood to be easier to manage. She shared that the lessons taught changed her life."

***

Business Links

Visit the Product store at https://www.cma-ent.com/cma-media-products

Learn more at
https://www.cma-ent.com

Be sure to collect your FREE giveaway!

Viola Edward
GRIT Academy
Nicosia, Cyprus
viola@violaedward,com

Chapter 48
Your GRIT is your Foundation

Founder/CEO of GRIT Academy. Multi-awarded personal & corporate advisor/mentor. Transcultural psychotherapist, mentoring & breathwork trainer. Global connector. Humanitarian, social entrepreneur. Partner of Creative Women Platform and Ugivme Startup.

She has been pioneering and developing emotional well-being and mental health fitness in the workplace since the nineties, bridging the space between breathwork therapy and business management. She now works internationally with individual and corporate clients in cross-pollination between self-development, management, and leadership. As a creative entrepreneur, she is a synergist, developing innovative schemes, her latest is Managing by Emotions. She is the co-creator of BQ – Breath Intelligence and GRIT Method. Author. Board member. Caring alliances to achieve the SDG's goals. Ambassador for Human Rights.

Mission and Vision

"We believe that positive impact in the world starts with self-transformation. At the GRIT Academy we make self-development, personal, and professional growth simple, accessible, and meaningful.

Our purpose is to enable millions of people to learn and practice the GRIT Methodology so that they can be healthier, happier, resilient, and at service.

Starting from Scratch

You may have lost many things in life but you still have yourself. Organic resilience is about standing up more nurtured and wiser. The best of it is that you can share this knowledge and wisdom with others. You are a very important key for all evolution.

Resilience

Inheriting my mother's resilience, I became a woman living a meaningful and loving life as I have been on a continuous path of growth. I have been a migrant frequently in my life, recreating myself each time, learning new languages and ways of how to get smoothly into the new culture while getting over the grief of what was left behind and, in some cases, never being able to return because of a political regime or a war.

Exploring, learning, and expanding in a sustainable way has been my passion since age 13 when I interrupted my formal schooling and started working for a living to help my mother and sister; my father passed away when I was 3. Non-formal education has been and still is my best companion, having led me to the delight of creating teaching spaces that enable people to develop, grow and sustain, individually and in groups.

To survive in the best way possible, learn from the experience, and mentor others with what I learned and mastered. I had the glory to read "Man Search for Meaning" by Dr. Viktor Frankl at a very early age, maybe at 11 or 12, and at that age, this is how I interpreted it, and I keep following those steps.

Big Why
Emotional Well-being

I was a thoughtful child. I loved reading. I started reading Freud at 11 years old, and I discovered the power of emotional freedom.

This knowledge didn't save me from experiencing chaos in my life but what it did for me is give me the power to ask for help to get out of the chaos and get my full freedom as an adult. My big why is now to be of service to others to identify, discover, and obtain their emotional freedom in life and therefore in business. I am here to remind you to take care of your emotional well-being. Make sure to reach out and ask for help. I am here for you so reach out for support and join my community to thrive and be who you are meant to be. You are not alone.

Aha Moment Epiphany
Freedom

When I was 27, I was a successful marketing manager of an Insurance Broker company, I had already been working for 14 years. By then, my family and I had migrated twice with a lot of grief, and losses, and with every immigration, we lost our social stages. I had long-term grief in my life that I went into an addiction to silence grief. Silencing my grief was not a good thing. I was young, good-looking, intelligent, and with a tremendous passion to learn and advance in life...BUT with the same intensity to self-destruction. My aha moment was when I was 27 years old when a person told me that I was the freest person that he had ever met. In that instance, I understood that I was not free, I had huge grief holding me back and I was an addict. Then I felt the strongest, the root of my family, energy, and chose life. It is when I asked for professional help.

My love for freedom made me choose life. I promised to honor life until my last breath and help others to do so. Then I got seriously into psychotherapy studies and work. I am a mentor and psychotherapist.

If you find yourself in my shoes or in a similar situation, you need to stop, reflect, observe, and learn to ask for help.

Secret Formula
Continuous Self-Development and Sharing

I dare to follow my intuition and purpose and ask mentors to help me when I need it. I always keep learning while sharing with others the changes and the discoveries of my journey. This is my formula. I help people understand their behavior, and the layers of emotions under their behaviors to become emotionally immune.

You must learn to breathe consciously, remember as you are breathing you are alive; therefore, you have infinite possibilities to transform. From being emotionally immune, you will be able to follow your purpose, and vision, thrive, and be successful therefore naturally be ready to serve others. I am learning and teaching/mentoring all the time wherever I am.

This formula took me wide and high to so many countries, companies, and new spaces such as publishing my first book in 1998 "Breathing the Rhythm of Success" when publishing was so difficult. I was so humbled by the opportunity I got, so I always shared it.

My book was like a diplomatic passport when I moved from Venezuela to Cyprus., I had something to say and to share., I had published a book.

Your GRIT is your Foundation

Steps to Build Success from Scratch
I am here because I dare.

If you dare to work on yourself, truly and deeply you will dare to follow your dreams. Maybe even you will support others to do so. Below you will find simple steps to start and/or continue your conscious successful journey:

- 1st: to know who I am, the bright and the shadow. I learned to dance between them. My self-discovery and emotional well-being was helped by mentors and therapists; then I became a psychotherapist and mentor.
- 2nd: to learn how to BREATHE in a conscious breath and connected way. Breathing is synonymous with a life of life, caring about how we breathe and taking it to another level is caring about how to live fully. I became a Breathworker.
- 3rd: to forgive the self and others and, of course, to amend.
- 4th: To be in gratitude
- 5th: is to have a vision, purpose, and objectives for short and medium terms and several action plans
- 6th: to be able to let go without forgetting the bigger purpose of being at service for a greater good

First Sign of Success

Success started when I healed from being a victim; it was automatic. I was 34. Finally, I was awakened, alert, and relaxed, sure of who I am... filled with energy that I used in a sustainable way. Then, fame and prosperity came, I learned learn, applied the theories, and proved what worked and what did not. Mainly, it was a simple dynamic meaningful slide into holistic success and it continues now. Remember the ultimate goal is the end but to enjoy the process and keep learning what life presents us.

Ultimate Solution
Breathe the Joy of Life as Emotional Balance is Happening

My first clients were m: My therapist/mentor and a business consultant that I admired much. Both paid me double of my fee. I still keep their blessing and support.

I have wonderful mentors in life. My vision is that everyone could have mentors.

Mentors lived an experience and managed to learn from it and, capitalized it into wisdom. They are trained professionally to support you in elaborating the maps to make it easier and more effective to go on your journey.

I am almost sure that you have learned how to manage objectively and surely by values...Now is the time to add to these fundamental areas how to manage my emotions. Yes, emotional well-being is a key factor in every business's health and success, to strengthen and expand in a sustained way and with the social responsibility required nowadays. Almost 30 years in this field will be at your service.

It doesn't matter what your gender, age, ethnicity, trauma, or drama, you have the possibility to heal and thrive. If I achieve it, you will, too.

Let's connect to help you gain clarity and tap into your success. I am just a breath away from you. I believe you have everything you need to thrive.

Free Gift

I connect amazing humans to one another and connect people to life-changing opportunities. **The free** gift is a semi-scholarship to the GRIT Star program. If you are serious and ready to dive into self-development join my GRIT Star program which is a seven-week long program and two hours a week. If you are committed to change, expanding, and transforming, it is my honor to present you with this amazing scholarship.

Accolades and Achievements

I am blessed and honored to have been internationally recognized and awarded. I am a Mentor by heart and by profession, and I like the human being I have become, All of the recognitions are very important and the ones here are representing all the others—.
The Outstanding Contribution to Mentoring and the Honorary Causa Mentoring. Aspirational Woman Award and the Leadership and humanitarian Honoris Causa Doctorate.
Thank you Always

See What They Are Saying...

I am a lawyer by profession, I got trained as a Breathwork-Mentor with Viola and the team. Besides learning the technique, I was coached, mentored, and supported to get through my personal challenges and negative patterns. We had wonderful group dynamics. Viola was amazing in navigating between teaching and helping each one of us individually and in a group.

**

My journey started 15 years ago with this woman who makes me happy with my existence and with this philosophy I have taken the path of joy and success. I was on my own and now I am married and the mother of two beautiful souls. She is always next to me and all of her clients. I don't know how she can do this successfully, being professional and having her own family at the same time.

***

How I feel about having Viola in my life, and the joy and freedom I am living as a result of our paths meeting. Viola is a pure shining embodiment of love, light, and support. She has supported me in healing my heart, encouraged me to exceed my limits and step out of my comfort zone, and held the space for me to overcome my fears and step into my courage and into my light. She is the epitome of the divine feminine in action and has taught me what true sisterhood and support look like, enabling me to cultivate and grow authentic relationships at a deeper level.

Books and Business Links
Man Search for Meaning Dr. Viktor Frankl

Https://linktr.ee/ViolaEdward
https://apps.apple.com/tr/app/qr-me-contact/id1412627381

Dr. Professor Caroline Makaka
Founder of Ladies of All Nations (LOANI)
Northhampton, UK
loanipr17@gmail.com

Pulling It All Together - Closing Remarks
Starting from Scratch Leads to Unreachable Heights

The second volume of "100 Successful Women in Business---Starting from Scratch" was professionally written by some of the most talented international lady entrepreneurs. Maria Renee Davila, Al Otero, and I selected women who have worked hard, dreamed bigger, and thus have achieved much success. We want to thank them for their inspiring and educational chapters of wisdom.

These incredible business leaders openly shared their stories so others could learn how to overcome hardships and failures. Each lady stated her Mission and Vision for her business and why her business was a dream she had to pursue. Success did not happen overnight. The ladies share how they started from scratch and through their personally designed steps to build successful businesses also discovered a secret formula and their ultimate business solution they open-heartedly shared with you readers. Reading about their "Aha Moments" and their "First Signs of Success" clearly showed how their passions for their businesses brought them happiness and the continued motivation to strive to make their businesses the best they could. Their prestigious Accolades and Achievements speak for themselves. These ladies have deservingly been recognized and rewarded for the services provided by their businesses. Their impressive

Testimonials confirm their true and enormous impact on their present and past clients or customers.

Women have always been a pivotal part of any society. In any capacity at all, they have always brought about peace and happiness. These ladies are no exception. Many are world leaders in their industry. Entrepreneurship is an important piece of the puzzle to create conditions that will bring stability to communities and foster peace. This is the point where women entrepreneurs become a massive building block in creating these conditions that promote peace.

Female Entrepreneur leaders serve as important role models. The business ladies in this book also provide a source of employment, and they also shift expectations about what is possible for a woman or a girl to do. These women entrepreneurs can provide economic opportunities for other women. They can provide stability and at the same time work to eradicate the deep barriers to opportunities that women face. These women offer new perspectives on how to remove constraints and disadvantages that may be the root cause for instability. All these concepts point towards the fact that women who are entrepreneurs have a pivotal role in world peace as well as in their businesses.

Through this book, these women all came together from a diverse creed, race, religion, sexual preference, age, ethnic identity, color, and gender to create a better world and take a step on the path to furthering successful female-owned businesses. They wish to create a world where people can get all the help and support, they need.

Please contact them if you need their assistance. They have offered special FREE GIFTS and ADVICE. Take advantage of these and learn from their amazing business experiences.

I, Dr.Caroline Makaka, am the Founder/President of Ladies of All Nations International (LOANI), a world record holding organization that reaches beyond boundaries by focusing on sustainability and corporate social responsibility through matchless contribution to humanity and uniting a Global Diverse Cultures from various nationalities across the world to drive change, peace, stability and development of a better future. My other titles and positions of leadership include the following:

Global Partner of 100 Successful Women in Business,

Co-Founder of World Peace Leaders

Creator of We are the Change World Movement

Chief Executive Officer of World Wide Leaders Association

USA International Chairperson for Global International Alliance University which covers the Department for The Global of International Alliance School Programs for all new international students that apply to the program in the USA.

Global leadership and international management professor for The Global Women and Leadership International development Programme.

Expert advisor and professor for Institute of Global Professionals

Board member and strategic chief advisor for several non- profit and social enterprise boards.

I am also a No. 1 international best seller and co-author of "100 Most Successful Women around the World".

My areas of expertise encompass a wide range of skills such as Global Leadership, International Management Executive Leadership, Diversity, Equality and Inclusion, philanthropy, Coach, Youth Leadership, charities, non-profit organizations, international project management, human resources, Group and Individual Counseling, Women and Girls Empowerment, Cultural Exchange Facilitator and Recognition Awards.

I was selected to represent The United Kingdom as part of The 80 Countries around The World to send a well-wishers message to the 2022 Beijing Winter Olympics.

I have humbly received prestigious awards and honors for my dedication to create a better world. Below are some of my major accolades and achievements:

Selected as 2022 Woman of The Year

Global Chairperson of the year

UK Humanitarian of The Year

Wise Woman Leader of The Year

Top 50 inspiring Black Women in United Kingdom

Influential Role Model of the year

Received Volunteer Lifetime Achievement Award from The USA President Joe Biden and Vice President Kamala Harris

Received Citation Recognition Award from the New York Mayor Eric Adams

She was featured at the New York Billboard Times Square.

Received Her Majesty the Queen platinum Jubilee volunteer Medal Diversity and Inclusion influential Leader Community Award

In addition to these notable merits, I have devoted a significant amount of my time and proficiency, serving the underprivileged. I have volunteered, facilitated charity events, and funded educational seminars and workshops to empower the impoverished specifically in third world countries.

"As we grow, we continue with *our* mission of creating positive change. More importantly we join hands with various communities, supporting each to create a pathway for a better future whilst raising awareness for a better tomorrow." (Prof. Dr. Caroline Makaka)

www.loaniglobal.org

LinkedIn: Professor Caroline Makaka

Instagram: loaniglobal

Citations

Baum, F. (1900) You've always had the power, my dear, you just had to learn it for yourself." – the Wicked Witch, The Wizard of Oz.

Brown, B. (October 9, 2018) Dare to lead - Random House Publishers.

Leonhardt, M. (Dec. 3, 2020) retrieved from August 2, 2022 Make it CNBC https://www.cnbc.com/2020/12/03/millions-of-working-mothers-in-the-us-are-suffering-from-burnout.html

Miller, S. (June 17, 2021, SHRM.org) retrieved from August 2, 2022 https://www.shrm.org/resourcesandtools/hr-topics/benefits/pages/lack-of-flex-arrangements-keep-moms-from-returning-to-work.aspx

Mujeres Violeta SAS, https://mujeres-violeta.com/

Porter, M. (N.D). BrainyQuote. Retrieved July 10, 2022, from **https://www.brainyquote.com/quotes/michael_porter_396281**

Psalms, 34 verses 2-4. It says "My soul **shall** make her boast in the Lord: the humble shall hear thereof, and be glad. Come magnify the Lord with me, come let us exalt his name together, I sought the Lord, and he heard me and delivered me from all my fears."

Pelzer, K. (August 19, 202) retrieved from August 2, 2022 *https://parade.com/1074913/kelseypelzer/nelson-mandela-quotes/*)

Signo Plast S.A., https://www.signoplast.com.ar/

Citations

"The future belongs to those who believe in the beauty of Mandela quote from: https://parade.com/1074913/kelseypelzer/nelson-mandela-quotes/
their dreams." Eleanor Roosevelt.

Made in the USA
Columbia, SC
31 August 2022

66381915R00196